Plague?

Habent sua fata libelli

Volume XXVIII
of Sixteenth Century Studies

Charles G. Nauert, Jr., General Editor

Plague?

JESUIT
ACCOUNTS
OF EPIDEMIC
DISEASE IN THE
16TH CENTURY

A. LYNN
MARTIN

Sixteenth Century Journal Publishers
1996

This book has been brought to publication with the generous support of Truman State University.

Library of Congress Cataloging-in-Publication Data

Martin, A. Lynn.
    Plague? : Jesuit accounts of epidemic disease in the sixteenth century / A. Lynn Martin.
        p. cm. —(Sixteenth century essays and studies ; v. 28)
    Includes bibliographical references and index.
    ISBN 0-940474-30-1 (alk. paper)
    1. Plague—Europe—History—16th century. 2. Jesuits—Europe—History—16th century.   I. Title. II. Series.
    [DNLM: 1. Plague—history—Europe. 2. Plague—epidemiology—Europe. 3. Disease Outbreaks—history—Europe. 4. History of Medicine, 16th cent.—Europe. 5. Religion and Medicine.   WC 355 M379p 1994]
RC178 .A1M37 1994
614.4'94'09031—dc20
DNLM/DLC
for Library of Congress   94-21215
                                                                                              CIP

To Robert M. Kingdon

CONTENTS

—◆—

TABLES AND GRAPHS

———

———

HUMAN RESPONSE TO EPIDEMIC disease exhibits basic similarities despite vast differences in historical, geographical, and cultural environments, as well as differences in the disease itself. Throughout history people have considered epidemic disease to be contagious, spreading from person to person, and they have consequently believed that the best method of avoiding the disease was flight. Another common feature is the conviction that God used the epidemic to punish people for their sins. In apparent contradiction to this belief in the divine origins of disease was the tendency to seek scapegoats for the calamity by blaming others, usually outsiders such as Jews. In spite of these common features and similarities, the responses have taken different forms as a result of differences in the social, political, intellectual, and religious contexts.[1]

Jesuit accounts of epidemic disease in the sixteenth century reveal both the similarities and the differences. Jesuits and their contemporaries encountered a disease, now identified as bubonic plague, which they considered highly contagious, even though modern studies of the plague indicate that it is not contagious but spreads to humans from the black rat through the bites of the rat flea and that a necessary accompaniment to an epidemic of plague is the deaths of rats. A tempting conclusion would be that Jesuits and others were

---

[1]See the excellent Introduction by Paul Slack in *Epidemics and Ideas: Essays on the Historical Perception of Pestilence*, ed. Terence Ranger and Paul Slack (Cambridge: Cambridge University Press, 1992), 1–20.

mistaken in their perceptions and naive in their diagnosis. However, Jesuits were sophisticated observers of their environment; they did not notice the deaths of any rats, and their accounts document chains of infection that indicate a highly contagious disease. A careful analysis of these accounts has forced me to place the question mark in the title of this book and to abandon the word "plague" in my discussion of Jesuits' perceptions of the disease. Instead of "plague" I use *pest*, a variant of the word used by the Jesuits to denote the disease whether they wrote in Latin, Italian, Spanish, Portuguese, or French.

The Jesuit response to an epidemic also demonstrated the common pattern of flight to escape it, behavior which is not surprising in view of their perceptions regarding the contagious nature of the disease. If unable to flee, Jesuits often practiced a form of what could be considered internal flight in their residences and colleges, that is, segregation from all outside contacts to avoid infection. What is surprising in this flight, be it external or internal, is that the founder of the Society of Jesus, Ignatius Loyola, had gained a reputation for service to the sick and had urged his followers to emulate his example. As noted by John W. O'Malley, the author of the best recent study of the Jesuits, the primary thrust of the Society was "to help souls," and Jesuits helped souls through their ministries.[2] During an epidemic their ministries would include hearing the confessions of the sick and giving them communion as well as caring for their physical needs. In the very early years Jesuits did follow the example of their founder, but as the Society developed its educational ministry, the focus turned to establishing and staffing colleges. To preserve this aspect of their ministry, when an epidemic threatened a college the Jesuit superiors, the young novices, and most of the teaching staff would usually flee to safety. On the other hand, the Society never completely abandoned Loyola's commitment to the sick, and the typical pattern was for the majority to flee while a few remained to serve the sick.

Jesuits also shared the common view that God sent epidemics to punish people for their sins. Protestants, those archenemies of the Jesuits, subscribed to the same opinion on the cause of an epidemic but had divergent views on possible remedies. In addition to the moral reform, prayer, and fasting promoted by Protestants, Jesuits and other Catholic clergy could offer to those threatened by epidemics the spiritual help of confession and communion,

---

[2]John W. O'Malley, *The First Jesuits* (Cambridge, Mass.: Harvard University Press, 1993).

processions and pilgrimages, miracle-working relics and the intervention of the saints. Jesuits also had a more complex view on the divine origins of epidemic disease than the notion that it was punishment for sin; God also sent epidemics to select and to warn the faithful and to purge and confound His enemies. Another way in which Jesuits and Protestants shared common features in their response to epidemic disease was their search for scapegoats, but rather than blame the Jews they blamed each other.

As noted by Slack, "Past epidemics continue to throw a peculiarly sharp light on the ideologies and mentalities of the societies they afflicted."[3] So it is with the epidemics encountered by the Society of Jesus in the sixteenth century. First and foremost they throw light on the ideology and mentality of the Jesuits and, second, those of their contemporaries. In addition, an examination of Jesuit accounts of epidemic disease helps reveal the nature of epidemic disease itself.

* * *

My acknowledgments are a series of tributes; the first and the last are the most important. My first tribute is to the late Father Edmond Lamalle, S.J. He was archivist of the Jesuit Archives at Rome when I began research there as a graduate student in 1968. As a result of his paternal concern and assistance I happily returned to Rome and the Jesuit Archives again and again. He was never too busy to offer his help with a difficult paleographical problem, and he freely gave researchers the benefit of his enormous knowledge of the Society's history and its Archives.

To my friends in the international community of scholars, Frederic Baumgartner, Robert Bireley, S.J., Thomas Cohen, Stephen Large, John Law, Thomas M. McCoog, S.J., and especially Francis Brooks, J. Patrick Donnelly, S.J., and Gernot Heiss, for their interest and stimulation.

To my colleagues in the Department of History at the University of Adelaide and its former head, Frank McGregor, for their support.

To the students in my honors and postgraduate seminar for their help and their challenging provocation, especially Connie Held, Jennifer Jones, and Sara Warneke.

---

[3] Slack, Introduction in *Epidemics and Ideas*, 3.

To Margaret Hosking and Patricia Scott, the subject librarians for history at the Barr Smith Library, for their diligent quest for materials on the plague, the rat, and the flea.

To Noreen, Nancy, Kristin, and Andrew, my wife and children, for their patience and companionship.

The last tribute is to Robert M. Kingdon, teacher, supervisor, mentor, model, and friend. I dedicate this book to him.

—

ONE

INTRODUCTION

MODERN MEDICAL KNOWLEDGE of the plague and its application to the past form a complex topic. An examination of this topic is necessary to come to terms with historical accounts of epidemic disease, especially with accounts of outbreaks of "plague" in the sixteenth century. The major problem for historians is that historical descriptions of the plague do not always conform to the modern experience of the disease. Scholars have reacted to this discrepancy by suggesting a variety of solutions: that the epidemic was not the result of the bubonic plague but of another disease, that the disease was a variant form of the plague that behaved in a different manner, or that the historical descriptions are wrong or at best incomplete. The descriptions contained in Jesuit accounts of epidemic disease in the sixteenth century likewise do not conform to the modern experience. A discussion of these accounts, primarily contained in the huge corpus of Jesuit correspondence, indicates their value for historians attempting to understand epidemic disease in the past.

PLAGUE?

During an outbreak of bubonic plague at Hong Kong in 1894 the French scientist Alexandre Yersin discovered the bacillus responsible for the disease, a bacillus now known as *Yersinia pestis* in honor of the discoverer but then named *Pasteurella pestis* in honor of Louis Pasteur. Shortly after this discovery Yersin expressed his suspicions regarding the role of the rat in the spread of the disease. The entry in his diary for June 23, 1894, states, "I search and find the organism in the corpses of dead rats, and there are many throughout the city."[1] The epidemic at Hong Kong was one of the first serious manifestations of the modern pandemic of bubonic plague that spread from East Asia to Australia, the Asian subcontinent, the Middle East, Africa, Europe including England, and the Americas. The Plague Research Commission, established to study the pandemic in India, confirmed Yersin's suspicions regarding the role of rats as a vector of the disease and identified another vector, the rat flea. The Commission's work not only led to the acceptance by the international medical community of the role of rats and rat fleas but also to the identification of a particular species of rat, the black rat or *Rattus rattus*, and a particular species of rat flea, *Xenopsylla cheopis*, as the most important vectors. Thereafter discussions of outbreaks of the bubonic plague always had to confront the unholy trinity of culprits, *Y. pestis*, *R. rattus*, and *X. cheopis*.[2]

To begin this discussion with an exception, the variant form of bubonic plague known as pneumonic or pulmonary plague does not require the presence of *R. rattus* and *X. cheopis* to spread from person to person. As suggested by its name, pneumonic plague affects the lungs and spreads through airborne droplets when the victim coughs, sneezes, or even talks.[3] Several other characteristics of the pneumonic form of plague distinguish it from the bubonic form: it has a short incubation period of from one to three days, its characteristic symptom is not the appearance of painful boils or buboes but the coughing or spitting of bloody sputum, and it has a mortality rate of almost 100 percent in untreated cases. Another difference concerns the seasonality of the epidemics. While bubonic plague normally occurs during warm weather, the pneumonic form usually develops in winter, especially in poorly ventilated and crowded housing.[4] Historians have identified accompanying outbreaks of

---

[1] Quoted in R. Pollitzer, *Plague* (Geneva: World Health Organization, 1954), 297.

[2] I have attempted to write what follows so that the nonspecialist can understand the medical aspects of plague and have accordingly defined medical terms and avoided technical discussions that I consider irrelevant to my purposes. Pollitzer's *Plague* remains the standard treatment, while a shorter, more recent medical discussion of plague is Jack D. Poland, "Plague," in *Infectious Diseases: A Modern Treatise of Infectious Processes*, ed. Paul D. Hoeprich (Philadelphia: Harper and Row, 1983), 1227–37.

[3] To complicate the situation somewhat, flies can spread the bacillus to humans from the bloody sputum, and the victims of pneumonic plague can be a source of infection for fleas; see M. Bahmanyar and D. C. Cavanaugh, *Plague Manual* (Geneva: World Health Organization, 1976), 60.

[4] Pollitzer, *Plague*, 211–12, 440–42, 504–15, and Leonard Fabian Hirst, *The Conquest of the Plague: A Study of the Evolution of Epidemiology* (Oxford: Clarendon Press, 1953), 221–26, contain good descriptions of pneumonic plague.

pneumonic plague during the epidemic of bubonic plague now known as the Black Death, which first struck southern Europe in 1347 and in the following years spread throughout the Continent, reaching England in late June or July 1348 and Sweden in mid-1350. One of the best sources for the existence of pneumonic plague at this time is the observation of Gui de Chauliac, physician to the pope at Avignon, who wrote, "The mortality...was of two types. The first lasted two months, with continuous fever and spitting of blood, and from this one died in three days."[5] The other type, as described by Chauliac, had the characteristic buboes. However, historians doubt that the pneumonic form of plague had a significant role in the epidemics of the sixteenth and seventeenth centuries; in fact, the evidence indicates that it was not present during this period.[6]

Bubonic plague pure and simple cannot spread from person to person but requires the presence of rats and rat fleas, so much so that experts state that no rats and no rat fleas mean no plague. Bubonic plague is a disease of rats that incidentally affects humans via the rat flea. The black rat is but one of almost two hundred different species or subspecies of rodents that are susceptible to *Y. pestis* and consequently capable of spreading the disease.[7] While *R. rattus* is extremely susceptible to *Y. pestis* and dies in great numbers from plague, what makes it such a dangerous vector is its relationship with humans, a relationship that has resulted in another name for it—the house rat. The gregarious *R. rattus* lives close to people and has never been found more than two hundred meters from a human habitation.[8] As a poor burrower and a good climber it infests walls and roofs; as a native of warm climates it requires the warmth of human dwellings to survive the northern winters.

When a flea bites a rat infected with plague, it ingests bacilli into its stomach. In some fleas the bacilli then multiply in the stomach to such an

---

[5]Quoted from Philip Ziegler, *The Black Death* (Harmondsworth: Penguin Books, 1970), 19.

[6]Paul Slack, *The Impact of Plague in Tudor and Stuart England* (London: Routledge and Kegan Paul, 1985), 9; Leslie Bradley, "Some Medical Aspects of Plague," in *The Plague Reconsidered: A New Look at Its Origins and Effects in Sixteenth- and Seventeenth-Century England*, Local Population Studies Supplement (Matlock, Derbyshire: "Local Population Studies" with the S.S.R.C. Cambridge Group for the History of Population and Social Structure, 1977), 13.

[7]R. Pollitzer and Karl F. Meyer, "The Ecology of Plague," in *Studies in Disease Ecology*, ed. Jacques M. Mays (New York: Hafner Publishing Company, 1961), 436.

[8]Jean-Noël Biraben, "Current Medical and Epidemiological Views on Plague," in *Plague Reconsidered*, 31.

extent that they block the proventriculus, the organ that acts as a valve at the entrance to the stomach. As a result the flea is incapable of digesting any blood; it becomes a "blocked" flea. Such fleas remain quite hungry and in consequence are likely to bite any warm-blooded creature, including humans, again and again. Moreover, after the infection kills the host rat, and as the temperature of the cadaver cools, the flea leaves the rat and seeks an alternate host. When a "blocked" flea bites its new host, it sucks blood into its stomach, but the blockage forces the flea to regurgitate some of the blood into the host, in the process infecting it with the bacilli from its stomach. The human flea, *Pulex irritans*, is an inefficient vector of the disease because it has no proventriculus and therefore seldom becomes blocked; normally it can only transmit the bacilli through its proboscis. *P. irritans* spreads plague when it is present in large numbers and when a person's infection is septicemic, that is, when *Y. pestis* multiplies in huge numbers in the bloodstream.[9] The most efficient vector is one of the fleas that infect rodents, *X. cheopis*, so efficient in fact that, according to Leon Fabian Hirst in his book *The Conquest of the Plague*, "No epidemic of human plague...has ever occurred anywhere during the course of the recent pandemic in the absence of an adequate density of *X. cheopis*."[10]

Once a person is infected, the incubation period is from one to six days. The initial symptoms include a fever of 39° or 40°C and perhaps the appearance of a blisterlike carbuncle at the point of infection. Two or three days following the initial symptoms a hard, painful swelling, varying in size between an almond and an orange, develops in the lymph nodes closest to the point of infection. This is the bubo, the most characteristic sign of bubonic plague, although in some cases no bubo appears, especially in the rare, variant form of plague known as septicemic, which bypasses the lymph nodes and concentrates in the bloodstream. The most common location of the buboes is on the thigh or groin, but they also often occur on the neck or under the arm, sometimes elsewhere, occasionally in several places. Studies of the location of buboes during recent epidemics have indicated the distribution shown in table 1.

[9]Bradley, "Some Medical Aspects," 12; Michael W. Dols, "Geographical Origin of the Black Death: Comment," *Bulletin of the History of Medicine* 52 (1978): 118.

[10]Hirst, *Conquest of the Plague*, 302. More recent works, while still stressing the importance of *X. cheopis*, do not exclude the role of other fleas; see, for example, Bahmanyar and Cavanaugh, *Plague Manual*, 47.

TABLE 1: LOCATION OF BUBOES DURING RECENT EPIDEMICS[a]

Site	%
Femoral (thigh)	31
Inguinal (groin)	23
Axillary (armpit)	22
Cervical (neck)	9
Other sites	2
Multiple	13

a. *Source*: My combinations of the statistics in Pollitzer, *Plague*, 420.

TABLE 2: SYMPTOMS OF PLAGUE IN VIETNAM IN 1970[a]

Symptom	Patients	
	No.	%
Fever	40	100
Chill	16	40
Painful bubo	40	100
Headache	34	85
Prostration	30	75
Anorexia	13	33
Vomiting	10	25
Abdominal pain	7	18
Cough	10	25
Chest pain	5	13
Skin rash	9	23

a. Source: Thomas Butler, "A Clinical Study of Bubonic Plague," *American Journal of Medicine* 53 (1972): 271.

Other physical symptoms include headache, nausea, diarrhea, abdominal pain, and spots (petechiae) and blotches on the skin, while the victim's response ranges from apathy to delirium and coma.[11] Table 2 shows the symptoms recorded during an outbreak of plague in Vietnam in 1970. If untreated, the case-mortality rate of bubonic plague is from 60 to 90 percent, not as high as the almost always fatal pneumonic plague, but still high enough to make it one of the most deadly diseases that afflict humans. Death usually occurs within three to five days of infection, although some victims die after more than a month.[12]

Historians have identified two pandemics of plague in the past, one occurring in the early Middle Ages from the sixth to the eighth centuries, the other beginning with the Black Death of 1347–1352.[13] For the earlier pandemic one of the best sources is Gregory of Tours, whose description is almost as revealing as the one written by Gui de Chauliac eight centuries later: "Death was very sudden. A snakelike wound appeared in the groin or in the armpit and the poison affected the patients in such a way that they gave up the ghost on the second or third day. Furthermore, the power of the poison robbed people of their senses."[14] Historical demographers have not attempted "guesstimates" of the mortality figures from the earlier pandemic, but according to Jean-Noël Biraben and Jacques Le Goff, plague performed a "severe demographic pruning" and "caused a catastrophic demographic slump."[15] The effect of the Black Death was more severe; some historians put the mortality as high as 50 percent, some favor a figure as low as 20 percent, and others opt for the safe middle ground of 30 to 40 percent.[16] Even the low figure of 20 percent

---

[11]Poland, "Plague," 1233.

[12]Pollitzer, *Plague*, 418; Slack, *Impact of Plague*, 7; cf. Biraben, "Current Medical Views," 28.

[13]Some historians note a third pandemic of antiquity—the Plague of Athens, but the identification of this disease is impossible according to J. F. D. Shrewsbury, "The Plague of Athens," *Bulletin of the History of Medicine* 24 (1950): 1–25. Some scholars suggest that it was toxic shock syndrome; see Graham I. Twigg, "The Black Death in England: An Epidemiological Dilemma," in *Maladies et société (XIIe-XVIIIe siècles): Actes du colloque de Bielefeld, novembre 1986*, ed. Neithard Bulst and Robert Delort (Paris: Editions du CNRS, 1989), 76.

[14]Quoted from Jean-Noël Biraben and Jacques Le Goff, "The Plague in the Early Middle Ages," in *Biology of Man in History*, ed. Robert Forster and Orest Ranum (Baltimore: Johns Hopkins University Press, 1975), 57.

[15]Ibid., 62.

[16]See the discussion in Robert S. Gottfried, *The Black Death: Natural and Human Disaster in Medieval Europe* (New York: The Free Press, 1983), xvi, 77.

translates into over ten million deaths. Following the initial outbreak between 1347 and 1352, plague became a recurrent feature of Europe's epidemic history for the next three and a half centuries. In his monumental study of plague, *Les hommes et la peste*, Jean-Noël Biraben states that plague was present somewhere in Europe during every year from 1347 to 1670 with the exception of two years, 1354 and 1355.[17] The last significant manifestation of this pandemic in England was the Great Plague of London in 1665; on the continent, the outbreak at Marseilles between 1720 and 1722.

Although the first pandemic has not received much attention from historians, the second has produced an abundant bibliography that testifies to the popularity of "plague" among professional as well as the a mateur historians and of course the lay reader. As noted by the epidemiologist Major Greenwood, the term "plague" has an emotional color that separates it from all other diseases and provides it with a morbid fascination.[18] So abundant is the literature on plague that the indefatigable Fernand Braudel had to confess to the failure of his attempts to master it; "the over-plentiful documentation defeats the historian's good intentions by its very quantity."[19] A good indication of the quantity is Biraben's bibliography—215 pages of printed sources,[20] and many more books and articles have appeared since its publication in 1976.[21]

Historians who use modern science to examine the pandemics of the past are engaged in regressive history, that is, the study of the present to understand the past. *Y. pestis, R. rattus, X. cheopis*, and bubonic plague in man—in the words of Emmanuel Le Roy Ladurie, a *ménage à quatre*[22]—are the

[17]Jean-Noël Biraben, *Les hommes et la peste en France et dans les pays européens et méditerranéens*, 2 vols. (Paris: Mouton, 1975–1976), 1: 104–5.

[18]Major Greenwood, *Epidemics and Crowd-Diseases: An Introduction to the Study of Epidemiology* (London: Williams and Norgate, 1935), 289. Of course, Greenwood wrote before the outbreak of AIDS.

[19]Fernand Braudel, *The Structures of Everyday Life: The Limits of the Possible* (London: Collins, 1981), 84.

[20]Biraben, *Les hommes* , 2: 196–410. For other bibliographies see R. Pollitzer, "A Review of Recent Literature on the Plague," *Bulletin of the World Health Organization* 23 (1960): 313–400; and Arthur L. Bloomfield, "A Bibliography of Internal Medicine: Plague," *Stanford Medical Bulletin* 15 (1957): 3–13. My bibliography only contains works cited in this book and those which provided information for the appendix.

[21]One of the easiest ways to keep abreast of recent literature on plague is to consult the *Current Work in the History of Medicine*, published quarterly by the Wellcome Institute for the History of Medicine. It indexes medical articles in historical journals and historical articles in medical journals.

[22]Emmanuel Le Roy Ladurie, "A Concept: The Unification of the Globe by Disease (Fourteenth to Seventeenth Centuries)," in *The Mind and Method of the Historian* (Chicago: University of Chicago Press, 1981), 31.

discoveries of modern science used by these historians. To explain the higher death rates among the poor than among the wealthy, J. F. D. Shrewsbury could point to the differences in their housing. The black rat could not make itself at home in the stone and brick houses of the wealthy; on the contrary, "It was in the medieval, 'soft-walled' dwelling-house, with its thatched roof, its dark, unventilated, humid interior, and its earthen floor, that R. rattus and X. cheopis found mutually congenial conditions for their subsistence and multiplication."[23] To explain the spread of outbreaks in England, Paul Slack could point to the introduction of plague by ships through infective fleas or infected rats, the movement from town to town along the main trade routes through infective fleas that infected local rats, the spread of the disease within a town as a result of the deaths of its rats, and the transmission of plague among the residents of a household by fleas.[24]

Because Paolo Preto understood the role of rats and rat fleas in the spread of plague he could point out the fatal limitations of contemporary measures to prevent the transmission of the disease.[25] To determine which epidemic disease caused a large number of deaths in the English village of Colyton between November 1645 and November 1646, Roger S. Schofield could analyze the clustering of deaths in households and conclude that the pattern was unlikely to be the result of airborne diseases such as influenza, contagious diseases such as dysentery, or diseases caused by human parasites such as typhus; "[r]ather it points to a disease whose distribution is largely determined by ecological factors, and the most promising candidate would seem to be bubonic plague with the rat flea as the significant vector."[26] Finally, the climatic conditions favored by Y. pestis, R. rattus, and X. cheopis help historians to identify epidemics occurring in late summer and early autumn as outbreaks of bubonic plague and those occurring in winter as pneumonic plague.[27]

---

[23]J. F. D. Shrewsbury, *A History of Bubonic Plague in the British Isles* (Cambridge: Cambridge University Press, 1970), 35–36.

[24]Slack, *Impact of Plague*, 313–15.

[25]Paolo Preto, *Peste e società a Venezia nel 1576* (Vicenza: Neri Pozza Editore, 1978), 47.

[26]Roger S. Schofield, "An Anatomy of an Epidemic: Colyton, November 1645 to November 1646," in *Plague Reconsidered*, 104–8.

[27]See, for example, Gottfried, *Black Death*, 44, 49, 50, 55, 57, 64, 66, and idem, *Epidemic Disease in Fifteenth-Century England: The Medical Response and the Demographic Consequences* (New Brunswick: Rutgers University Press, 1978), 139.

One gigantic problem with this regressive use of Le Roy Ladurie's *ménage à quatre* is that no evidence exists definitely proving the role of *Y. pestis*, *R. rattus*, and *X. cheopis* during any of these earlier pandemics. No one can be certain that the bacillus discovered by Yersin at Hong Kong in 1894 was the same bacillus responsible for the Black Death. Although the statements by Gregory of Tours and Gui de Chauliac are good descriptions of plague symptoms, the historian has no way of proving that the disease they describe was the result of that unholy trinity of culprits. Furthermore, epidemics of plague in the past quite often had characteristics that differ from those resulting from modern observations of the disease. For example, the transmission of modern bubonic plague from one person to another is so difficult that multiple cases in a single household are rare.[28] Yet the evidence from the second plague pandemic often reveals multiple cases within a household, as entire families succumbed to the disease. So intractable are some of the problems associated with the regressive application of the *ménage à quatre* that Graham I. Twigg, a zoologist specializing in rodents, has argued that the Black Death was not an epidemic of plague but one of anthrax.[29]

Most historians nonetheless accept the classic plague model and insist on the reliability of their diagnoses. Paul Slack, for example, when writing about Tudor and Stuart England, affirms, "We can be sure...of the predominance of plague in its bubonic form and of its general clinical picture in our period,"[30] Ann G. Carmichael in her study of epidemics in Renaissance Florence asserts, "Bubonic *Y. pestis* was certainly part of the complex of disease in these recurrent fifteenth-century plagues,"[31] and Stephen R. Ell states, "The Venetian plague of 1630–1631 was...clearly predominantly an outbreak of the infection produced by *Y. pestis*."[32] Many, including Slack, Carmichael, and Ell, admit the difficulty in diagnosing particular epidemics or individual victims,[33]

---

[28]Pollitzer, *Plague*, 379–80.

[29]Graham I. Twigg, *The Black Death: A Biological Reappraisal* (London: Batsford Academic and Educational, 1984), 212–22. More recently he has argued that the Black Death in England resulted from "an airborne organism of high infectivity and virulence, having a short incubation period and being spread by respiratory means"; see Twigg, "Black Death in England," 98.

[30]Slack *Impact of Plague*, 9.

[31]Ann G. Carmichael, *Plague and the Poor in Renaissance Florence* (Cambridge: Cambridge University Press, 1986), 21.

[32]Stephen R. Ell, "Three Days in October of 1630: Detailed Examination of Mortality during an Early Modern Plague Epidemic in Venice," *Reviews of Infectious Diseases* 11 (1989): 131.

[33]Ibid., 130–31; Carmichael, *Plague and the Poor*, 8, 18–19, 59; Slack, Introduction in *Plague Reconsidered*, 6.

and they would in these cases accept the advice of J.-P. Goubert: "The retrospective diagnosis that [the historian] can make often belongs to the realm of the likely, at best that of the probable, and rarely to that of the irrefutable."[34]

One of the difficulties in making diagnoses for particular epidemics or individual victims is the generic use of the English terms "plague" and "pestilence" and their equivalents in other European languages, usually derivatives of the Latin *pestis*. During the second pandemic, people could use these terms to signify different epidemic diseases—typhus, dysentery, smallpox, and influenza. On the other hand, Paul Slack has discerned a tendency in England during the sixteenth century to use "plague" in a more discriminating manner to denote a specific disease.[35] To complicate the picture further, at times accounts of an epidemic disease did not put any label on it but merely noted its most prominent symptom such as "carbuncles," "tumors," or "petechiae."[36] Another problem encountered when diagnosing particular epidemics and individual cases is the possibility of confusing the symptoms of plague in all its variant forms with those of other diseases, a possibility that continues among modern medical practitioners. When physicians in New Mexico encountered cases of plague in the 1960s, they made the following initial diagnoses: "tularemia, cat scratch fever, streptococcal adenitis (swollen glands), venereal disease, viral meningitis, rickettsial infection, cellulitis, gastroenteritis, appendicitis, and incarcerated hernia."[37]

[34]J.-P. Goubert, "Twenty Years On: Problems of Historical Methodology in the History of Health," in *Problems and Methods in the History of Medicine*, ed. Roy Porter and Andrew Wear (London: Croom Helm, 1987), 51. Sölvi Sogner poses the question, "May [*sic*] an analysis of the death-structure in an epidemically based crisis make it possible to specify the disease in question?" He concludes that the question "cannot as yet be answered." See Sölvi Sogner, "Nature and Dynamics of Crises (Including Recent Crises in Developing Countries)," in *The Great Mortalities: Methodological Studies of Demographic Crises in the Past*, ed. Hubert Charbonneau and André Larose (Liège, Belgium: International Union for the Scientific Study of Population, 1980), 321. For another discussion of the problem see Jean-Charles Sournia, "Discipline du diagnostic rétrospectif," in *Maladies et société (XIIe-XVIIIe siècles): Actes du colloque de Bielefeld, novembre 1986*, ed. Neithard Bulst and Robert Delort (Paris: Editions du CNRS, 1989), 57–64.

[35]Slack, *Impact of Plague*, 64.

[36]Vicente Pérez Moreda, *Las crisis de mortalidad en la España interior (siglos XVI-XIX)* (Madrid: Siglo Ventiuno Editores, 1980), 64.

[37]John T. Alexander, *Bubonic Plague in Early Modern Russia: Public Health and Urban Disaster* (Baltimore: Johns Hopkins University Press, 1980), 4.

Many other diseases, including ergotism and other mycotoxicoses, present symptoms that make diagnostic certainty impossible in the absence of laboratory tests.[38] One of these diseases, tularemia, not only has a comparable incubation period (two to ten days) and symptoms (buboes and carbuncles) but also spreads as a result of the bites of insect vectors (ticks, deerflies, and horseflies) that transmit the disease from mammals (rabbits, squirrels, woodchucks, muskrats, and beavers).[39] The final problem in making diagnoses for plague results from the nature of the disease and its bacillus; the disease has three variant forms and the bacillus has several different strains. The leading expert on plague, R. Pollitzer, asserts that the disease is so variable that every general rule concerning it has exceptions and that scientists should never generalize from observations made in only one or two areas.[40] None of these diagnostic problems of course proves that *Y. pestis* was not responsible for the first two "plague" pandemics, but they do stress the necessity of caution in reaching conclusions.

Since *R. rattus* is much more visible than *Y. pestis* its existence during the earlier pandemics should be easier to prove. Here, however, the historian encounters silence. According to the classic model of bubonic plague, deaths of house rats had to precede an epidemic, deaths numbering in the millions when taking into consideration the enormous human mortality of the Black Death. The silence of the European sources is all the more remarkable in view of the evidence from elsewhere; in East Asia, the Asian subcontinent, and Africa the death of rats was a harbinger of plague and led to the abandonment of villages.[41] A sacred poem in Sanskrit warned people in Hindustan to flee their homes whenever rats fell from the roofs and died, and a Chinese poem entitled *Death of Rats* from the late eighteenth century made the connection between rat mortality and the death of humans:

> Few days following the death of the rats,
> Men pass away like falling walls![42]

[38]John T. Alexander, "Reconsiderations on Plague in Early Modern Russia, 1500–1800," *Jahrbücher für Geschichte Osteuropas* 34 (1986): 245.

[39]Thomas Butler, "Plague and Tularemia," *Pediatric Clinics of North America* 26 (1979): 355–66.

[40]Pollitzer, "Review of Recent Literature," 355, 361.

[41]Graham I. Twigg, "The Role of Rodents in Plague Dissemination: A Worldwide Review," *Mammal Review* 8 (September 1978): 84.

[42]Quoted from Pollitzer, *Plague*, 296.

In contrast to this popular wisdom and these literary warnings, the European evidence is slight. According to the Greek historian Nicephore Gregoras, "rats in the houses died"—as well as dogs and horses—during an outbreak of plague in 1348 and 1349 on islands in the Aegean,[43] but historians have to wait until the seventeenth century before encountering other writers who comment on rats in conjunction with an epidemic of plague. These writers, far from singling out rats, included moles, birds, dogs, cats, mice, serpents, conies, and foxes.[44] Of course, this lack of evidence is not proof that *R. rattus* was not there in Shrewsbury's "'soft-walled' dwelling-house, with its thatched roof, its dark, unventilated, humid interior, and its earthen floor," but when European observers made meticulous descriptions of other environmental factors that might help explain or predict the outbreak of epidemics, the historian is entitled to marvel at the silence on rats. Europeans moreover had a long tradition of looking for omens, signs, and portents in nature; the behavior of animals could predict the future. Hence, people could believe that ravens were an indication of plague,[45] but no one ever noticed that the death of rats heralded an epidemic.

When confronted by this silence of the sources, Slack states, "Black rats *must have been common* [my emphasis] between the floors and in the roofs of wooden or wattle-and-daub houses."[46] Shrewsbury adopts a similar argument by citing evidence that rats seldom die in the open and by asserting that the thatch roofs "undoubtedly hid the carcases of many plague-rats"—hardly a convincing argument to anyone who has ever smelled a dead rat. So confident is Shrewsbury in his diagnosis that he claims that Englishmen such as Samuel Pepys were so familiar with the house rat that they "did not consider it worth a mention."[47] All this indicates the hold that the classic model of plague—*Y. pestis*, *R. rattus*, and *X. cheopis*—has on many scholars. One of the best illustrations of this comes from James Rackham's article, "*Rattus rattus*: The Introduction of the Black Rat into Britain." Rackham believes that to prove the

---

[43]Le Roy Ladurie, "A Concept," 36.

[44]Hirst, *Conquest of Plague*, 127; David E. Davis, "The Scarcity of Rats and the Black Death: An Ecological History," *Journal of Interdisciplinary History* 16 (1986): 465–67.

[45]Keith Thomas, *Religion and the Decline of Magic: Studies in Popular Belief in Sixteenth- and Seventeenth-Century England* (Harmondsworth: Penguin Books, 1973), 747.

[46]Slack, *Impact of Plague*, 11–12.

[47]Shrewsbury, *History of Bubonic Plague*, 4, 14.

existence of the black rat in an area he just needs to point to an outbreak of bubonic plague.[48] Quite a different perspective comes from a recent article by David E. Davis, an article entitled "The Scarcity of Rats and the Black Death: An Ecological History." Davis argues that the black rat could not have survived in the climate of northern Europe; only temporary colonies could exist in port towns with a good supply of grain. Shipping could reintroduce colonies of black rats in the north, but they became established in rural areas solely in southern Europe. Davis concludes: "*Rattus rattus* was rare or absent in most of Europe where Black Death spread and hence was not responsible for the epidemic."[49] Shrewsbury deserves the final word on rats: "The historian seeking to identify a particular pestilence as an epidemic of plague must produce convincing evidence that the house-haunting rat was established in the afflicted society at the relevant time."[50]

If historians have not been successful in finding *R. rattus*, their efforts to locate *X. cheopis* are likely to yield even less evidence. Nonetheless, most of the recent controversies surrounding plague focus on the role of the rat flea in the transmission of plague. No evidence documents the presence of *X. cheopis* during the previous pandemics,[51] so historians under the influence of the classic plague model have to assume, in the words of Hirst, "an adequate density of *X. cheopis.*" This flea shares with the black rat an origin in a warm climate, can only survive northern winters in heated buildings, and is at present rare in Europe. Pollitzer notes that colonies of *X. cheopis* recently discovered in Europe were living in basements of steam-heated buildings and doubts that similarly suitable environments existed in the houses of medieval Europe, and Graham Twigg claims that the climatic conditions in much of Europe were

---

[48]James Rackham, "*Rattus Rattus:* The Introduction of the Black Rat into Britain," *Antiquity* 53 (1979): 116.

[49]Davis, "Scarcity of Rats," 456; see also the comments by Twigg, "Black Death in England," 81–83. Scattered archaeological discoveries document the presence of *R. Rattus* in Europe, particularly from the eleventh century; Frédérique Audoin-Rouzeau, "La peste et les rats: Les réponses de l'archéozoologie," in *Maladies et société (XIIe–XVIIIe siècles): Actes du colloque de Bielefeld, novembre 1986*, ed. Neithard Bulst and Robert Delort (Paris: Editions du CNRS, 1989), 65–71.

[50]Shrewsbury, *History of Bubonic Plague*, 6.

[51]According to Pollitzer, *Plague*, 330, the earliest flea specimens found date from the early nineteenth century. I would imagine that since the publication of this book in 1954 modern archaeological techniques have discovered older flea specimens, but I am not aware of any studies that cite such discoveries.

unsuitable for the survival and proliferation of *X. cheopis.* Some historians, including Hirst, nonetheless argue that *X. cheopis* was formerly widespread in Europe, widespread enough to play its role during the Black Death, but the replacement of *R. rattus* by another species of rat, the grey rat or *Rattus norvegicus,* resulted in the disappearance of *X. cheopis.* Pollitzer's verdict on this theory is that it is fascinating but unacceptable.[52] If Davis is correct in doubting the widespread presence of *R. rattus* in Europe, and if Pollitzer and Twigg are correct in doubting the widespread presence of *X. cheopis* in Europe, the classic model of plague must be inapplicable to preindustrial Europe.

Some scholars have advanced an alternative plague model for the pandemics of preindustrial Europe, a model based upon interhuman spread of the bubonic variant of plague via the human flea *P. irritans.* The two scholars associated with this model are the Frenchmen M. Baltazard and Jean-Noël Biraben; they are the leading proponents of what Emmanuel Le Roy Ladurie has called the French human flea school opposed to the English rat flea school, led by Shrewsbury.[53] The French school bases its argument on the research of the Institut Pasteur in Iran and Morocco, research that demonstrated the importance of the human flea in the spread of plague. Baltazard, in short, rejects the dogma "no rats, no plague" for "plague without rats."[54] According to Biraben, the classic model of plague might be appropriate for tropical areas where the inhabitants wear little clothing, but in areas where layers of clothing could increase the number of fleas, interhuman transmission of plague via *P. irritans* was the appropriate model and applicable to the previous pandemics.[55] The

---

[52]Ibid., 330–32; Twigg, "Black Death in England," 84–86.

[53]Le Roy Ladurie, "A Concept," 32–36; see Michael W. Flinn, *The European Demographic System, 1500–1820* (Baltimore: Johns Hopkins University Press, 1985), 56–57; idem, "Plague in Europe and the Mediterranean Countries," *Journal of European Economic History* 8 (1979): 134–38; and Dols, "Geographical Origins," 116–19, for good discussions of the controversy. The dispute began early in this century, and the first thorough application of the approach of the "French human flea school" was the German Ernst Rodenwaldt's *Pest in Venedig, 1575–1577: Ein Beitrag zur Frage der Infektkette bei dem Pestepidemein West-Europas* (Heidelberg: Springer, 1953). See also Stephen R. Ell, "Interhuman Transmission of Medieval Plague," *Bulletin of the History of Medicine* 54 (1980): 497–510.

[54]M. Baltazard, "Déclin et destin d'une maladie infectieuse: La peste," *Bulletin of the World Health Organization* 23 (1960): 254. For a study of a recent outbreak of plague that appeared to result from interhuman spread via *P. irritans,* see F. Marc Laforce et al., "Clinical and Epidemiological Observations on an Outbreak of Plague in Nepal," *Bulletin of the World Health Organization* 45 (1971): 693–706.

[55]Biraben, "Current Medical Views," 30.

scholars supporting the classic model acknowledge that the human flea (as well as other insects including lice, bed bugs, ticks, and flies) is capable of spreading plague, but they claim that it is an inefficient vector without a prominent role in spreading the disease.[56]

One factor in favor of the French school's model is that it helps explain the spread of epidemics in the past. Since black rats are reluctant travelers and seldom leave their home territory, modern cases of the spread of bubonic plague over distance among communities of black rats reveal a very slow rate; in one case cited by Pollitzer it took six weeks for plague to travel ninety meters.[57] During the Black Death in France, however, plague spread at a rate of from one to four kilometers a day.[58] Interhuman spread of plague via *P. irritans*, moreover, better accounts for many of the multiple cases of plague within a single household than does transmission via the rat flea, and it corroborates the widespread impression among contemporaries that the second pandemic plague was a highly contagious disease. The French model makes humans the carriers, and all human gatherings—fairs, processions, markets, inns, armies—could result in the transmission of plague.[59]

If the French model solves some problems it creates others, the foremost being the seasonality of plague epidemics; bubonic plague often occurred in summer or early autumn and declined with the onset of cold weather, but increased layers of clothing and decreased bathing during winter would result in an increase in the numbers of *P. irritans*.[60] Another problem concerns the relationship between interhuman spread of plague and rats; even the proponents of the French human flea school admit that an epidemic initially requires the presence of plague among rats, and Baltazard agrees with James Rackham's assertion that the presence of plague is proof of the presence of *R. rattus*.[61] Although the French model can explain multiple cases within a household, it fails to explain other aspects of plague epidemics, as noted by Paul Slack:

[56]Pollitzer and Meyer, "Ecology of Plague," 470–72.

[57]Pollitzer, *Plague*, 300.

[58]Biraben, *Les hommes*, 1: 90.

[59]Biraben, "Current Medical Views," 30.

[60]Flinn, "Plague in Europe," 137–38.

[61]Baltazard, "Déclin et destin," 260; see Dols, "Geographical Origin," 118–19.

First, there is the concentration of plague mortality in towns and, within towns, in separate neighbourhoods, often on the outskirts and not in the centre where the chances of contact between infected and non-infected humans might be expected to be greatest.... Secondly despite the frequency of multiple cases of plague within single households, it has not yet been shown that mortality rates were related to size of household, as one might expect if the human flea was the significant vector. Finally these clusters of cases in households need not necessarily imply direct transmission between humans: their temporal distribution suggests that they could be explained by successive and multiple deaths of rats.[62]

O. J. Benedictow in his article "Morbidity in Historical Plague Epidemics" points out further problems with the French model. Interhuman spread of plague would result in sudden but geographically erratic outbreaks within a community, as human contacts quickly spread the disease to people in different parts of the town. Where records have permitted a reconstruction of an outbreak, such as in the small north German town of Uelzen in 1597 and in the Jordan quarter of Amsterdam in 1617 and 1624, the reverse is true, that is, plague spread erratically in time but contiguously in space, "house by house, street by street, parish by parish, and quarter by quarter," as the disease slowly spread from one community of rats to another.[63]

Benedictow's argument against interhuman spread of plague is a sophisticated one, and it has the support of two of the conclusions of the Indian Plague Research Commission:

1. A direct spread of the infection from bubonic patients was most unlikely....

2. There was no convincing evidence to show that the human flea played an important role in the conveyance of the infection to man.

On the other hand, much of the evidence from the second plague pandemic does not support the other five conclusions:

3. Those attending bubonic plague patients remained singularly free from infection....

---

[62]Slack, *Impact of Plague*, 10–11.

[63]Ole Jøregen Benedictow, "Morbidity in Historical Plague Epidemics," *Population Studies* 41 (1987): 423–30. Benedictow cites the work of J. G. Dijkstra on Jordan and E. Woehlkens on Uelzen.

Jesuit Accounts of Epidemic Disease in the Sixteenth Century

Begun by a Spaniard in France in 1534 and approved by an Italian pope six years later, the Society of Jesus had origins that heralded its international destiny. By the end of the sixteenth century the Society was operating colleges that stretched from Vilnius in Lithuania to Angra in the Azores, from Slovenian Ljubljana to Netherlandish Maastricht. Outside Europe, Jesuits undertook missions to the far corners of the globe, to the inhabitants of the New World and the Old, to the East and West Indies, China and Brazil, Japan and Peru. These missions fit "The First Sketch of the Institute of the Society of Jesus," written by its founder and first general, Ignatius Loyola, in 1539. Loyola proclaimed that those who joined the new religious order must be willing to follow the commands of the pope, "whether he sends us to the Turks or to the New World or to the Lutherans."[77] On the other hand, "The First Sketch" gave no indications of the dominant role of colleges in the Jesuit missions in service of the papacy. The only mentions of education in the document concerned the instruction of children and the uneducated in the rudiments of Christianity.[78] Eight years after Pope Paul III formally established the Society in 1540, it opened its first college for non-Jesuits at Messina in Sicily. Between then and his death in 1556 Loyola approved the establishment of another thirty-eight colleges, and in 1575 the Society had 130 colleges, seminaries, and universities. Poland serves as a good example of this extraordinary expansion. The Society opened its first college in Poland at Braniewo in 1564; by the end of the century the Polish province had five hundred members operating eleven colleges and one university.[79] In the words of Martin Harney, the Society was "the first religious order to adopt this education of youth as a special ministry whereby it might attain its end, the glory of God and the salvation of souls."[80]

---

[77]Published in *The Autobiography of Saint Ignatius Loyola with Related Documents*, ed. John C. Olin (New York: Harper and Row, 1974), 107.

[78]Ibid., 107–8.

[79]Wieslaw Müller, "Les jésuites en Pologne aux XVIe et XVIIe siècles," in *Les jésuites parmi les hommes aux XVIe et XVIIe siècles* Association des publications de la Faculté des lettres et sciences humaines (Clermont-Ferrand, 1987), 324–25.

[80]Martin Harney, *The Jesuits in History: The Society of Jesus through Four Centuries* (Chicago: Loyola University Press, 1962), 192–93.

The glue of this multinational corporation of educational institutions was correspondence. An endless stream of directives came from the general's office in Rome to the superiors in the provinces and colleges. In turn, the provincials of provinces and the rectors of colleges wrote monthly reports to the general, weekly if they were near Rome,[81] and official visitors on periodic tours of inspection added to the flow of letters. To help establish institutional solidarity or, in the words of Ignatius Loyola, "to cement the union of the members among themselves,"[82] he devised a system of exchanging letters between the various Jesuit missions and institutions. These letters were the *quadrimestres;* at the end of every four months each Jesuit mission and institution had to send reports containing "edifying" information to their superiors, who then distributed them to all the other missions and institutions.[83] The burden imposed by this system soon became obvious as the Society's recruitment of new members failed to keep pace with the demands for more and more colleges. As a result, superiors abandoned the *quadrimestres* in 1565 and replaced them with a system of annual reports. Then in 1571 the Society adopted a system of annual reports from each province rather than from each mission or educational establishment, a system that still endures.

This correspondence provides the historian with a rich source of information, not just on the Society of Jesus but also on the religious, cultural, political, social, and epidemic history of the period. Despite the suppression of the Society from 1773 to 1814, a large number of letters have survived, and these are available to scholars at the Jesuit Archives in Rome, the *Archivum Romanum Societatis Iesu.* The historian of the sixteenth century has an advantage over those of later centuries, for after 1600 the Jesuit superiors in Rome no longer preserved incoming correspondence.[84] Even so, the sixteenth-century correspondence contains many gaps. For example, the Archives hold forty-nine volumes of letters in the series *Italia* that cover the twenty-three years

[81]Ignatius Loyola, *The Constitutions of the Society of Jesus,* ed. George E. Ganss (St. Louis: Institute of Jesuit Sources, 1970), [674]. I follow here the standard practice of reference by a number enclosed in brackets; the number refers to an article rather than a page and thus permits a person to consult the passage regardless of edition.

[82]Ibid., [671].

[83]Ibid., [675].

[84]Edmond Lamalle, "L'archivio di un grande ordine religioso: L'Archivio Generale della Compagnia di Gesù," *Archiva Ecclesiae* 24–25 (1981–1982): 96–97 and notes. Father Lamalle was the archivist; his article is the best introduction to the Jesuit Archives.

from 1555 to 1577, yet the next seven volumes cover twenty-eight years, from 1578 to 1605. The correspondence from France has a similar gap; the series *Epistolae Galliae* has twelve volumes for the years 1557–1579 but three for the next twenty years.[85]

The starting place for an examination of Jesuit correspondence is not the Jesuit Archives at Rome but the *Monumenta Historica Societatis Iesu*. This is the series of edited documents primarily from the Jesuit Archives. Thus far 145 volumes have appeared in the series. Relevant to the search for Jesuit accounts of epidemic disease in the sixteenth century are the volumes devoted to Nicolás Bobadilla, Francis Borgia, Paschase Broët, Peter Canisius (appearing outside the *Monumenta* series), Jean Codure, Pierre Favre, Claude Jay, Diego Lainez, Ignatius Loyola, Jerónimo Nadal, Juan Polanco, Pedro Ribadeneira, Simon Rodriguez, and Alfonso Salmeron, as well as other collections entitled *Epistolae Mixtae, Fontes Narrativi, Monumenta Hungariae, Monumenta Paedagogica*, and of course *Litterae Quadrimestres*—eighty-five volumes in all. In addition, for the purposes of comparison I looked for accounts of epidemic disease in another thirty-six volumes on Jesuit missions in Brazil, Peru, Mexico, Florida, India, and the East Indies. The focus of the search, however, was the collection of correspondence at the Jesuit Archives. There I managed to look at most of the volumes relevant to the sixteenth century; I have listed all 277 of these in the bibliography even though I did not find any accounts of epidemic disease in many of them.[86] The national histories of the Society are also useful since the authors visited local archives and discovered documents not available at Rome. These historians include Antonio Astrain for Spain,[87] Bernard Duhr for Germany,[88] Henri Fouqueray for France,[89] Alois Kroess for Bohemia,[90] Alfred Poncelet for the Low Countries,[91] Francisco Rodrigues for

[85]See the bibliography, p. 232.

[86]Because all manuscript sources cited in this book come from the Jesuit Archives I do not mention the Archives in the notes. The abbreviations used in the notes are listed in the bibliography.

[87]Antonio Astrain, *Historia de la Compañia de Jesús en la Asistencia de España*, 7 vols. (Madrid: Sucesores de Rivadeneyra, 1902–1925).

[88]Bernard Duhr, *Geschichte der Jesuiten in den Ländern deutscher Zunge*, 4 vols. (Freiburg im Breisgau: Herder, 1907–1928). Also useful is Joseph Hansen, ed., *Rheinische Akten zur Geschichte des Jesuitenordens, 1542–1582* (Bonn: H. Berendt, 1896).

[89]Henri Fouqueray, *Histoire de la Compagnie de Jésus en France des origines à la suppression (1528–1762)*, 5 vols. (Paris: Librairie Alphonse Picard et Fils, 1910–1925).

[90]Alois Kroess, *Geschichte der böhmischen Provinz der Gesellschaft Jesu*, 2 vols. (Vienna: Ambr. Opitz, 1910–1927).

[91]Alfred Poncelet, *Histoire de la Compagnie de Jésus dans les anciens Pays-Bas*, 2 vols. (Brussels: M. Lamertin, 1927–1928).

Portugal,[92] and Pietro Tacchi Venturi and Mario Scaduto for Italy.[93] Finally, a few sixteenth-century Jesuits published relevant material; in 1577 Paolo Bisciola wrote an account of the pest at Milan,[94] Peter Michael Brillmacher included a prayer for the pest in a devotional book,[95] and Antonio Possevino published anonymously a book on the causes and remedies of the pest.[96]

The earliest account of an epidemic disease in these sources occurred in a letter from Nicolás Bobadilla. Written on November 1, 1546, the letter described how Bobadilla contracted the pest at Regensberg; he was so sick that many thought him dead, "but," he piously proclaimed, "the Lord Christ saved me from the pestiferous infection."[97] I found almost 1,500 letters that mentioned an outbreak of epidemic disease, the majority concerning the pest. These letters document 572 epidemics in 215 places, resulting in the death of almost 500 Jesuits. Some of the documentation is thin to say the least; Jesuits merely noted that an epidemic was occurring in a neighboring village. Juan Vitoria's account of an epidemic at Poznan in November 1563 is one of the briefest: "Some are dying from the pest here."[98] Other accounts, such as the

[92]Francisco Rodrigues, *História da Companhia de Jesus na Assistência de Portugal*, 4 vols. (Pôrto: Apostolado da Imprensa, 1931–1950).

[93]Pietro Tacchi Venturi and Mario Scaduto, *Storia della Compagnia di Gesù in Italia*, 4 vols. (Rome: Società Editrice Dante Alighieri and Edizioni La Civiltà Cattolica, 1938–1974).

[94]Paolo Bisciola, *Relatione verissima del progresso della peste di Milano: Qual principiò nel mese d'agosto 1576 e sequì sino al mese di maggio 1577* (Ancona: Alessandro Benacci, 1577).

[95]Peter Michael Brillmacher, *Serta honoris et exultationis, ad catholicorum devotionem ornandam et exhilarandam* (Cologne: Apud Gervinum Calenium et haeredes Joannis Quentelli, 1589).

[96]Antonio Possevino, *Cause et rimedii della peste, et d'altre infermità* (Florence: Appresso i Giunti, 1577). Carlos Sommervogel listed two other relevant publications in his nine-volume *Bibliothèque de la Compagnie de Jésus* (Paris: Alphonse Picard, 1890–1900): Emond Auger, *Epitre consolataire aux catholiques de Lyon, atteints de peste avec une priere à Dieu* (Lyon, 1564) and Gaspar Loarte, *Antidoto spirituale, contra la peste, dove si contengono alcun avisi, et rimedii spirituali, che possono giovare per la preservatione, et curatione di questo morbo* (Genoa, 1577). However, I was unable to locate either one, and Jean-François Gilmont, *Les écrits spirituels des premiers jésuites: Inventaire commenté* (Rome: Institutum Historicum Societatis Iesu, 1961), 268, 299, similarly states that he could not find them. For a general discussion of contemporary accounts of the plague during this period see Miguel Parets, *A Journal of the Plague Year: The Diary of the Barcelona Tanner Miguel Parets, 1651* ed., James S. Amelang (New York: Oxford University Press, 1991), 5–7; see also idem, Appendix II, "A Select List of Autobiographical Plague Accounts," 103–5.

[97]Nicolás Bobadilla, *Bobadillae monumenta, Nicolai Alphonsi de Bobadilla, sacerdotis e Societate Jesu, gesta et scripta* (Madrid: Gabrielis Lopez del Horno, 1913), 109.

[98]*Monumenta antiquae Hungariae*, 3 vols., ed. Ladislaus Lukács, 3 vols. (Rome: Institutum Historicum Societatis Iesu, 1969–1981), 1: 166, to Lainez, November 9.

longest, an eleven-page description of an epidemic at Rome in 1566,[99] provide detailed information. The best-documented epidemic is the outbreak of pest in Italy from 1575 to 1577. This began at Messina in June of 1575, swept through Sicily, arrived at Venice in November, and in the following year struck Mantua, Padua, Reggio in Calabria, Milan, and Brescia. The Jesuit Archives contain almost 350 letters with information on this epidemic.

I have used all the available evidence from Jesuit sources to construct a chronology of epidemic disease (see the appendix), modeled on the one included in Jean-Noël Biraben's *Les hommes et la peste*.[100] Biraben's seventy-five-page chronology includes outbreaks of "plague" in Europe from the sixth to the nineteenth centuries. The Jesuit sources document a large number of outbreaks in the sixteenth century not included in this chronology as well as outbreaks not mentioned in recent local studies.[101] One criticism of Biraben's chronology is that it is not rigorous enough in distinguishing between epidemics of "plague" and other diseases. My chronology attempts to overcome this problem by noting the terms used by Jesuits to describe the epidemic. If they noted that it was an epidemic of pest pure and simple (about half the cases), I have not included that information. I have included the term pest when the account included it with other terms. Another feature of this chronology is my attempt to indicate the months that the epidemic was active at a particular place rather than just note the year, as occurs in Biraben's chronology.

I make no claims that this chronology indicates the complete record of Jesuit encounters with epidemic disease in the sixteenth century. I could have missed some accounts in the 277 volumes at the Jesuit Archives and the eighty-five volumes of the *Monumenta*, although the indices in the *Monumenta* make this less likely. Furthermore, the gaps in the correspondence and the disappearance of huge numbers of letters make any claims to completeness impossible. A

---

[99]ROM 126a: 234–39, partially translated in chapter 2, p. 39.

[100]Biraben, *Les hommes*, 1: 375–449.

[101]For example, Jesuit sources note three epidemics not mentioned in the "Chronologie des Epidemies (1544–1636)" in Guy Cabourdin, *Terre et hommes en Lorraine (1550–1635)* (Nancy: Université de Nancy, 1977), 101; and they document the presence of the pest during 1553, 1560, 1561, 1571, and 1572, years not included in the chart prepared by Boris and Helga Velimirovic, "Plague in Vienna," *Reviews of Infectious Diseases* 11 (1989): 810. Similarly, Jesuit sources document a large number of outbreaks of pest not included in Edward A. Eckert, "Swiss Communities Reporting Plague Outbreaks," appendix in "Boundary Formation and Diffusion of Plague: Swiss Epidemics from 1562 to 1669," *Annales de démographie historique* (1978): 78–80.

good illustration of this is Sardinia. According to Biraben's chronology "plague" was present on this island from 1579 until 1583, but the correspondence from Sardinia during this period contains only two letters written between July 1579 and January 1585, and neither mentions any epidemic.[102] Another problem results from the unevenness in the survival of letters from different places; the Archives might contain copious correspondence from one college, almost none from another. The Jesuits established their college at Mauriac in 1563, at Chambéry in 1565; only a few letters from Mauriac have survived compared with more than 150 from Chambéry. Even when many letters from a college survive they might contain no mention of any disease although other sources indicate that the area was suffering from an epidemic. One reason for this is that many letters had a single purpose, reporting on the scandalous behavior of a member, recommending a pilgrim on his way to Rome, or seeking approval for a policy. Although these letters have survived, others from the same college that might contain information on an epidemic have not. The survival of so many accounts of epidemic disease is remarkable; public officials usually ordered the destruction of all letters (as well as other items) arriving from a pest-stricken area. As a result of this policy, on occasion Jesuits did not even try to inform their superiors of an outbreak of epidemic disease. Those who did, however, left posterity a valuable source of information on sixteenth-century society.

The huge amount of printed material on the Jesuits is just as daunting as the mountain of literature on plague. Each volume of the *Archivum Historicum Societatis Iesu*, the journal devoted to the history of the Society, includes a bibliography of recently published books and articles relevant to the history of the Jesuits; since 1983 the number of bibliographical entries in each volume has exceeded one thousand. The secondary sources on the Society of Jesus have frequent references to outbreaks of epidemic disease, usually focusing on Jesuit assistance to the sick and the dying and the subsequent death of many Jesuits—the so-called "victims of charity." On the other hand, the literature on sixteenth-century epidemics seldom mentions the Society or its members. Paolo Preto's *Peste e società a Venezia nel 1576*, for example, does not contain a single reference to the Jesuits, and A. Francesco La Cava's book on the Milanese epidemic of 1576 only mentions them twice.[103] A few local studies of epidemics

---

[102]The volume is SARD 15, containing correspondence for the years 1573–1585.

[103]A. Francesco La Cava, *La peste di S. Carlo: Note storicomediche sulla peste del 1576* (Milano: Editore Ulrico Hoepli, 1945); La Cava mentions (141) a devotional book written by the Jesuit Gaspare Loarte and (143) the deaths of two unnamed Jesuits.

do contain the odd reference to the Society,[104] but J. de Pas and M. Lanselle's article on an epidemic at Saint-Omer in 1596 is almost unique in its use of Jesuit sources.[105]

As already noted, Jesuit correspondence contains valuable information relevant to epidemics, and a book utilizing this information can contribute to an understanding of the history of disease in the sixteenth century. On the other hand, the focus of the letters was Jesuit affairs—the diseases and deaths of Jesuits and their friends and enemies, the measures taken by Jesuits to avoid infection, Jesuit assistance to the sick and dying, and the impact of the epidemic on the colleges. This focus on Jesuit affairs means that a book utilizing these letters can also contribute to an understanding of the Society of Jesus by demonstrating the Jesuit reaction to epidemic disease in the sixteenth century. Use of the Jesuit correspondence to obtain an understanding of both epidemic disease and the Society of Jesus does create a methodological problem for the historian however. Just as the *quadrimestres* contained "edifying" information, so other letters served other purposes, and the letters reveal the rhetorical tradition that influenced all forms of Jesuit communication. It is easier to observe this rhetorical tradition by reading relatively complete letters than by reading the odd snippet from them. It is also the best way to appreciate Jesuit accounts of epidemic disease.

[104]Examples include Andreina Zitelli and Richard J. Palmer, "Le teorie mediche sulla peste e il contesto veneziano," in *Venezia e la peste, 1348–1797,* 2d ed. (Venice: Marsilio Editori, 1980), 27; and Madeleine Saint-Eloy, "Quand la peste régnait à Nevers, 1399–1628," *Bulletin de philologie historique* (1966): 349, 357. A general survey that also mentions Jesuits is Lynn Thorndike, "The Blight of Pestilence on Early Modern Civilization," *American Historical Review* 32 (1927): 464.

[105]J. de Pas and M. Lanselle, "Documents sur la peste de 1596 à Saint-Omer," *Bulletin de la Société Française d'Histoire de la Médecine* 23 (1928): 206–16.

RELATIONE
VERISSIMA DEL PROGRESSO DELLA PESTE DI MILANO.

QV AL PRINCIPIO' NEL MESE D'AGOSTO
1576. e segui fino al mese di Maggio 1577. scritta dal R. D.
Paolo Bisciola Prete della compagnia del Iesù in
Milano, nella Chiesa di San Fedele.

Doue si raccontano tutte le prouisioni fatte da Monsignor Illustrissimo
Cardinal Borromeo, & di Sua Eccellenza; Senato, & Signori depu-
tati sopra la Sanità.   Doue si può imparare, il vero modo d'un per-
fetto Pastore amator del suo gregge: e come vn Principe deue go-
uernar vna Città, nel tempo di peste, cosa molto vtile.

Con vn raguaglio, del seguito della sua liberatione per fino
alli 20 . di Luglio. 1 5 7 7.

Stampata in Ancona, Et ristampata in Bologna, Per Alessandro
Benacci.   Con licenza de' Superiori, M D L X X V I I.

TWO

SOME ACCOUNTS

THE PURPOSE OF THIS chapter is to permit readers to sample some of the Jesuit accounts of epidemic disease. Aside from the intrinsic interest of these accounts, variety was the main criterion for inclusion, variety in the nature of the disease, in the intensity of the epidemic, and in the reactions by Jesuits and others. Time and place form another type of variety; included are accounts from Coimbra in 1558, Paris in 1562, Trier in 1564–1565, Rome in 1566, Seville in 1568, Prague in 1569, Vilnius in 1571–1572, Graz in 1575, Palermo in 1575, Venice in 1577, Avignon in 1577, Cluj in 1587, and Ljubljana in 1600.

COIMBRA, A PESTILENCE WITHOUT A NAME

Nicolau Gracida to Manuel Lopez　　　　　　　　　　*February 14, 1558*[1]

In the parish of São Justa, either because it is too close to the river or because a pond is next to it, Our Lord willed an outbreak of very devastating fevers like *modorra*.[2] The bishop called it a pestilence without a name. It began in São Justa and spread to neighboring parishes, but the focus of the disease remained in São Justa, and it spread so much that when it entered a house it struck everyone; quite often a man, his wife, and children were all sick in their house. Seven or eight were in bed sick in one small house, and this was not unusual.

---

[1]Gracida never dated what follows except to note that it was winter. Because this letter was one of the *quadrimestres*, that is, the letters detailing the activities of the last four months of the year, I assume the events he described took place in December 1557.

[2]For *modorra* see p. 68.

The colleges that are next to our own had so many sick that they did not have a choir or anyone to say mass. In the college of Saint Augustine the fevers affected everyone from the porter to the rector and from the vice rector to the cook. In the college of the Carmelites brothers had to come from Lisbon to help, because everyone was sick with such severe fevers that no one gave them many days to live.

Everyone was terrified to see so much death in front of their own eyes, because you did not hear anything all day except the tolling of the bells for the dead, now here, now there. From one side you heard someone mourning, from another the office of the dead. If you walked through the streets you encountered nothing but the dead. Seven deaths in one day were not unusual, and five or six shared the same funeral since there was not enough time for everyone to have their own. While the husband was dying, the wife was receiving extreme unction, and the son was confessing his sins, because there was not enough time for everything. Entire houses became completely empty. If you went through the streets you encountered no one, and if by chance you encountered someone it was not a man but the figure of a man, because everyone was yellow and discolored, incapable of standing, and terrified of death. And the stench was so bad that, according to what was said, they found toads in the houses.

During this time our fathers and brothers coped with much work in assisting the sick and dying. Some were in the middle of a meal when as a result of an urgent request they had to leave the table. Others while on their way to a house had to stop at four or five other houses before reaching their destination, because other people would stop them in the streets, and when they left the sick at one place they were brought to another. On many occasions when they arrived at a place they had to begin by listening to others who were waiting for them. Father Don Inácio and Father Miguel de Sousa, despite their other duties, worked with diligence during this time. This was very edifying to the people, since they could not find confessors anywhere except here.

Despite the strength of this disease as a result of the mercy of Our Lord only one teacher became sick. Other teachers did become sick due to the extreme cold of winter, but by the goodness of God they never missed a single lesson. As for the others, not nearly as many were sick in comparison to those in other places, but as a result of the closeness of the inferior college to São Justa we could not completely shut the door to illness. As some became sick they began to fill the infirmary. According to the doctors, to a great extent this resulted from the location of the inferior college, so the sick moved to the superior college. So many were consequently there that they filled a very large building. The weather was very cold, and beds so stretched from one side to another that it appeared to be a hospital, but they still did not have room for everyone here. The sick also filled the old infirmary, and even this was not enough until they took large parts of other houses, in such a manner that it was pitiful to see. The number in bed reached more or less thirty, and aside from these another twelve or fourteen and at times twenty were convalescing. Those convalescing seemed to be contesting the beds with the sick, because as one rose another fell in his place....

The sick always received very careful attention, for two doctors, the best, continually came to visit them. Every two of the sick had at least one brother to give them special care and to stay with them day and night. These brothers engaged in a holy combat with each other to find the best means of consoling their patients. Aside from all this Father Jorge Rijo left...his tasks in the inferior college to give special care to the sick in accordance with his customary charity and prudence in such affairs. His care visibly improved the health of the majority, and because of his great virtue he still does not relinquish this care for whoever becomes sick even now. Of all these sick no one died, for which we owe much praise to Our Lord.... No one remains in bed except for one brother named Luis Sigurado.[3] He is very sick, and we need to commend him to Our Lord. Eight are still convalescing, and none of these are in danger of a relapse. One of the convalescents has already received holy orders; he escaped death through the mercy of the Lord.[4]

PARIS, EVEN THE CATS DIED

Ponce Cogordan to Diego Lainez   *Noyon, September 29, 1562*
On the 14th of September, which was a Monday, at 11:00 at night our good Father Provincial Paschase Broët passed from this world to eternal life. Seventeen days before this, which was the 29th of August, Father Otto [Briamond]

---

[3]According to Josephus Fejér, *Defuncti Primi Saeculi Societatis Jesu, 1540–1640*, 2 vols. (Rome: Institutum Historicum Societatis Iesu, 1982), 2: 218, a Luis Segurado died at Lisbon in 1560.

[4]*Litterae quadrimestres ex universis praeter Indiam et Brasiliam locis in quibus aliqui de Societate Jesu versabantur Romam missae*, 7 vols. (Madrid and Rome: Augustinus Avrial, La Editorial Ibérica, and A. Macioce e Pisani, 1894–1932), 5: 949–51.

from Flanders died,...and a few days before this, that is, on the 25th of August, our good brother Jean de Savoie died.... On the 22nd of September, after the death of our Father Paschase, our brother Jean the cook died all alone without anyone to mourn him, and they all died from the pest.... Our house in Paris is so infected by the pest that even the animals and the cats are dead. Our brother Jean Cornilleau, our Father Master Nicolas [Bellefille], and I are still alive and together, and we have fled to Noyon.... I sent Claude [Matthieu] from Lorraine, who had cared for Jean de Savoie until he died, with five *écus d'or* on pilgrimage to Notre-Dame de Liesse so that he might survive. In addition to protectives against the pest, I gave him some remedies that he ought to use en route....

[On the Friday after the feast of Notre Dame (August 15)] seven of us left Paris on account of the pest to go to Saint-Cloud, in accordance with the opinions of our Father Paschase and everyone. On Saturday about 9:00 in the evening the pest struck Jean de Savoie.... He spent the night in the room where I slept, and during the previous night he had slept with me in the same bed. When he became ill I heard him wailing and complaining, so I asked him what was wrong. Soon afterwards I got up and put some angelica in his mouth,[5] thinking that it was only a fever. I got up again, talked to him, and decided to send him secretly with Claude to some village where no one would suspect his condition and where he could obtain care. I gave him enough to meet their needs and had them leave the house at Saint-Cloud before dawn to preserve the others. I dressed him in a white shirt, consoling him and touching him all over, and I heard both their confessions before their departure. After that Jean de Savoie lived only another thirty-six hours or thereabout. They buried him in profane ground because they could not carry him to holy ground; since everyone had fled, the only person for two leagues surrounding Saint-Cloud was a poor old woman who helped the unfortunate Claude dig the grave and carry the corpse. He gave her three livres.

After this, as I stated, I decided to send Claude to Notre Dame de Liesse. [Claude desired above all else to serve the sick at the Hôtel-Dieu at Paris.[6] I forbade him by virtue of holy obedience and ordered him to undertake the pilgrimage. He told me that he had special devotion to Saint Sebastian and asked

[5]Angelica was a herb widely used as a medicine.
[6]A hospital.

me to let him go to Paris,[7] saying, "I will die, for no one escapes once they have been with someone infected by the pest." Nonetheless, he had as much pluck as I have ever seen in a young lad.][8] [I decided to] send Master Otto with Guillaume [Lescaffette] to Tournai until the pest had ceased. They were quite happy with this decision, and Master Otto said that it would be tempting God to remain at Paris or in its environs and that only his oath of obedience held him here. Yet he asked for a day in Paris before departing.... I did not want them to pass through Paris at all for fear that they would trouble the house or infect it, ... but he said that he wanted to pick up his writings.... Before they had arrived at Paris Master Otto became ill with the pest and did not last forty hours. And poor Master Paschase and Guillaume cared for him and buried him. [Father Paschase also sent our brother Guillaume to Notre Dame de Liesse to join our brother Claude. We know nothing of them, where they are, or if they are dead.][9]

We heard this at Saint-Cloud, and because the pest was already assailing this village from all sides as a result of the large number of students and other people taking refuge there, I decided that Master Nicolas, Jean Cornilleau, and I would leave Saint-Cloud and flee a long way from Paris. The pest had infected every place for twelve to fourteen leagues all around Paris. I wrote this to our Father Paschase, informing him that we had no money and asking him to send us some. He arranged to meet me at the Bois de Boulogne, near Saint-Cloud, and brought me two hundred livres. I begged him several times to take the money from the house and to close up the house, because if something happened to him we would lose him, the house, and everything in it. He always responded that we need not fear and that he could take care of himself....

When we had the two hundred livres we went to Noyon, as I said. Our friends sent me a messenger who told us that Master Paschase was dead, that Jean was all alone, that he could come to harm, and that thieves could rob the house. I then left with traveling companions, for fear of brigands, and found the good Jean dead and a man inside the house guarding it. For guard duty of

---

[7]Saint Sebastian was widely regarded as a protector from the pestilence, but the context of Claude's devotion to the saint seems to indicate that Claude felt obliged to care for the pest-stricken.

[8]The passage in brackets occurred earlier in the letter, but I have included it here to preserve the continuity of the narrative.

[9]Idem.

fifteen days I promised him six écus d'or. I promised fifteen sous a day to a widow who had served both Master Paschase and Jean and had done the washing and cleaned the drapes in the hall. I had given some advice to Master Paschase so that I could find what was in the house should anything happen to him. When he realized that he was touched by the pest, he wrote me two similar notes, one of which I am sending to you. As you will see, he commends himself to you, to the entire Society, and to all of us who are scattered. But I have not found either the signs indicating the location of the keys or the money, if there is any, so that we face great troubles from all sides…. Meanwhile, all of us who are scattered beg you to pray and to have others pray to God for us, for we have great need of it and are in great dangers from everywhere.[10]

> I, Paschase Broët, after being touched by the pest, did not go into the pantry, and I did not touch anything. Nor did I go into the old refectory, and I did not touch any books from the library. In my room I touched some handwritten books of devotion and three or four other printed books, such as the breviary, the herbal, and the little book against the pest. I touched some money, part of which is in this wooden coffer near the window of the stall in the library. I gave the rest to Jean the cook. I commend my soul to the most reverend Lord God and to all the court of heaven, and to our reverend Father General, and to all the Society, and to all of you scattered by the pest, begging you to pray to the Lord God for me that He may forgive me for all my sins. I ask all whom I have offended to pardon me. I hope in God that by means of the prayers of the Society the Lord God through His mercy will pardon me.
>
> On the 11th of September 1562.
>
> Paschase Broët
>
> P.S. The main keys are to the right of the mat in the tailor's room.[11]

---

[10]Diego Lainez, *Lainii monumenta, epistolae et acta patris Jacobi Lainii secundi praepositi generalis Societatis Jesu*, 8 vols. (Madrid: Gabrielis Lopez del Horno, 1912–1917), 6: 416–21.

[11]Paschase Broët et al., *Epistolae P.P. Paschasii Broeti, Claudii Jaii, Joannis Codurii et Simonis Roderici Societatis Jesu* (Madrid: Gabrielis Lopez del Horno, 1903), 194. According to one account, Broët was "wounded by the pest behind both ears," that is, he had buboes behind the ears; see Lainez, *Lainii monumenta*, 6: 450, Polanco to Christopher Madrid, Trent, October 22, 1562.

Trier, Processions and Prayers, Confession and Communion

Anton Vinck to Lainez   *October 7, 1564*

We are all well, thank God, although the contagious mortality is so widespread in this city that I think no street is free from it, and it is opposite the college in the house of a bookseller. During the past few days four have died there, the mother, two children, and a maid, who was the first to die. However, we do not hear anything more. As for the environs of Trier, about fifteen days have passed since anyone died. On the advice of the archbishop we have sent home all the boarders except for two, one from Erfurt and another from Frankfurt; they are now staying in the house of Father Bertrand until the Lord disposes otherwise.

Father Andreas Valkenburg and Father Peter Haupt have been appointed confessors during this period, to their own consolation. They hear confessions in our church, where some people come who actually have the pest. They are also called to the homes of the sick and are prepared to go whenever it is necessary. They live in the house where the boarders used to stay with the nephew of Father Peter Fahr, who is the pastor of Saint Gangolf, and they have a youth who serves them. We provided them with everything they need from the kitchen of the college, and they take care to use preservatives, such as perfume in the church and in the house, and also to take them orally. They are both well and comforted by the grace of the Lord. In that same house they are preparing a room to serve as an infirmary in case (may God through his infinite mercy avert) they or any of us become sick.... We continue with the lessons in the school although with few students except for the two lowest classes, which have a large number of little boys.[12]

October 12, 1564

As for the pest, it still spreads in this city and affects almost every street. However, the number who die is not large, and many recover their health. Four died in a house opposite the college, and I have heard that some infected houses are not far away on the other side.... Thus far we are all well, thank God, and we are all extremely animated not only to receive a visit from the Lord whenever it might happen but also with a desire, should obedience permit it, to serve the sick. Some, especially among the novices, have begged me many times to permit them to go and exercise charity toward those sick

[12]GERM 145: 225.

with the pest, offering not only to beg for themselves (because I told them that they should not come to eat or sleep in the college) but also to beg for the sick....

As for the future of the pest, we hope for the best. Almost all the people have already twice confessed and taken communion. They have also gone on processions, in particular one on the 28th of September. Beginning at the cathedral, they went to the church of the Madonna where they all together on bended knee begged forgiveness. From there they went to a church outside the city called Die Heilige, that is, where Saint Agroecius, whom Pope Sylvester sent to Trier, deposited the seamless robe of the Lord, part of the holy cross, a nail, and the body of Saint Matthew the Apostle. There likewise everyone knelt and again begged forgiveness. Next they went to the church of Saint Matthew where mass was celebrated and Father Herman delivered a sermon. From there they then returned to the cathedral where for a third time they begged forgiveness and humbled themselves. All this was the result of the preaching on behalf of the senate and on behalf of the chapter of the cathedral canons, which encouraged everyone to undertake this wholeheartedly by means of charity toward the poor, prayer, and above all else confession and holy communion. Afterwards the pest did not seem to spread as much as before, and we have heard that at Cologne and Mainz, by the grace of the Lord, the pest does not do as much harm as before. In those days so great were the crowds at holy confession that nine priests were not enough to hear them in our church, although other priests also heard confessions in all the parish churches and in all the monasteries. I believe that not as many people confessed at Easter. Hence, we hope in the Lord that He will look at these people and at this city with the eyes of His mercy.[13]

December 14, 1564

We thank you very much for your charity in having prayers said in all the houses of the Society for us and for the other colleges where there is an outbreak of the pest, and thus by a singular benefit of the Lord we find ourselves healthy. The pest has not yet stopped spreading in this city, but it does not have much fury. Nonetheless, some continue to die from it. During all this time we have never stopped our usual work in the church and in the school.[14]

[13]Ibid., 230–30v.
[14]Ibid., 266.

January 8, 1565

Thanks to the Lord we are all well, and we hope that God has freed this city from the pest. Already we have heard nothing about it for several weeks. For about the past twenty-four days we have had very cold weather, with extremely calm air, so much so that not only the Mosel River but also the Rhine is so frozen that you can walk from one side to the other.[15]

Rome, The Blessed Angels of God

Anonymous   *[1566][16]*

Toward the end of last summer Rome suffered a very great and dangerous disease caused, we believe, by the infection of the water. Although the disease did not spread throughout the entire city, it nonetheless extended through a very large part of it that contains four thousand houses or more, that is, from the Madonna del Popolo to Piazza Colonna and from the Trinità [dei Monti] to the river. In the middle of this area a large amount of stagnant water collected around some vegetable gardens and became infected by some manure lying nearby. The water then slowly penetrated underground throughout all this area, which was not less than a mile long and a half mile wide, and in that manner it poisoned all the wells. In consequence everyone who drank this water [was] poisoned. In confirmation of [the belief that the water was poisonous], when twenty-five men were put to work filling in the ditches that contained the water, that evening all of them were sick and seven or eight died....[17]

One parish in this area, which was close to the gardens, felt the effects of this infection before the others. Since those who were sick were for the most part also poor, they died as a result of sheer hardship, and as a result some went to a certain gentleman who lived in the same parish, a very rich man named Paolo del Bufalo, to ask his help. The good gentleman did all he could

[15]GERM 146: 17v.

[16]According to a letter from Polanco to Juan de Vitoria, Rome, October 21, 1566, the events described below took place in September and October 1566; Juan Polanco, *Polanci complementa: Epistolae et commentaria P. Joannis Alphonsi de Polanco e Societate Jesu*, 2 vols. (Madrid: Gabrielis Lopez del Horno, 1916–1917), 1: 604.

[17]This opinion was not unanimous; according to one *avviso* heat and wind "that burned the day and night" were the causes of this epidemic. See Ludwig von Pastor, *The History of the Popes from the Close of the Middle Ages*, 40 vols. (London: Routledge and Kegan Paul, 1949–1953), 17: 106, n. 4.

to help, but seeing that he could not help the many who daily became ill, especially since his own household was full of the sick, he appealed to Cardinal Amulio [Marcantonio da Mula], who was the protector of that parish, to send some trustworthy people there to attend the needs of the poor … and others to administer the sacraments…. The cardinal felt that we would be good for both of these tasks, and he accordingly asked Our Father [General Francis Borgia] if he would send some priests. Our Father willingly agreed and sent two, who went with that gentleman and a parishioner from house to house. They did not find in the entire parish more than two healthy people who could walk through the streets; all the rest were sick. In one monastery that had one hundred nuns they found more than ninety in bed, and the ten who were not in bed were also sick, but they had left their beds to serve those who were worse. Throughout the parish in all the private houses they found five, ten, fifteen, and more sick in each house, without a single healthy person to help them. Aside from the infirmity, however, the misery was so extreme that you could not describe it; they lacked beds, medicine, food, and people who would visit them and give them even a glass of water, as a result of which they even found people who died as beasts without the sacraments…. In particular, one sick man was alone in a little house, and, because he could not help himself or ask help from others, he died miserably without the sacraments, nor would anyone have known he was dead except for the stench. They found two or more other dead people who were lying in their own filth….

As the priests and their two companions visited the sick house by house, one always distributed alms after first determining their needs, another wrote down the names of the sick, and the other consoled them and encouraged them to confess. This visit from house to house was also necessary to obtain information regarding the people who were so forsaken that they could not ask for help, … and they found very many in this condition who were just waiting hour after hour to die shut inside their own house. And it happened I do not know how many times that when they knocked on the door of a house before entering and not hearing anything were ready to leave, they remembered those who died so miserably by themselves, forced the door, and found inside ten or twelve people, husband, wife, and children, more dead than alive, lying naked on the ground since they had no bed nor even a mat on which to lie. The happiness of the sick was so great that it would be impossible to describe, for they thought those who entered their house were angels sent by God to help them in their extreme need, having lost hope in human assistance. In consequence many recognized the beneficence of God, and they could not contain their tears. Others went down on their knees, saying, "You are blessed angels of God who have today plucked our souls from hell and our bodies from the grave," and other similar words.

Although as a result of the distribution of these alms the sick appeared to have some respite, the need was nonetheless so great that more help was necessary, such as doctors, medicine, food, and people to care for them, and other similar things. Hence, it seemed appropriate to advise His Holiness [Pope Pius V]... of these needs. [With the assistance of the pope, other prelates and nobles, and the Roman government, the Jesuits organized a large relief operation.] Now I will explain the method that was established to help the sick and the results obtained from it through the goodness of God.... The area was divided into a certain number of streets, fifteen in all, and two of us had the responsibility for each street. Early every morning and again right after dinner the two went with a doctor from house to house according to the numbers marked on the doors. They wrote down the doctor's advice regarding each patient's food and then proceeded to one of the three kitchens that had been established in the three largest houses in the area. In each kitchen were one of our priests and a cook with his assistants. The two would find everything in order, and they would take a squad of twelve or more persons to carry the provisions and distribute them according to the advice of the doctor.... They all left [the kitchens] in good order with their load; one carried a sack of bread on his shoulders, one the flasks of wine, one the pot of meat, one the *pisto*,[18] one the sugar, and others the medicine, etc. At the same time you could see one of these squads in every street with such order, charity, and modesty that it astonished everyone....

According to the judgment of the doctors, more than a thousand people would have undoubtedly died without this help.... For the sake of brevity I will leave out other things. I will only say that with these results and other similar ones from this work we have much cause to thank the goodness of the Lord.[19]

---

[18] *Sic*, possibly a variant of *pesto*, but I doubt that the Jesuits brought this spicy Genoese sauce to the sick; perhaps more generally condiments.

[19] ROM 126a: 234–39, untitled. The complete account is much longer than my translated version.

SEVILLE, AN EPIDEMIC OF TUMORS[20]

Juan Loarte to Francis Borgia   *July 16, 1568*

At the end of Lent they began to say that some people here had become sick and died from tumors, but they were so few in number and so low in rank that it seemed nothing. Then, when it increased dramatically, the municipal council undertook to provide a house for the sick outside the city where the wounded[21] could receive care. When the first house established for this purpose proved inadequate, the Count of Monte Agudo, who is the royal officer here,... managed to send the sick to the hospital of La Sangre, which is outside the city in a very large and comfortable building. He was very diligent in arranging for all the wounded to go there because they could receive treatment with less trouble and danger to the city. He sent barber-surgeons, apothecaries, and nurses, all with good salaries, to attend to their physical health and arranged for priests to attend to their spiritual health. Although some of us helped, because the number of the wounded was so large we could not provide enough assistance for all.

If my memory is correct, more than twenty-five hundred persons died before the feast of Saint John [June 24]. Many more would have perished had the council not taken so much trouble in removing the sick from the city; although many left the city and fled to neighboring places (where also some people began to be infected), nonetheless Seville has such a very large population and the heat was so severe that the mercy of the Lord seemed to quell the fire of this illness. Almost all the sick and dead have been women, children, slaves, and a few men, all poor people. I do not believe that twenty died among the principal people and the middling sort. From the feast of Saint John to the feast of Saints Peter and Paul [June 29] the situation did not improve. Then the situation became worse until the past five or six days, when it seemed to improve a great deal, because in the hospital where previously twenty to thirty people died every day, in the past four or five days only two people died even though the hospital contained more than three hundred. The sick convalesce and recover their health more than before, which indicates less virulence than

---

[20]That is, *landres,* meaning tumors or in modern Spanish swellings in the lymph glands, or possibly buboes. In this letter Loarte does not use the Spanish term *peste* to describe this epidemic, but some Jesuits did, while others used the term *pestilencia.* See, for example HISP 108: 278, Diego Avellaneda to Borgia, Granada, June 28, and 109: 109, Fonseca to Borgia, Seville, October 22.

[21]*Heridos,* that is, wounded with a tumor.

previously. Moreover, they have removed fewer wounded people in these four or five days, since before they removed thirty or forty a day, whereas in those four or five days of improvement they have not removed fifteen. In consequence, we definitely believe that as it ceases Our Lord wishes to use His mercy with this city, giving it spiritual health combined with the physical....

At first they were uncertain about the nature of this disease, because most of the doctors who were consulted said that it was not tumors. As a result the priests went to hear the confessions of the sick with little fear and precaution. This was the reason, as they say, why Father Alonso de Velasco contracted this disease from a sick person whose confession he heard. He immediately felt much heat in the arm and hand that he had placed over the tumor[22] of the sick at the time of saying the gospel, and the heat developed into a fever and produced a tumor[23] in the [groin].[24] After four days Our Lord took him to Himself on the 19th of May. We had taken great care, but the house was so full of new people with so little room in such great heat that Father Gregorio de Mata...immediately arranged to send some of us to the other colleges of the province. He began with the novices and the old who seemed to be at greater risk.... Nine fathers [who] were stronger [and] less likely to contract this disease remained with fifteen brothers, so in total we number twenty-four.[25]

Prague, Waiting out an Epidemic

Annual letter by Georg Ware   *August 30, 1569*

Although as a rule the climate in Prague is very healthy, every year a tendency to pestilential disease is noticeable, either because very many people of the most varied type come here or for other reasons. During the past summer and winter the pest fiercely raged for a long time both here and in other cities. As a result we had to close the school from August 2 to January 3. Even though previously high dignitaries and some good friends had advised our superiors to close the school, for a long time they could not decide to do so on account of their zeal for the advancement of the students in piety and wisdom. Finally, the

---

[22]Instead of *landre* Loarte here uses *postema.*

[23]*Landre* this time.

[24]Loarte stated that Velasco had a tumor in *la vedeja*, a word now meaning forelock, an unlikely location for a tumor; two other accounts state that the tumor was in *la ingle*, that is, the groin. See HISP 108: 254, 278, Avellaneda to Borgia, Granada, June 3 and 28.

[25]Ibid., 339–39v.

superiors prudently resolved to dismiss the students and to keep all of us in the college. They reached this decision because a great danger threatened us; a student at the college contracted this disease and suffered from it for two months, and most of the boarding students either willingly stayed away or were summoned by their parents.

As long as the destructive power of the pest threatened, we could not perform the normal ministries of the Society. The few Catholics here had already received the sacraments in our church before the pest had struck, and the others were unfortunately heretics who had no desire for this help. Moreover, almost all of those with whom we could have had useful discussions to the greater honor of God had left Prague. For these reasons we became concerned and troubled that we could not harvest as much in the salvation of souls this year as we had in past years. Because the infinite wisdom of God had so ordered it in the meantime we decided to concentrate on establishing virtue more firmly in our souls....

When soon after this we learned that the pest had quickly killed a novice, we began to think a bit about death. Our superiors spared no pains in their diligence and care; they closely followed the advice of the doctor, who is very devoted to us, and agreed on many appropriate precautionary measures—it would take too much space to list them all here. Through frequent confession and communion and through incessant prayer we wanted to prepare ourselves so that the Lord might find us watchful. In doing this we did not neglect to preserve our bodies to the honor of God by means of various remedies. All this rather astonished some Bohemians; in the face of the contagion, confident in God's predestination, many of them not only stood around the corpses of the dead but even embraced and kissed them.

After a break of one month a second person became sick in the house and succumbed to the violence of the disease. Now the remaining members of the Society could not only imagine death but also with their own eyes gaze upon the face of the recently expired brother, while they still kept busy with the above-mentioned tasks. Then just when it appeared safe, a third Jesuit, who had appeared to be the strongest of all and who had helped the other in his illness, became sick and died after only a few days. At the end of October at last the Lord brought an end to the pest in our college, although in Prague and in the surrounding countryside the number dying was still rather high, and a great solitude reigned in the streets and squares of the city since none of those who had sought safety in flight had returned. We remained shut in the rooms of our house, and we received in the house of God the sweet nourishment of the body and blood of Christ. We continued to fortify and prepare ourselves with properly founded virtues so that when the time came to mix with others once again we would not be contaminated.[26]

Vilnius, A Jesuit College in Heaven

Francisco Sunyer to Jerónimo Nadal   *October 25, 1571*

On the 16th of October I wrote to you of my arrival in Vilnius. Now I am forced to write to you of my flight from Vilnius on the 22nd with fourteen brothers, because the Lord took Father Lucas [Crassovius] on the 21st about 9:00 at night. They believe that he died from the pest because he became sick on the 19th and died on the 21st, and they afterwards found the sign of the pest, which had not fully emerged on the surface, making his death sudden and unexpected. We think that he contracted that disease from hearing confessions in the church. In the college I left Father [Stanislaus] Varsevic, who did not want to leave with the others because he has been preaching ever since the beginning of the pest. With him is Father Ivan Conar, whom I brought from Pultusk to study; he is taking the place of Father Lucas, preaching after dinner and hearing confessions when needed. I left seven brothers with these two, while Father Balthassar [Hostovinus] and two others are with the bishop. Now twenty-three of us are at a farm belonging to the bishop, wondering with much solicitude about those left in Vilnius and also uncertain about what the Lord wants to do with us, since we all stayed in an infected house.

If only Father Varsevic had written to me well before my arrival in Vilnius, informing me of the situation and the danger there and telling me where I and my companions should go, but instead he wrote that we could safely enter Vilnius. When I arrived with my company on the 7th of this month, the bishop was not a little annoyed, and he wrote to me that if I had not already left Vilnius I should do so at once. I did this the day after I received his letter, since Father Lucas had died in the meantime. Now that the bishop has heard of our arrival at his farm he has again written asking me to come to him, but for good reasons I have excused myself.

---

[26]Alois Kroess, *Geschichte der böhmischen Provinz der Gesellschaft Jesu*, 2 vols. (Vienna: Ambr. Opitz, 1910–1927), 1: 182–84.

On the 18th Paulus Sarbinius and Balthassar Gersius arrived from Pultusk with the news that on the feast of Saint Matthew [September 21] the school at Pultusk was closed on account of the pest that had begun to spread in that city. Hence, you can see that we have reached those last days when the Lord threatens His Gospel. You can also see the loss of a priest that we have suffered in Vilnius at a time when we want many more priests. Although most of those who were in Vilnius have departed, I do not know what might happen to those who remain there, and I am not a little concerned for them.... I hope that the cold weather which follows will stop this disease, and that they will open the schools at both Vilnius and Pultusk at least after Christmas, if not before.[27]

February 9, 1572

On the 19th of January all the brothers who had scattered on account of the pest were back in the college. When we thought we were safe and able to recover a bit from the past troubles, it pleased the Lord to take Vincenzo Cassio from us on the 24th. He had cared for the two who died from the pest.[28] Not content with this, the Lord wanted to go further and take Stanislaus Mielecki from us on the 7th of February. He was an excellent brother from an illustrious family. He died after only two days of illness, and the signs indicate that he died from the pest. May God be praised for everything, for we do not doubt that He has done this for our instruction and help, and before strengthening this college on earth He wanted first to establish one in heaven so that with such great benefits we are more animated to respond in our vocation to whatever great task the Lord imposes on us.[29]

GRAZ, JESUIT SORCERERS

Heinrich Blessem to Lorenzo Maggio   *March 5, 1575*

An acute and malignant fever rages somewhat at Graz. It disturbed the synagogue of the Lutherans in particular, for three of their teachers and the rector died, and it threatened the life of other teachers and about eighty students. As a result they closed their school and dismissed their students. They attempted to blame the Jesuits for causing this infection, evidently by poisoning their well,

[27]GERM 152: 120–20v.

[28]In addition to Father Lucas Crassovius, Grzegorz Jurgiewicz, a coadjutor, died on September 19.

[29]GERM, 134 I: 82.

but careful cleaning revealed nothing. A certain teacher, before he died, blamed the Jesuits for causing his death. Whence the rumor circulates again that Jesuits are sorcerers who are able to poison and to kill people just by looking at them. This teacher had once spoken to some of us, and recently he had even taken part in a debate with us. As a result one of their teachers, namely Marbachius, a man in most respects learned, eloquent, and modest, but an infamous Lutheran, had proposed to speak to us and to confer with us concerning religion, but this rumor terrified him, and in consequence he and many others do not dare come near us, even those who are greatly at odds with their colleagues for not being, as they say, pure Lutherans. However, these rumors concerning us have already vanished, and the doctors and other serious men consider it a mystery that this disease struck almost only the Lutherans, when neither in the city nor among their neighbors did it appear notable. May the most holy God deign to direct all things according to His glory.[30]

Palermo, A Chronicle of Death and Divine Providence

Paolo Achille to Everard Mercurian   *July 5, 1575*

The rumor of the pest continues to increase, although some people do not want to call it the pest. The city has established a hospital for it outside the city where they carry the sick people whom they suspect of having this disease. They have asked me for at least one priest to hear the confessions of the sick there, and with the advice of my consultors I sent Father Paolo Mantovano with a novice as a companion. They have been there seven days, and they are well, thank the Lord. In the college we are well as far as this disease is concerned, but Father Giovanni Domenico Candella, master of the novices, has had a fever since Sunday. We have large crowds at confession, and we are called to different parts of the city to hear the confessions of the sick, whom we have not neglected, thank the Lord.[31]

July 16, 1575

In my last letter I wrote that as a result of a request from the magistrate and councilors of this city, with the advice of my consultors I sent Father Paolo Mantovano to hear confessions at the hospital which they had established for

---

[30]GERM, 136 I: 146.
[31]ITAL 148: 46–46v.

the care of those who have the pest. At the end of ten days it pleased the Divine Beneficence to put an end to his labors and to conduct him, as we piously hope, to eternal rest. When he was sick it seemed to my consultors that we should send another priest to help with the confessions, and at present this priest is very sick from the pest and in great danger, and the companion whom I sent with Father Paolo, a novice, is also sick at present with a very high fever; may Our Lord Jesus Christ be thanked for everything. In this college we are all well, thank God. The confessors are very busy hearing the confessions of the healthy who come to our church and those of the sick in different parts of the city. By order of the magistrate we have closed the school. Until now we have preached in our church, but the Lord President told me the other day that he thought we should stop preaching for a few days, and so we have suspended it for now.[32]

August 2, 1575

When the city requested some priests to hear the confessions of the sick, ... I sent two, Father Paolo Mantovano and Father [Diego] Martinez, and in the space of twenty days both finished their labors and went to enjoy, as we piously hope, that eternal rest which Our Lord has promised to those who labor here through His love. Moreover, the city has ordered that some of the sick stay in their houses, and it urgently requested that we send some priests to hear the confessions of these people. Since my consultors were of the opinion that we could not neglect this charitable duty, we sent two priests, Father [Francesco] Costantino and Father Gabriele [Puteo], who now live separately from us. We hope that Our Lord will preserve them through His immense mercy. All this has been, however, of much edification to the Lord and to the entire city; may the glory be to Jesus Christ Our Lord. In this college of Palermo we are all healthy, thank the Lord.... Over the past two days it seems as if the pest has declined, may the most holy will of Our Lord God be done in all things, for He disposes and orders everything in accordance with great wisdom and goodness. More people confess and take holy communion in our church than ever before. May Jesus Christ Our Lord be thanked for everything.[33]

[32]Ibid., 89–89v.
[33]Ibid., 151–52.

Achille to Alfonso Salmeron   *August 9, 1575*

[The two priests whom I sent] to hear the confessions of the sick in their homes...stay separately in a place apart from this college but next to it. They are well, thank the Lord, and every day they go to hear the confessions of the sick throughout the city. This is a great spiritual help to those poor, sick people and of edification to the entire city. May everything be to the glory of Jesus Christ Our Lord. In the city the disease now increases, now diminishes; eight or ten a day die from it. Many others are taken to the hospital for those with the pest....

P.S. During the three days since I have written this letter the pest has greatly declined, because they have not taken more than four to the hospital, and our fathers have not heard the confessions of more than five sick people in the city. We hope that it will further decline with each passing day, with the grace of Jesus Christ Our Lord.[34]

Achille to Mercurian   *August 17, 1575*

It has pleased Our Lord to take to Himself Father Francesco Costantino, who was hearing the confessions of the sick in the city,...and he died from the pest after an illness lasting three days. He was staying separately with another priest and their companions. May the blessed God be glorified for everything. We are thinking of sending the others away from that place to another outside the city for their health.... In the city the pest has diminished greatly, for during the past four days they have only taken two to the hospital. We hope that Our Lord will free this city from this contagious disease through His infinite mercy. In our church we have had large crowds of penitents especially on feast days. On the day of the Assumption of the most glorious Mother of Our Lord [August 15] eight hundred people communicated there, and two hundred on the day before, which was a Sunday. May everything be to the glory of Jesus Christ Our Lord. We are also called to confess the sick throughout the city, but we take care of ourselves as much as possible with the grace of the Lord.[35]

[34]Ibid., 182–83.
[35]Ibid., 200–200v.

September 12, 1575

After the death of Father Costantino his four companions, one priest and three brothers, were sent to a place outside the city reserved for those suspected of having the pest. There the priest heard the confessions of many of these people and gave them communion every Sunday. This priest, whose name is Father Gabriele Puteo from Mallorca, and two of those brothers fell sick with the pest four days ago. Today they are in good spirits, but we do not know what will be the outcome of their illness; may the Lord be thanked for everything. In the college we have ten sick people but not with a contagious disease, thank the Lord....

P.S. The situation regarding the pest in the city is not going very well.... Every day they are taking eight, ten, or twelve to the hospital.[36]

September 19, 1575

I previously wrote about Father Gabriele Puteo who was sick with the pest; he rendered his soul to his creator last Friday, and we hope in the infinite Divine Beneficence that he will receive his rest in paradise. He was a good servant of the Lord especially endowed with the virtue of obedience. May Jesus Christ Our Lord be glorified in everything. The other two brothers, companions of that father, are still sick with the pest but better, and we hope that they will recover through the grace of the Lord. The situation regarding the pest in this city continues much the same as I have written previously, that is, varying, now increasing, now diminishing, in such a manner that even the doctors remain mystified and do not know what to say. The air is not corrupt;... may the most holy will of blessed God be done in all things.... Our confessors are very busy hearing confessions of the healthy in our church, especially on feast days, and the sick throughout the city; may everything be to the glory of His Divine Majesty.[37]

October 18, 1575

In this college we have had many sick, but through the grace of the Lord all are better except for one novice, whose illness caused some suspicion of contagion, but we soon saw that it was not the case, may the Lord be praised. Those

---

[36]Ibid., 320–20v.
[37]Ibid., 340–40v.

two brothers who were the companions of those fathers who heard the confessions of the *sick*... are better, although they have not completely recovered their health; thanks to Jesus Christ Our Lord.... The contagious disease in the city always varies, now increasing, now diminishing; during the past three days it has increased somewhat; may the most holy will of Our Lord be done in everything.[38]

November 1, 1575

One of those who is at the hospital for those with the pest is very sick; it was necessary to cut once again the wound of the pest. The other is all right; thank the Lord for everything. The pest in the city has not gone well for the past four days; it always varies, now good, now bad. May the most holy will of Our Lord be done in all things.[39]

November 10, 1575

Brother Giovanni Antonio Olivieri, who was the companion of Father Costantino and Father Gabriele, had finished the time of purgation (as they call it here)[40] to return to the college. On the same day that he was supposed to come to the college, which was last Monday, he rendered his soul to his creator. His illness was a fever that did not last more than forty hours; it started Saturday night... and lasted until the 21st hour of Monday. We do not know if he had the pest. He left much good edification in both the college and that place where he remained for two and a half months. May Jesus Christ Our Lord be thanked for everything.... The situation regarding the pest in this city has been good for the past four days; during the past week it was very bad. May the most holy will of the blessed God Our Lord be done in all things.[41]

Venice, Finally a Clean Bill of Health

Domenico Cosso to Mercurian   *January 18, 1577*

I have written to you more than twenty-one times, by means fair and foul, especially after the death of good Father Cesare Helmi, which was on the night

---

[38]ITAL 149: 26–26v.

[39]Ibid., 79–79v.

[40]Obviously a type of quarantine for those infected with the pest.

[41]ITAL 149: 108–8v. The pest at Palermo continued for another half year until May 1576; see ITAL 151: 106, Achille to Mercurian, May 14.

before the feast of Saint Peter in Chains, the 1st of August, when I had to take over the government of this house, as ordered and desired by that father.[42] I immediately wrote of this to you and to the provincial, informing you of the state of all of us and our affairs and of the condition of this poor and very afflicted city, as prudently as I could and should in these calamitous times, with all the routes surrounding this city strictly closed and guarded day and night with such diligence that no one of whatever rank, status, and condition could pass. Even the letters went straight into the fire without respect or possibility of remission, and whoever had enough courage to approach the blockades had to have artillery....

Now through the mercy and grace of God Our Lord the epidemic has abated so much that ever since the 1st of January we have had a clean bill of health [*carta bianca*]. We moreover hope that this situation will continue, if it pleases His Divine Majesty, although we do not a little fear of the coming spring, especially since we do not see that change in the manner of living, which ought to accompany such a great and terrible scourge sent by the blessed God to achieve such a change. We are all praying that it will please the Lord to look at us with the most merciful eyes of His Divine Majesty.

Because I heard that the couriers have started to operate, I decided to write this to you, greeting you and all the other fathers and brothers in Rome and giving you news of the clean bill of health and of all of us in this house. We are here, Father, through the pure goodness and singular grace of the most merciful God Our Lord, all alive and safe and sound, always provided, governed, guarded, and strengthened almost miraculously by His Divine Majesty, with the continual and very particular care of an excellent and most loving Father, amid such continuous troubles and dangers and in such terrible events and horrendous skirmishes. This very potent epidemic (with the permission or wish of the omnipotent God Our Lord) has caused such mortality and such slaughters in this poor and afflicted city that the number of dead from the beginning of the pest until now between the city and the lazaretto (according to those who have kept us diligently informed) is 140,000,[43] including fifty-

---

[42]Cosso either left the Society in 1578 or was dismissed from it for (I suspect) usurping the authority of the rector Helmi upon his death; see ITAL 153: 100, Mario Beringucci to [Mercurian], Venice, February 6, 1577.

[43]An exaggeration for the population of Venice at this time was 180,000. According to Paolo Preto, "Peste e demografia: L'età moderna: Le due pesti del 1575–77 e 1630–31," in *Venezia e la Peste, 1348–1797,* 2d ed. (Venice: Marsilio Editori, 1980), 97, the number of dead was 46,721.

eight of the best physicians, twenty-eight parish priests, and more than two hundred other priests.

Oh what very great compassion and grief, together with fear, to see the houses, the shops, and the churches closed and barricaded with crossed planks across the doors as a sign and a barrier! The city was almost deserted, so that it was unusual to see some poor men in a street, each fleeing the others as if they feared their shadows. There were very few masses, and you could not find a confessor, nor could you even find hosts to purchase for the sacrifice of the altar; some of the few priests here came to our house asking for them. So many, many barges full of dead bodies packed like sardines [*composti come le sardelle*] and so many barges full of infected goods passed by that the wind brought a great stench and stink, even from the lazaretto as a result of the multitude of bodies and the burning of infected goods. People consequently had to close all the windows and doors on that side, because the danger of infection was great, and many were infected in this manner, which caused great fear among everyone.

With all this and with only four poor priests, namely, Father Bartolomeo Monaco, Father Francesco Allegri, whom I chose to help me govern the house, Father Bartolomeo Franci, and myself, Father Domenico Cosso, through the singular grace and help given us by God through His mercy we have never failed to help others with the usual exercises of our Society, confessing, communicating, saying mass, and exhorting, with the church open every day. Almost all the other churches were closed and barricaded and hence deprived of masses and confessors, but we even heard confessions when we were barricaded, for with the permission of the magistrates we kept the church open and listened to confessions, the penitents standing almost in the middle of the church behind a barricade made with benches. We said mass every day, and even those with the pest came to us for confession; we spoke to them face to face as if we did not know of their condition. God through His grace wanted to preserve us safe and happy, and He took much particular care of us.

Oh, my dear Father, I have seen and experienced that a very great difference truly exists between doing the meditation on death from a distance with your imagination and doing it with death before your eyes day and night, every hour, every moment, but the wretched person that I am did not profit from this as much as he should.[44]

[44]ITAL 153: 52–52v.

AVIGNON, PEST?

Jean Pionneau to Annibal Coudret *September 2, 1577*

This serves to inform you of the visit that Our Lord was pleased to make to this college just recently, giving us every occasion to recognize His power and to hope that His mercy will spare us more abundantly after having endured the afflictions that He was pleased to send us…. Some soldiers from the camps engaged against Nîmes and Montpellier wanted to come to this town to recover, some from wounds and others from fevers. The town willingly received those who could fit in the space available at the hospital…. This gave us another opportunity to exercise the ministries of the Society, and we therefore in the first place gave them what physical assistance we could, not forgetting the spiritual assistance as well…. There was never any suspicion, much less any appearance of contagion, because they only had long-lasting fevers, but experience has shown the contrary, for those of us who had more often visited them, the servants at the hospital, and several people of quality who had visited and cared for them fell very sick. No one could ever presume that any danger could come from contagion since these were ordinary illnesses, but in the end we discovered that this fever had I know not what poisons.

There you have what according to my judgment is the cause and origin of what happened in less than ten days; that is, from the 5th to the 14th of August fourteen of ours fell grievously ill. The air itself seemed to generate such fevers, for several who had not had any contact with the sick also became ill and continue to become ill from the same disease. Among us the illness has been a continual fever, violent and intense, which on the seventh or at the latest on the fourteenth day resulted in the death of several. The first was Louis [Masert] who died on the 12th of August; we believe that God has given him a beautiful grace, drawing him to Himself to keep him from withdrawing from His sacred service.[45] The second was Father [Pierre] Rostille who died on the 20th in a very violent frenzy. The third was Father Mathieu [Thomas] who died on the 25th, the feast of Saint Louis, to whom he was greatly devoted, and his departure occurred by means of an election of the saints. The fourth was Pierre Gaillard, who died on the 26th. The fifth was Master Jacques Chaulet, who died yesterday, the 1st of September. The sixth was Vincent Pregert, who died today. I believe that not for a long time or perhaps never has a college of

[45]Apparently Masert was going to leave the Society.

the Society suffered six deaths in the space of twenty-two days. But to those of us who are here it seems that we have received much grace from Our Lord, who is content with these six, for all the others who were sick except for me, who have been sick for fifteen days, were in very evident danger of death according to the judgment of several doctors.... By God's grace we have not forgotten anything that could assist the sick in any way possible, for ordinarily we have two doctors and very often three who visit us. Nor have we spared anything in obtaining all that was necessary, and we have hired five or six servants to care for the sick.[46]

Pionneau to Mercurian   *September 19, 1577*

The situation does not improve because many people continually become sick and die, so that during the past two months more than seven hundred people have died at Avignon. The multitude of children who die proves that the air must be infected, because they are more likely to receive the corruption. However, it is certainly not the pest, and in consequence no one flees, which is why it would not be permissible or expedient for us to leave. We would be reproved for being the first to flee, and by fleeing we would indicate that some danger of contagion existed among us and in our house. Besides it is not safe to leave the city, for yesterday one league from here, Huguenots took all the mules, twelve in all, of the Cardinal of Armagnac. I believe that God has used this stratagem in not sending the pest to Avignon but only this acute fever, so that everyone would voluntarily remain here [and not risk capture by the Huguenots]. May His name be blessed in eternity.[47]

Pionneau to Coudret   *October 7, 1577*

After God had given us some respite for ten or twelve days,... Father [Jean] Beautricet became ill and two days afterwards Caliste [Felin] did the same. Already our college was battered and afflicted from all sides, for some were sick, others convalescing, and others suffering from such long labors that we scarcely had time to breathe.... It is difficult to find someone to care for the sick, and besides all this Charles Lingonet and Jehan Bernardices became ill at the same time.... We sent them to their relatives and thus got rid of them. We

[46]GAL 89: 271–72.
[47]Ibid., 285.

then saw in addition that this disease carries its contagion with it, and in a short time God called to Himself Father Beautricet and Caliste, one on the 11th and the other on the 13th day of their illness. The town has experienced these scourges everywhere to such an extent that from the 1st of August until the 1st of October one estimates that fifteen hundred people have died in Avignon.... We have moved the sick to a garden for a change of air.... There they receive help from one of ours and from some women of the village who are accustomed to working in such service, for men are not available here for this work.[48]

Pionneau to Mercurian   *Pont-à-Sorgue, October 15, 1577*
Several days ago I came here with seven or eight of ours to a castle called Pont-à-Sorgue, a league and a half from Avignon, in the house of the Monsignor of Santo Sisto, which is the same palace of the ancient popes. Today another of ours became ill; he had cared for many others, and we brought him here for a change of air, but now we had to send him back to Avignon. Five are sick now, and this infirmity reigns throughout the town. They fear that it might change to the pest.[49]

Pont-à-Sorgue, October 31, 1577
By the grace of God we now have in our house a bit of respite from the diseases. I do not know if it will please Him to recommence them a third time. His will be done. In the city the illnesses always continue. We are divided into five places, three in the college to guard it and keep it clean, three all-healthy or half-healthy in a garden of the Guadagni, another three already free from continual fever except one in another garden, two at Vaison[-la-Romaine], and ten at Pont-à-Sorgue, where our intention is, with the help of God, to recover the relics of Israel.[50]

Pont-à-Sorgue, October 31, 1577[51]
The disease has been and still is universal throughout the entire city, but none of our friends who often came to visit our sick became ill, and an infinity of

---

[48]Ibid., 298, to Coudret.
[49]Ibid., 310.
[50]Ibid., 332.
[51]Pionneau wrote two letters to Mercurian on October 31, the second one *soli*, that is, only for the eyes of General Mercurian; ibid., 333v–34.

other people whom we do not know have died and still die every day. Moreover, I am certain that of the approximately fifteen persons who have during this entire period cared for those of us who were sick (some of whom still continue to do so) none has become sick by the grace of God, nor have any had anything wrong with them. What is more, our sick all died on the 7th, 9th, 11th, 13th, 17th, and 21st days of their illness, and many others in the city died on the 4th, which is a more apparent sign of the pest. Nonetheless, the deputies of health and other councilors have considered us many times in their deliberations, and they have decided to quarantine us in our college as infected with the pest, without any consideration for the others in the college. When five of ours died, they wanted to make people believe that twelve or fifteen died. They spread a rumor throughout the city that we had welcomed one of ours who came with the pest from Lyon, that we had buried him at night, and that this person had been responsible for spreading the disease throughout the city.

Cluj,[52] Twenty Dead

Mateusz Strus to Claudio Aquaviva   *February 12, 1587*

As soon as I had recovered from the pest, I seriously thought I would write something to you concerning our situation. However, the difficulties in sending letters and the uniqueness of the occasion impeded me. Before the month of July in the year 1586 there were thirty persons in this college; twenty are now missing from that number, for in the space of two months the pest killed eighteen, except for one who died from consumption. Of the remaining two, one died in October from paralysis, and the other in January from the aftereffects of the pest. Although I do not doubt that you have already heard of the time and manner of these deaths, nevertheless, because I was present, partly active and partly passive, during these events by no means do I want to neglect to send you a catologue of all the dead. Therefore, the dead are:

1. Georg Alman on July 17 at almost 3:00 in the afternoon, pest under the armpit and petechia.

2. Paulùkus Kiniscovic, Lithuanian, a scholar in the course of philosophy, on July 19 about the time of vespers, pest in the groin and petechia.

3. Albert Volucki, Polish, professor of syntax, on July 20 about 10:00 at night, pest in the groin and petechia.

---

[52]In Romania, formerly Kolozvár and Klausenburg, Latin Claudiopolis.

4. Albert Brantmaier, Prussian, scholar in the course of philosophy, on July 28 at 9:00 in the morning, pest in the groin and petechia.

5. Johan Burman, Prussian, professor of superior grammar, on July 29 at dawn, pest in the groin.

6. Urban Schipper, Prussian, carpenter,[53] on the 29th of July at 6:00 in the afternoon, pest in the groin.

7. Father Johan Ardulph, German, prefect of the novices, etc., on July 31 about noon, pest in the groin.

8. Father Ferdinando Capecio, Italian, rector of the college, on July 31 at 5:00 in the afternoon, pest in the groin, two carbuncles on the right shin, and black petechia.

9. Michael Viller, Prussian, carpenter, on August 1 about the time of vespers, pest in the groin.

10. Johan Elbing, Prussian, a scholar in the course of philosophy, financial assistant to the prefect of the seminary, on August 3 at dawn, carbuncle on the breast and petechia.

11. Jonas Credik, Prussian, professor of humanities, on August 4 at 10:00 at night, carbuncle on the groin, arm, foot.

12. Adam Tensier, Prussian, carpenter, on August 5 at 4:00 in the afternoon, pest in the groin.

13. Jan Psarski, Polish, tailor, on August 6 at 7:00 in the afternoon, pest in the groin, carbuncle under the knee, who ... died because of the pain in passing urine.

14. Mateusz Zaleski, Polish, professor of inferior grammar, on August 7 at 7:00 in the afternoon, pest in the groin and petechia.

15. Kazimierz, Polish, coadjutor, on August 8 at 6:00 in the morning, carbuncle on the groin, neck, shin, and violent bleeding from the nose.

16. Michal Ripinensis, Polish, prefect of the seminary and professor of poetry and rhetoric, on August 14 about 7:00 in the afternoon, pest in the groin.

17. Father Girolamo Fanfoni, Italian, professor of the course of philosophy, on August 17 at dawn, pest in the groin.

---

[53] *Arcularius,* more precisely a casket maker. The carpenters or casket makers would have been Jesuit temporal coadjutors, or lay brothers.

18. Father Peter Silvanus, Hungarian, on July 18 about the middle of the night, consumption.

19. Father Jorge Torres on October 28, paralysis.

20. Wawrzyniec Horoschow, Polish, coadjutor, about 11:00 at night on January 22. He was miserably sick for almost six whole months from the pest that he contracted in August, for the tumors and carbuncles, with which he was burdened on both feet, were not purged well, and his entire right foot wasted away.[54] This was the cause of extreme and long-lasting pain. However, the unexpected flowing of the pus,[55] not the negligence of the surgeon, …impeded the sufficient purgation of the tumors and carbuncles. After this, besides the intolerable pain in his foot, his wounded flesh putrefied in many places on account of his continual reclining (for he could do little else), so that he was a living corpse. This was the result of divine will and preordination, for when he was outside the Society he sought to oppose the Lord God, so that in this life he suffered for his sins.[56]

LJUBLJANA, A ZEALOUS LUTHERAN AND THE PERSECUTING ANGEL

Henricus Vivarius to Aquavia   *January 10 1600*

During the last year our college endured many difficulties, for many of us suffered from varied and long-lasting diseases, and these gave us much trouble for almost the entire year. Two brother coadjutors, Johan Waltz and Ludovicus Messerius, were weakened by disease and at last piously went to sleep in the Lord…. Besides this trouble with diseases among ourselves, another greater disaster, completely lamentable and quite deadly, prevailed for a long time, affecting not only us but also the entire Duchy of Krain. A pestiferous epidemic, which a zealous Lutheran introduced during the previous winter…, lay hidden in the corners of one or another house until the beginning of summer, when it erupted very seriously and spread so far and wide that scarcely a corner in the entire duchy of Krain remained safe. It so consumed everyone in

---

[54]Necrosis, meaning the death or decay of body tissues, is a symptom of the bubonic plague. See Jack D. Poland, "Plague," in *Infectious Diseases: A Modern Treatise of Infectious Processes*, ed. Paul D. Hoeprich (Philadelphia: Harper and Row, 1983), 1235, for a graphic portrayal of this symptom.

[55]Strus uses the Latin *materia*.

[56]*Monumenta antiquae Hungariae*, ed. Ladislaus Lukács, 3 vols. (Rome: Institutum Historicum Societatis Iesu, 1969–1981), 3: 11–12.

a miserable way that more than three hundred of our students died. Very many sensibly fled; the image of death and mourning was everywhere. At least in our Ljubljana the pest has now waned a little. In the countryside, however, the persecuting angel has not yet ceased, because the harshness of the cold during this winter is unusual for these parts. Grave damage occurred to our school from the pest since it remained closed throughout the summer. We closed the college and sent ours to safer places in Carinthia and Styria; all the youth vanished.[57]

[57]GERM 179: 10.

THREE

———

EPIDEMIC DISEASE

THE SOCIETY OF JESUS encountered a variety of diseases, some of them restricted to its own members and some affecting the wider community and hence making them epidemic. Jesuit descriptions of epidemic disease often lacked enough precision for retrospective diagnoses, but the evidence indicates probable outbreaks of influenza and possible outbreaks of typhus and smallpox. Most of the epidemics were of pest, that is, the Latin *pestis* and its equivalent in other languages. An analysis of these epidemics demonstrates that while many aspects of the disease concur with the modern scientific knowledge of the bubonic plague, other aspects reveal a disease that does not fit this knowledge. The most significant of these aspects is the contagious nature of the disease, spreading from person to person in a manner that suggests the absence of rats as well as fleas, be they rat fleas or human fleas.

MORBIDITY AMONG THE JESUITS

Jesuits often discussed their illnesses and outbreaks of epidemic disease in letters to superiors. One reason for the frequency of these accounts of morbidity is Ignatius Loyola's concern for the physical well-being of his followers. As noted by W. W. Meissner, after his conversion and during his pilgrim years Loyola "ruined his health and destroyed his body in his impatient and immoderate zeal for self-abnegation and severe penances." As founder and first general of a new religious order he did not want his followers to make the same mistake and render themselves unfit for an active life of Christian service.[1] Loyola accordingly devoted an entire chapter of his *Constitutions* to "The Preservation of the Body," where his instructions stated, "a proper concern about the preservation of one's health and bodily strength for the divine service is praiseworthy, and all should exercise it." Loyola also charged Jesuit superiors with the task of promoting the health of their subordinates as well as caring for them when they became sick.[2] As a result provincials and rectors often reported on the health of Jesuits, the precautions taken to avoid illness, the ailments of individuals, the remedies applied to cure them, and the outbreaks of threatening epidemics.

Another reason for the frequency of such accounts is the high level of morbidity in preindustrial society; people were sicker more often with a wider variety of diseases than they are today.[3] Atypical but indicative of the situation was Cesare Dainotto's report from Palermo in September 1563: "We have experienced the goodness of Our Lord God,... for we have had a winter and a summer... with almost no one sick,... and everyone is amazed."[4] A similar situation existed at Paris in September 1570 when the provincial, Oliver Manare, proudly announced to General Francis Borgia that the Jesuit college was an island of good health in the middle of a "great multitude of sick people."[5] At the other extreme were the conditions in the Jesuit communities at Nola in southern Italy and at Sassari on Sardinia. According to Mario Morselli's report from Nola in December 1569, the college had endured "the continual infirmities of many for almost the entire year,"[6] and Guido Bellini's letter from Sassari in August 1570 complained of the excessive heat of summer, the great cold of

---

[1]W. W. Meissner, *Ignatius of Loyola: The Psychology of a Saint*, (New Haven: Yale University Press, 1992), 223.

[2]Ignatius Loyola, *The Constitutions of the Society of Jesus*, ed. George E. Ganss (St. Louis: The Institute of Jesuit Sources, 1970), [292–306]; see also Ignatius Loyola, *Sancti Ignatii de Loyola, Societatis Jesu fundatoris, epistolae et instructiones*, 11 vols. (Madrid: Gabrielis Lopez del Horno, 1903–1911), 4: 494–95, to the superiors of the Society, Rome, November 2, 1552. Loyola's concern for the health of Jesuits is the topic of a book by J. A. de Laburu, *La salud corporal y San Ignacio de Loyola* (Bilbao: Mensajero del Corazón de Jésus, 1956).

[3]James C. Riley, *Sickness, Recovery and Death: A History and Forecast of Ill Health* (Iowa City: University of Iowa Press, 1989), argues against the notion that people were sicker in the past than now. The evidence from Jesuit correspondence does not support his argument.

[4]SIC 182: 68, *quadrimestris*, September 1.

[5]GAL 83: 137, 142, September 17 and 20.

[6]NEAP 193: 138, annual letter, December 11.

winter, and the bad air of autumn, all of which combined to produce "extremely dangerous and very long illnesses."[7]

The French Jesuit Annibal Coudret provides a good illustration of both the high level of morbidity and the comments of the superiors on the sicknesses of those in their care. Between 1572 and 1574, when he was rector of the Jesuit college at Toulouse, Coudret's letters chronicled the illnesses of his subordinates and his own bout with recurrent fevers. During this period one of the Jesuits at Toulouse had a gruesome rash that would not disappear despite various remedies including bleeding, wet and dry baths, and medicine. Other Jesuits had cases of double tertian, erratic, continuous, and pestilential fevers. One Jesuit died from an unspecified illness and another from one of the continuous fevers, and Coudret suffered from catarrh and fevers that doctors diagnosed as quintan of the quartan type, an erratic quartan, then quintan with some tertian in the middle, erratic, and continuous.[8] The two deaths at Toulouse during these three years were minor compared to the mortality in other Jesuit communities. In the summer and autumn of 1573 Juan Cañas reported on the illnesses in the Jesuit province of Andalusia that resulted in the deaths of six Jesuits; especially troubled was the college at Seville where from July until November ten to twelve Jesuits were sick in bed.[9] The annual letter of the Jesuit province of Rome for 1575 noted that as a result of "grave and dangerous diseases" eight Jesuits had died at Loreto and another twelve at Rome.[10] In the spring and summer of 1594 the college at Fulda suffered the deaths of three Jesuits, one from "a most troublesome and lengthy disease of paralysis."[11]

Epidemic Diseases

The diseases that afflicted Jesuits at Toulouse and Fulda and in the provinces of Andalusia and Rome, although deadly, were not proper epidemics because they affected only a Jesuit community. To qualify for inclusion in this analysis of epidemic disease the sources must indicate that the disease was widespread

---

[7]SARD 14: 308, to Borgia, August 12.

[8]I discuss Coudret's chronicle of fevers in A. Lynn Martin, *The Jesuit Mind: The Mentality of an Elite in Early Modern France* (Ithaca: Cornell University Press, 1988), 153–56, 161.

[9]HISP 119: 83, 139, 239, to Mercurian, Granada, Cordova, and Seville, August 24, September 26, and November 15.

[10]ROM 126b: 94, by Benedetto Giustiniano, Rome, January 1, 1576.

[11]GERM 173: 31, Melchior Toxites to Aquaviva, August 14.

or epidemic to the world outside the Jesuit colleges and missions. The chronology in the appendix lists 572 such epidemics that were responsible for the deaths of not quite five hundred Jesuits. As indicated in table 3, of the 572 epidemics, Jesuits identified 67 percent as pest; another group, comprising 9 percent, consists of epidemics that had the stem *pest-* in the words describing them—pestilence, pestilential, and pestiferous; 2 percent were epidemics that combined pest with another disease such as dysentery; and 22 percent were epidemics not identified as pest. By combining the first three categories, pest accounted for 78 percent of the epidemics. Pest accounted for similar percentages of the 494 deaths: 73 percent were due to pest, 3 percent to the category of types of pest, 3 percent to unspecified epidemics (most of which were probably pest), and 22 percent to diseases not identified as pest.

TABLE 3: EPIDEMICS AND DEATHS IN JESUIT ACCOUNTS

	Epidemics	Deaths
Pest	382 (67%)	359 (73%)
Pest- as stem	52 (9%)	13 (3%)
Pest and other diseases	13 (2%)	—
Unspecified	—	15 (3%)
Non-pest diseases	125 (22%)	107 (22%)
TOTAL	572	494

These figures reveal only contemporary perceptions and diagnoses and cannot be an objective guide to morbidity and mortality. Jesuits did not always make their own diagnoses of epidemic diseases or the causes of deaths. They often relied on public opinion, much of it based on ill-informed and panic-driven rumor, or the advice of medical practitioners, which was not necessarily more reliable than public opinion. Hence, the diagnoses, based at times on a combination of Jesuit perception, public opinion, and medical advice, could be confusing. Angelo Sibilla's description of an outbreak near Bivona in August 1575 reveals such confusion: "the pest or, as others call it, an epidemic or a contagious disease."[12] Similar is Ottaviano Navaroli's account from Brno in Moravia (Czech Republic) in October 1597: many were dying from "the pest or dysentery or from some other disease, which they do not recognize and do not know how to treat."[13] More enigmatic is the "great infestation of the air almost like half a pest" that affected all of Le Marche in the summer of 1557.[14]

Stephen R. Ell doubts whether people considered "the concept of simultaneous epidemics" during this period.[15] The attitudes of seventeenth-century Florentine medical authorities provide support for Ell's doubts, for they believed that similar diseases could not exist at the same time.[16] The only evidence of this attitude in Jesuit accounts is a report from Venice in June 1577; according to Mario Beringucci the discovery of other diseases was an indication that the epidemic of pest was ceasing.[17] On the other hand, the 2 percent of the epidemics that combined pest with other diseases indicate that Jesuits, and presumably others, believed that simultaneous epidemics were possible. Some of these combinations could have resulted from changing diagnoses, but some accounts reveal perceptions of quite distinct diseases. Ponce Corgordan wrote in December 1562, "The pest still thrives at Paris in addition to a second disease called catarrh, from which many die,"[18] Lorenzo Maggio reported from Vienna in August 1575, "From time to time people die from the pest in this city; besides this a malignant fever and dysentery kills many,"[19] and Edmund Hay noted that during 1579 Pont-à-Mousson suffered from dysentery in July, August, and September and from the pest in the latter two months.[20]

---

[12]ITAL 148: 210, to Mercurian, August 21.

[13]GERM 177: 286v, to Aquaviva, October 20.

[14]*Litterae quadrimestres ex universis praeter Indiam et Brasiliam locis in quibus aliqui de Societate Jesu versabantur Romam missae*, 7 vols. (Madrid and Rome: Augustinus Avrial, La Editorial Ibérica, and A. Macioce e Pisani, 1894–1932), 5: 398, by Raffaele Riera, Loreto, October 5.

[15]Stephen R. Ell, "The Venetian Plague of 1630–1631: A Preliminary Epidemiologic Analysis," *Janus* 73 (1986–1990), 94.

[16]Giulia Calvi, *Histories of a Plague Year: The Social and the Imaginary in Baroque Florence* (Berkeley: University of California Press, 1989), 63.

[17]ITAL 154: 58, to Mercurian, June 1.

[18]Diego Lainez, *Lainii monumenta: Epistolae et acta patris Jacobi Lainii secundi praepositi generalis Societatis Jesu*, 8 vols. (Madrid: Gabrielis Lopez del Horno, 1912–1917), 6: 597, to Borgia, December 26.

[19]GERM 136 II: 327v, to Mercurian, August 14; see 445v, Emerich Forsler to Mercurian, October 17.

[20]GAL 90: 316v, to Mercurian, October 16; see GERM 157: 291, Balduin Dawant to Mercurian, Liège, October 15, 1579.

EPIDEMICS OTHER THAN PEST

Despite the evident ability to consider the "concept of simultaneous epidemics," the sixteenth-century taxonomy of disease as revealed in Jesuit accounts was imprecise and vague. When confronted with an epidemic other than pest, about one-third of the time Jesuits noted the presence of a widespread disease or a great infirmity, without specifying symptoms or attempting to label it. Jesuits reported on "continual and severe illnesses" at Plasencia in Spain in 1557,[21] "very severe illnesses" that killed many people at Vilnius in Lithuania in 1580,[22] "a new disease, as they call it," that killed three Jesuits at Trier in 1587,[23] and "an epidemic of diseases" at Evora in Portugal in 1592.[24] In February 1571 Paul Hoffaeus wrote to General Francis Borgia, "I know not what type of disease is spreading at Ingolstadt; the students have left."[25]

For another third of the epidemics Jesuits stipulated the most obvious symptom or occasionally symptoms, most often fever but also petechia and catarrh. In January 1558 "a certain type of fever" spread at Modena, killing many people and making a great many sick,[26] "many fevers" infested Valladolid in the autumn of 1565,[27] "a contagious catarrh" spread through Naples in December 1562,[28] and during the spring and summer of 1570 Brescia had "a great abundance of petechia" that killed many people.[29] As indicated by Ponce Cogordan's use of the term "catarrh," Jesuits sometimes used these "symptoms" as names of a specific disease. For example, in September 1558 Giovanni Filippo Casini reported that Siracusa was suffering from "an infirmity, which in Italy they call petechia, as a result of which many die, including important people."[30] The final third of the epidemics received names. For some reason

---

[21]*Litterae quadrimestres*, 5: 446, by Jerónimo Ximenez, November 30.

[22]GERM 158: 136, Sunyer to Mercurian, April 20.

[23]GERM 167: 321v, Oliver Manare to Aquaviva, Wurzburg, September 2.

[24]LUS 106: 158v, annual by Salvador Sautomaior, January 1, 1593.

[25]GERM 133 I: 75, Munich, February 14.

[26]ITAL 111: 78, Philippe Faber to Lainez, January 14.

[27]HISP 141: 73, annual by Antonio Torres, March 14, 1566.

[28]NEAP 193: 96, *quadrimestris* by Ignazio Balsamo, January 23, 1563.

[29]ITAL 139: 135, Giovanni Battista Peruschi to Borgia, August 2. The *quadrimestris* from Cordoba in September 1561 reported that one Jesuit worked at the hospital hearing the confessions of the sick, especially those with "buboes," that is, *bubas* in the Spanish version, but according to the Latin version of the letter they suffered from *gallico morbo*, French disease, a euphemism for syphilis even in the sixteenth century. *Litterae quadrimestres*, 7: 446 and note, by Pedro Acevedo, September 1.

[30]*Litterae quadrimestres*, 3: 575, to Lainez, September 29.

Jesuits in Spain were more likely to label epidemics than Jesuits elsewhere, and they identified many of them with names no longer in common use—*blancos*, *modorra* (occasionally as *modorilla*), and *tabardillo*.

Historians have identified a number of epidemic diseases other than pest that afflicted sixteenth-century Europe, most notably influenza, typhus, and smallpox. The characteristic symptoms of influenza, a respiratory infection sometimes confused with the common cold, are fever, headache, congestion, catarrh, and cough, and like the common cold it causes more illnesses in winter than in summer. Influenza usually produces a high level of morbidity but a low rate of mortality, that is, many people become sick but few die.[31] According to Ann G. Carmichael, influenza was present in Italy in the fourteenth and fifteenth centuries, and contemporaries were capable of distinguishing it from other diseases,[32] but Gerald F. Pyle claims that the pandemic of 1580 "was the first confidently identified as influenza."[33] Jesuit accounts provide evidence for the pandemic of 1580 and also furnish support for earlier outbreaks of influenza that reached at least epidemic proportions in 1557 and 1562–1563.

In 1557 Gian Filippo Ingrassia, a medical adviser to the city of Palermo, described the symptoms of an epidemic that he identified as influenza: "catarrh with heaviness of head and headache and blushing of the face."[34] The first indication of the epidemic among Jesuits is the letter from Svetonio Crescenzi at Tivoli in April that complained of a widespread disease which caused fever and aches throughout the body and was responsible for many deaths.[35] The arrival of warm weather brought some respite, but toward the end of summer so many Italian cities were reporting the disease that, according to the Vicar General Diego Lainez, "this influenza seems to be universal throughout Italy."[36] From Bologna came news of "catarrh with fever and

---

[31]K. David Patterson, *Pandemic Influenza, 1700–1900: A Study in Historical Epidemiology* (Totowa, N.J.: Rowman and Littlefield, 1986), 3; Gerald F. Pyle, *The Diffusion of Influenza: Patterns and Paradigms* (Totowa, N.J.: Rowman and Littlefield, 1986), 1, 5.

[32]Anne G. Carmichael, *Plague and the Poor in Renaissance Florence* (Cambridge: Cambridge University Press, 1986), 13.

[33]Pyle, *Diffusion of Influenza*, 23.

[34]Liborio Giuffré, "L'epidemia d'influenza del 1557 in Palermo e le proposte per il risanamento della città fatte nel 1558 da G. F. Ingrassia," *Archivio storico siciliano* 15 (1890): 181.

[35]ITAL 108: 22, to Polanco, April 5; see 38, Lorenzo Cavaliere to Lainez, Tivoli, April 11.

[36]Lainez, *Lainii monumenta*, 2: 334, to Anton Vinck, Rome, July 31.

headache,"[37] from Rome "certain catarrhs with some fever that struck everyone or almost everyone,"[38] and later in the year from Florence and Palermo came further reports of "influenza."[39] Some evidence indicates that the epidemic reached Portugal. At the beginning of November so many students suffered from such a fierce catarrh at Coimbra that according to Nicolau Gracida the resulting coughs made it impossible for the teachers and students to hear each other.[40] Finally, Baltasar Loarte reported from Plasencia in Spain of "the great catarrh that was widespread in the world and that killed many people."[41] More widespread than the influenza epidemic of 1557 was the one of 1562–1563, for in addition to Murcia and Avila in Spain, Coimbra in Portugal, the Italian cities of Rome, Nola, Loreto, and Naples, Messina on Sicily, and Sassari on Sardinia, Jesuit accounts indicate that it reached France, where it affected the Jesuit communities at Paris, Toulouse, and Rodez. The rector of the Jesuit college at Toulouse, Jean Pelletier, reported in February 1563, "A certain disease spreads here and attacks everyone with coughs, headache, fever, and a pain in the side"; it killed a Jesuit at Rodez.[42]

Pyle claims that the pandemic of 1580 spread from Malta to Sicily in July and then swept north through Italy by August,[43] but according to Giacomo Croce, rector of the Jesuit college at Turin, the disease came to northern Italy from Burgundy, sweeping through Savoy and Piedmont to Milan. Croce wrote on July 13, and his comments indicate that the disease had been prevalent in Turin for some time. He also described many of the classic characteristics of influenza: "The entire college has been very much troubled during these months by a certain influenza of catarrh with fever and extremely sharp headache and stomach ache.... Of six parts of the city five have been sick in bed, and some become sick two or three times.... If this disease was as deadly as it is contagious, Piedmont would be depopulated."[44] A report on the colleges at

---

[37]ITAL 109: 106, Francesco Palmio to Lainez, July 27.

[38]Lainez, *Lainii monumenta*, 2: 375, to Vitoria, August 14.

[39]Ibid., 3: 51, Lainez to Hurtado Perez, Rome, January 18, 1558, reporting on information he had received.

[40]*Litterae quadrimestres*, 5: 953, to Lopez, February 14, 1558.

[41]Baltasar Loarte, "A Curious Document: Baltasar Loarte S. I. and the Years 1554–1570," ed. Nigel Griffin, *Archivum Historicum Societatis Iesu* 45 (1976): 73.

[42]GAL 80: 8, to Salmeron, February 5.

[43]Pyle, *Diffusion of Influenza*, 23–24.

[44]ITAL 156: 120, to Mercurian.

Cologne, Mainz, Speyer, and Fulda in August claimed, "We have had a thousand sick, and all have not yet recovered,"[45] and the annual letter for the Jesuit province of Portugal complained of "that pestiferous contagion of catarrh" which took the lives of over twenty Jesuits, nine of whom were priests.[46] The epidemic even touched the Jesuit mission to Sweden; Johan Ardulph noted in the annual letter for 1580 that "we were almost all in bed" from the widespread disease which also invaded Italy, France, and other countries.[47] Fernando Lucero wrote from Alcalá de Henares in July 1593 that an outbreak of catarrh was as widespread "as the one in the year '80,"[48] but no other Jesuits mentioned it, and Jesuit accounts do not produce any obvious indications of other epidemics of influenza in the sixteenth century. Although retrospective diagnoses are seldom definitive, the evidence suggests that Jesuits encountered epidemics of influenza in 1557, 1562–1563, and 1580.

Retrospective diagnoses are more problematic for epidemics of typhus and smallpox than they are for influenza. Typhus is transmitted by body lice and hence was a threat amid poor sanitary conditions, in winter when people wore more clothes and bathed less often, and among soldiers. Typhus was an apparent newcomer to Europe in the late fifteenth century. The Italian physician Girolamo Fracastoro described its symptoms in his *De contagione et contagiosis morbis et eorum curatione, Libri III*, first published in 1546, and noted that the disease was known as lenticular fever because its spots look like little lentils—*lenticulae* in Latin.[49] The symptoms of typhus are fever, delirium, and the spots or petechiae.[50] Although smallpox apparently has a much longer history in Europe than typhus, the virulent strain of the *variola* virus likewise was a newcomer to Europe in the fifteenth and sixteenth centuries, when it caused sporadic epidemics, and then became dominant in the seventeenth century.[51]

---

[45]GERM 158: 260v, François de Costere to Mercurian, Fulda, August 28.

[46]LUS 53: 23, by Miguel de Souza, February 1, 1581.

[47]OPP NN 339: 91, Stockholm, October 1, 1581.

[48]HISP 136: 19v, to Aquaviva, July 20.

[49]Girolamo Fracastoro [Hieronymi Fracastorii], *De contagione et contagiosis morbis et curatione, Libri III*, trans. Wilmer Cave Wright (New York: G. P. Putnam's Sons, 1930), 101.

[50]For general comments on typhus, see Michael W. Flinn, *The European Demographic System, 1500–1820*, (Baltimore: Johns Hopkins University Press, 1985), 62; Carmichael, *Plague and Poor*, 23; Henry E. Sigerist, *Civilization and Disease* (Ithaca: Cornell University Press, 1944), 118–19.

[51]Ann G. Carmichael and Arthur M. Silverstein, "Smallpox in Europe before the Seventeenth Century: Virulent Killer or Benign Disease?" *Journal of the History of Medicine and Allied Sciences* 42 (April 1987): 147–48.

Smallpox shares with typhus the symptoms of fever, delirium, and petechiae, but the distinctive rash turning into pimples and then blisters, pustules, and scabs makes smallpox unmistakable. Jesuits did not mention lenticular fever, and the references to smallpox are surprisingly rare given the sporadic epidemics. According to Ann G. Carmichael and Arthur M. Silverstein, epidemics of smallpox occurred at Valencia in 1555, at Rome in 1569, Venice in 1570–1571, and Paris in 1580,[52] but the Jesuit sources are silent. Alfio Vinci, when reporting on the start of the epidemic of pest at Palermo in July 1575, observed, "Many have died, and many die every day; in some they find buboes, ... yet on the other hand almost all the children have *vailore* [*sic*] (as they call it here), and many of them die."[53] This reference to *variola* is the only one found in the correspondence of Jesuits in Europe; references to it are common, however, in the letters from the Americas and Asia, indicating that Jesuits were familiar with the disease.[54]

A modern authority has suggested that *modorra*, a Spanish and Portuguese term now meaning drowsiness or a disease that affects sheep, referred to typhus in the sixteenth century.[55] Although Spanish and Portuguese Jesuits reported on numerous outbreaks of *modorra*, their use of the term and description of the disease provide little information that would help identify it as typhus. They used the term to designate a precise disease, not a condition or a symptom, and they felt no need to offer any explanations in letters to superiors. Typical was Juan Suarez's report to Francis Borgia in July 1570: "In Seville people are dying from *modorra*."[56] Other comments indicate that the disease was contagious, dangerous, produced fierce fevers, and could result in death in a few days,[57] all of which could indicate typhus, but Jesuits never linked

---

[52]Ibid., 159–60.

[53]ITAL 148: 48, to Mercurian, July 5.

[54]For some examples see *Monumenta Braziliae*, ed. Serafim Leite, 5 vols. (Rome: Monumenta Historica Societatis Iesu, 1956–1968), 4: 178–79, January 8, 1565; *Documenta Malucensia*, ed. Hubert Jacobs, 3 vols. (Rome: Institutum Historicum Societatis Iesu, 1974–1984), 1: 242, 265, 449, February 13, 1558, March 9, 1559, April 15, 1564; *Documenta Indica*, ed. Joseph Wicki and John Gomes, 18 vols. (Rome: Monumenta Historica Societatis Iesu, 1948–1984), 9: 354, February 9, 1574, 16: 337–39, 745, November 15, 1593, November 7, 1594.

[55]Cited in Alfred W. Crosby, *Ecological Imperialism: The Biological Expansion of Europe, 900–1900* (Cambridge: Cambridge University Press, 1986), 94.

[56]HISP 114: 261, Burgos, July 8.

[57]*Litterae quadrimestres*, 5: 279, by Pedro Cabrera, Murcia, June 29, 1557; 358, by Pedro de Sahelizes, Cordova, September 1, 1557; HISP 141: 257, annual for Granada, January 3, 1570.

modorra to the characteristic petechia of typhus. In short, the evidence does not support the contention that *modorra* was typhus, and it seems improbable that a word now meaning "drowsiness" could in the sixteenth century mean a disease noted for producing delirium in its victims. A more likely candidate for typhus than *modorra* is *tabardillo*, the Spanish "spotted fever." Jesuits used *tabardillo*, as they used *modorra*, to indicate a specific disease, but they did not associate it with petechia, and the only evident characteristics that emerge from Jesuit discussions of *tabardillo* are its contagiousness and deadliness. It infected all the Jesuits accompanying a Spanish army to Flanders in 1574, and many soldiers died from it.[58] Two brothers caring for people with *tabardillo* in Santiago in 1586 contracted the disease and died as a result.[59]

According to Brian Pullan, the Italian *mal di petecchie* or "spotted sickness" likewise referred to typhus,[60] an identification more likely than either *modorra* and *tabardillo* simply because of the petechia. As already noted, Jesuits used the term petechia to designate a specific disease, and Jesuit descriptions indicate many of the classic symptoms of typhus. The best example of this occurred when two Jesuits on board galleys bound for Spain became so sick that they disembarked at Genoa in April 1572; their symptoms were "continuous delirium and frenzy,...a pestiferous fever, and petechia." One was "so out of his mind" that those caring for him had to tie him to his bed.[61] Other cases of petechia presented symptoms that indicate a different disease, such as that of a Jesuit brother at Florence who, in addition to petechia, vomited blood, had a headache and a pain in the left side, and did not display the characteristic delirium.[62] Some of the petechia described by Jesuits was probably typhus, but so many diseases, including plague, smallpox, chicken pox, and measles, present cutaneous manifestations that other diagnoses are possible.[63]

Regressive analysis of some of the other epidemics mentioned by Jesuits, such as the "poisonous water" that afflicted Rome in 1566, would produce a

---

[58]HISP 122: 128, Francisco Valdivieso to Mercurian, Madrid, October 11.

[59]HISP 132: 93v, Pedro Villalba to Aquaviva, Valladolid, July 28.

[60]Brian Pullan, *Rich and Poor in Renaissance Venice: The Social Institutions of a Catholic State, to 1620* (Cambridge, Mass.: Harvard University Press, 1971), 245.

[61]ITAL 143: 245, 260, Girolamo Gigli and Giulio Fazio to Nadal, April 18 and 25.

[62]ITAL 111: 349, Fulvio Androzzi to Lainez, March 19, 1558.

[63]See W. Christopher Duncan, "Cutaneous Manifestations of Infectious Diseases," in *Infectious Diseases: A Modern Treatise of Infectious Processes*, 2d ed., ed. Paul D. Hoeprich (New York: Harper and Row, 1977), 68–74.

range of possible diagnoses of only marginal utility to the historian. Some diseases noted by Jesuits defy modern taxonomy; Cologne endured an outbreak of "insanity of the head" (*capitis insania*) that accompanied an outbreak of pest in 1553,[64] and in 1571 many people at Munich were sick with the Hungarian disease (*morbus hungaricus*).[65] Jesuits at Evora in Portugal died from erysipilas, and one at Oradea in Transylvania died from "sacred fire" (*ignis sacer*), both of which are also known as Saint Anthony's fire, meaning either a skin disease or ergotism.[66]

One of the few generalizations possible regarding these epidemics is that they did not inspire as much terror as did an outbreak of pest. As indicated by Jean Pionneau in his account of the epidemic at Avignon in 1577 that killed eleven Jesuits, had people suspected the pest they, including the Jesuits, would have fled elsewhere. The statistics cited above, however, demonstrate that epidemics other than pest account for 22 percent of the total as well as nearly 22 percent of the deaths. In other words, Jesuits were just as likely to die in the midst of one of these other epidemics as they were in an epidemic of pest, and the best example of this is the eleven who died at Avignon. One possible explanation for this discrepancy relates to the perception of these other epidemics. Because Jesuits did not fear them as much, they were not as diligent in fleeing and did not take as much care in avoiding contagion during their pastoral work as they would have done during epidemics of pest. The rate of morbidity from some of these diseases could be very high; according to a report from Ferrara in 1569 more than ten thousand people were sick as a result of a "great infirmity,"[67] and the annual letter for the province of Venezia in 1581 claimed that the greater part of the 216 Jesuits in the province had been sick from "a certain type of very dangerous and serious disease."[68] Despite the high rates of mortality and morbidity from these other diseases, Jesuits still reserved their

---

[64]Juan Polanco, *Vita Ignatii Loiolae et rerum Societatis Jesu historia*, 6 vols. (Madrid: Typographorum Societatis and Augustinus Avrial, 1894–1898), 3: 265, Chronicon Societatis Jesu.

[65]GERM 133 I: 9, Dominique Mengin to Borgia, June 13.

[66]*Monumenta antiquae Hungariae*, ed. Ladislaus Lukács, 3 vols. (Rome: Institutum Historicum Societatis Iesu, 1969–1981), 2: 923, Peter Szydlowski to Giovanni Paolo Campana, May 21, 1586; LUS 71: 68v, Fernando Rebello to Aquaviva, Evora, February 2, 1592.

[67]VEN 100: 209, annual by Andrea Padovano, December 22, 1569.

[68]VEN 105 I: 141, by Beringucci, May 1, 1582.

greatest fears for the pest and often expressed their anxiety that an epidemic of another disease could turn into the pest.

PEST

Jesuits used a variety of terms to indicate an epidemic of pest. The best example of this occurred in the annual letter for the province of the Rhine for 1597. The author began by noting that the fire of pestilence almost destroyed the entire province: at Cologne and Speyer it was a pestiferous contagion; at Trier, where a Jesuit died from a pestiferous ulcer, it was a pestilential disease; at Mainz and Paderborn a pestilential epidemic; at Wurzburg a contagion; at Fulda a disease; at Erfurt and Koblenz a pest; and at Heiligenstadt a disease of pestilence.[69] The use of "plague"—the Latin *plaga* and its equivalent in other languages—was rare; it occurs only twice in the accounts, once in Spanish and once in Latin.[70] Jesuits occasionally used the Latin *lues*, which can mean plague or pestilence, but they used it as a generic term indicating a widespread illness, so epidemic is the best translation.[71] Some of the terms used to denote pest were euphemisms, as if Jesuits wanted to avoid the dreaded "p" word. When describing the epidemic at Seville in 1568, Juan Loarte did not use the term "pest" but wrote instead of a disease of tumors,[72] and during the widespread epidemic of 1575–1577 Italian Jesuits on occasion did not mention pest but instead wrote of "the disease."[73] In contrast to this use of euphemisms, Jesuits had no pejoratives for pest because the term conveyed horrible and dreadful attributes and in consequence was a forceful pejorative itself, as indicated by the Jesuit use of it to describe their enemies. Annibal Coudret likened the Huguenots in Paris to a pest,[74] Antonio Possevino stated that the Lutheran

---

[69]RH INF 48: 52–63v, by Joannes Hasius, January 24, 1598.

[70]Francis Borgia, *Sanctus Franciscus Borgia quartus Gandiae dux et Societatis Jesu praepositus generalis*, 5 vols. (Madrid: Augustini Avrial and Gabrielis Lopez del Horno, 1894–1911), 3: 538, to Lainez, Valladolid, August 2, 1559; Joseph Hansen, ed., *Rheinische Akten zur Geschichte des Jesuitenordens, 1542–1582* (Bonn: H. Berendt, 1896), 500, *quadrimestris* by Johann Reidt, Cologne, September 1, 1564.

[71]For a few examples see GAL 92: 231, Martin Rovelle to Aquaviva, Rodez, September 25, 1586; GERM 171: 27, Otto Eisenreich to Aquaviva, Augsburg, January 23, 1593; LUGD 28: 142v, annual letter for the province of Lyon, 1596.

[72]For other examples see HISP 141: 223, annual for Seville by Melchior de San Juan, January 17, 1569; 114: 74, Diego Avellaneda to Borgia, Seville, April 21, 1570.

[73]For two examples see ITAL 153: 45v, Beringucci to Mercurian, Padua, January 18, 1577, and 154: 275, Francesco Adorno to Mercurian, Ferrara, June 29, 1577.

[74]Lainez, *Lainii monumenta*, 6: 63, to Lainez, Saint-Germain, September 27, 1561.

reformer Matthias Flacius Illyricus was "pestilentissimo,"[75] and in December 1588 Giovanni Paolo Campana, provincial of Poland, assured General Claudio Aquaviva that the Jesuits were safe from the epidemic of pest then spreading in Transylvania, but they had to fight the *pests* of Arians and other heretics.[76] Jesuits also used pest in the modern sense of the term as a person causing trouble; the rector of the Jesuit college at Forlì, exasperated at the disruptive conduct of one Jesuit lay brother, wrote that he had become a pest to his brethren.[77]

Paul Slack has noted that in England "plague" was a generic term, but during the sixteenth century a tendency existed to use the term in a more precise manner denoting a specific disease.[78] Jesuits also used "pest" as a generic term; it could apply to any disease provided it met three criteria—it had to be widespread, contagious, and deadly. For example, at the beginning of 1556 Gil Gonzalez wrote from Alcalá de Henares, "A certain pest, raging far and wide, rushed not only into this city but all around among neighboring people, and it spread with much danger and carnage."[79] During the epidemic of influenza in 1562, Juan Polanco reported, "One says it is a type of pest, and the doctors order people to guard themselves from it as a contagious infirmity."[80] Cristóbal Leitão, writing from Cochin in February 1574, reported that the natives were dying from a "pest of smallpox."[81] On the other hand, the Jesuit use of "pest" mirrored the tendency in England to use plague to denote a precise disease. Jesuits on missions to the Americas and Asia provide good examples of this tendency as they struggled to come to terms with the strange diseases they encountered in foreign lands. Jesuits in South America and the East Indies noted "types" of pest.[82] In Brazil Jesuits encountered an epidemic that killed so

---

[75]OPP NN 329 I: 160v, to Roberto Bellarmino, Vienna, June 10, 1583.

[76]*Monumenta Hungariae*, 3: 255, Braniewo, December 15.

[77]ITAL 130: 5, Ortensio Androzzi to Cristóbal Rodriguez, June 2, 1566.

[78]Paul Slack, *The Impact of Plague in Tudor and Stuart England* (London: Routledge and Kegan Paul, 1985), 64.

[79]*Litterae quadrimestres*, 4: 7, to Loyola, January 1.

[80]Jerónimo Nadal, *Epistolae P. Hieronymi Nadal Societatis Iesu ab anno 1546 ad 1577,* 4 vols. (Madrid: Augustini Avrial and Gabrielis Lopez del Horno, 1898–1905), 2: 184, to Nadal, Trent, December 10.

[81]*Documenta Indica*, 9: 355, to the General, Cochin, February 9.

[82]Ibid., 7: 526, Lourenço Perez to Lião Anriquez, Malacca, December 3, 1568; *Monumenta Peruana*, ed. Antonio de Egana, 4 vols. (Rome: Monumenta Historica Societatis Iesu, 1954–1966), 2: 625, José de Acosta to Mercurian, Lima, April 11, 1579.

many Indians that "it appeared to be a pestilence,"[83] and from Mannar on Sri Lanka, Henrique Henriques wrote of a disease that "appeared a type of pest, although they do not have the pest in India."[84] In Europe one indication that people regarded the pest as a specific disease is their fear, as stated above, that an epidemic of another disease might change into the pest. Another indication is the tendency for disputes to occur among town authorities and medical practitioners at the beginning of an epidemic over whether the outbreak was the result of the pest or some other disease.

When Jesuits used the term "pest" to denote a specific disease, their descriptions reveal that the four primary characteristics of the disease were its contagious nature, high mortality, the quickness of death, and the appearance of the bubo. At the time of the Black Death, experience led people to the conclusion that the epidemic was contagious in the sense that it spread by personal contact, even though most of the medical profession clung to the belief that the disease resulted from the corruption of the air. The measures taken by political authorities during the fourteenth and fifteenth centuries to combat the introduction and the spread of the disease, measures such as the quarantine and the *cordon sanitaire*, indicate that they sided with popular opinion. By the sixteenth century the medical profession had accepted the theory of contagion without, however, rejecting the view that the corruption of the air played an important role.[85]

---

[83]*Monumenta Brasiliae*, 3: 415, António Blázques to Lainez, Bahia, September 1, 1561.

[84]*Documenta Indica*, 6: 145, to Lainez, January 11, 1564. Jesuits in the Americas and Asia provide some interesting evidence on the epidemics they observed there. Jesuits in the East Indies produced the first known reference to beriberi (*Documenta Molucensia*, 1: 255 and note, Francisco Vieira to the Jesuits in Portugal, Ternate, March 9, 1559); they encountered epidemics of cholera, which the natives called *modxi* (*Documenta Indica*, 7: 143, Jerónimo Rodriguez and Andrés Cabrera to their Jesuit colleagues, Cochin, December 13, 1566; 16: 340, annual for India by Francisco Cabral, Goa, November 15, 1593); and in the Americas they reported on severe epidemics of the native disease called *cocoliztli*, which the Spanish Jesuits rendered as *cocoliste* and which became the French and English coqueluche (*Monumenta Mexicana*, ed. Felix Zubillaga, 7 vols. [Rome: Monumenta Historica Societatis Iesu, 1956–1981], 2: 38, 503; 3: 25, 310, 496; 4: 322; 5: 99; 6: 327).

[85]Jean-Noël Biraben, *Les hommes et la peste en France et dans les pays européens et méditerranéens*, 2 vols. (Paris: Mouton, 1975–1976), 2: 18–19, 25–27; Darrel W. Amundsen, "Medical Deontology and Pestilential Disease in the Late Middle Ages," *Journal of the History of Medicine* 32 (1977): 403–21. See also Ann G. Carmichael, "Contagion Theory and Contagion Practice in Fifteenth-Century Milan," *Renaissance Quarterly* 44 (1991): 213–56, for an excellent discussion of the competing views. John Henderson, "Epidemics in Renaissance Florence: Medical Theory and Government Response," in *Maladies et société (XIIe–XVIIIe siècles): Actes du colloque de Bielefeld, novembre 1986*, ed. Neithard Bulst and Robert Delort (Paris: Editions du CNRS, 1989), 171, argues that the difference between lay and medical opinion on the contagious nature of the disease was not as marked as some historians have argued.

Judging from the many references to the corruption of the air, infected air, and the contagious nature of the air, at least some Jesuits concurred with contemporary medical opinion. For example, in a report on July 11, 1576, the Venetian medical authorities stated that one of the principal causes of the epidemic was the air;[86] on the 14th Cesare Helmi wrote, "Some people begin to believe that the air is infected,"[87] but then on August 6 came the opinion that "the air was not infected at all."[88] The view of some Jesuits was that an epidemic of pest was normally the result of contagion, that is, personal contact with the sick or with infected goods, but whenever the air became corrupt, infected, or contagious the disease had passed to a new, much more dangerous stage. When Emond Auger remained in Lyon during the epidemic of 1564 to help the inhabitants, he informed General Lainez that he would go elsewhere if the air became contagious.[89] Similarly, Giulio Cesare Mazzarino assured General Mercurian in April 1577 that the Jesuits could remain safe and sound in their seminary at Brera, "since we are certain that the disease does not come from the infection of the air, which is very good, but from contagion."[90]

This belief in the corruption of the air, far from invalidating the belief in the contagious nature of the pest, reinforces it, for whenever someone contracted the pest Jesuits expected to find evidence of contact with infected persons or infective goods; failure to find such contact left corrupted air as the only possible explanation.[91] As revealed by Ponce Cogordan in his comments on sharing a bed with the stricken Jean de Savoie and by Paschase Broët in his careful listing of everything he had touched after he became sick, Jesuits believed that contact with persons and items was dangerous. Cogordan also reported Claude Matthieu's belief that "no one escapes after they have been with the pest-stricken." According to Cogordan, even the house where Broët died was contagious, and he recommended that it remain empty for a year.[92]

---

[86]A. Canalis and P. Sepulcri, "Prescrizioni mediche ufficiali e altri provvedimenti di governo in Venezia nella peste del 1575–1576," *Annali della sanità publica* 1 (1958): 1211.

[87]ITAL 151: 312, to Mercurian.

[88]Ibid., 410v, *Avisi cavati da diverse lettere venute da Venetia.*

[89]GAL 80: 264, September 28.

[90]ITAL 153: 314, Genoa, April 8.

[91]For two examples of the search for contacts, see ITAL 154: 221v, Adorno to Mercurian, Ferrara, July 17, 1577; 155: 167v, Beringucci to Mercurian, Venice, October 12, 1577.

[92]Lainez, *Lainii monumenta*, 6: 427, 8: 566, to Lainez, Noyon and Paris, September 29 and November 13, 1562.

When a lay brother became sick with the pest at Trier in 1576, other Jesuits believed that he had contracted the disease at the house where he did the washing; to protect themselves they did not distribute the clean linen and clothing but immediately submerged them in water.[93]

Typical of the Jesuit attitude toward contagion is the case of Angelo Sibilla. According to the accounts of his death, Sibilla contracted the pest while hearing confessions in the Jesuit church at Messina during the epidemic of 1577. Jesuits normally took precautions to avoid unnecessary contact with the sick, but a pest-stricken woman came to confession without declaring her illness. Sibilla did not notice her condition until the end and, after giving her absolution, retired to his room immediately to avoid contact with anyone. Within days he was suffering from delirium and fever; then the bubo appeared on the day before his death.[94] The accounts of Sibilla's death indicate that Jesuits believed that the pest resulted from personal contact, and that to avoid infecting others, those exposed to the disease should segregate themselves from the rest of the community. During the epidemic at Messina in 1575 Brother Luigi Calligaris had the task of supervising the assistance given to those victims living in poverty whom the authorities had banished from the town. When Calligaris contracted the pest late in October, the rector, Giovanni Battista Carminata, put him in the care of another brother and segregated them both in the school in the room directly above the theology classroom. Carminata supplied them with everything they needed—from a distance— and several times during the day visited them to console them and to give them encouragement, shouting at them from the top of the stairs. Carminata continued his account: "An hour ago I was called in haste; I went and found Brother Luigi suffering but still conscious. I said a few words of comfort to him—from a distance—and he rendered his soul to his creator."[95] These comments do not fully demonstrate Jesuit opinion on the contagious nature of the pest; it is a topic that will recur on the pages below, but the best illustration of the opinion is Guy Roillet's comment that the pest which afflicted the Jesuit community at Ferrara in 1557 "always goes jumping from one person to another."[96]

[93]GERM 137 II: 252, Balduin Dawant to Mercurian, July 3.
[94]ITAL 154: 95, Giulio Fazio to Mercurian, Siracusa, June 15; 105, Giovanni Giacomo Basso to Mercurian, Naples, June 18.
[95]ITAL 149: 75–76, 90, to Mercurian, November 1 and 4.
[96]ITAL 110: 356, 111: 3, to Lainez, December 24, 1557 and January 1, 1558.

Another widespread belief among Jesuits was the deadly nature of the pest; the sick expected to die, and others expected them to die. In June 1577 Giovanni Giacomo Basso reported that of the fourteen Dominicans who had the pest at Palermo eight had already died, and "no one had any hope that the others would recover."[97] Those Jesuits who did recover from the pest believed that they had received a special providence from God. When Massimo Milanesi informed his superior that he had survived his illness, he began his letter with, "I live, Reverend Father, through the mercy of God."[98] In addition to Milanesi the accounts document another twenty-eight cases of recovery from the pest. Since the accounts indicate 372 deaths attributed to the pest, the resulting rate of mortality is 93 percent, which is higher than the plague mortality rate of 60 to 90 percent cited by modern medical authorities. Jesuits were more likely to mention a death than to record a recovery, however,[99] so the total number of recoveries was higher than indicated by the twenty-nine documented cases.

More reliable than the figures on recovery are the figures on the number of days between the appearance of the symptoms and death, as shown in table 4. As indicated by the table, the pest killed quickly, usually within two to four days from the appearance of symptoms. Just as people believed in the contagious nature of the disease, so also did they recognize that death soon followed the first symptoms.[100] Once again Jesuits concurred with public opinion; to prove that the Jesuits at Avignon in 1577 did not die from the pest Jean Pionneau believed he need only point out that they died on the 7th, 9th, 11th, 13th, 17th, and 21st days of their illness. Other Jesuits also used the length of illness as a diagnostic aid. Because Vincenzo Cascovio died after eight days and Mateusz Dembinski after two weeks, their superiors doubted that they had

---

[97]ITAL 154: 105, to Mercurian, Naples, June 18.

[98]*Monumenta Hungariae*, 2: 985, to Campana, September 1586.

[99]For example, in a letter to Aquaviva from Liège, dated February 28, 1583, Balduin Dawant merely noted that those stricken with the pest at Douai had recovered; he gave no names or numbers; GERM 161: 50.

[100]See the discussion in Carlo M. Cipolla, *Fighting the Plague in Seventeenth-Century Italy* (Madison: University of Wisconsin Press, 1981), 108–9; also Biraben, *Les hommes*, 2: 48.

TABLE 4: NUMBER OF DAYS BETWEEN THE
APPEARANCE OF SYMPTOMS AND DEATH

Number of Days	Number of cases
1 ½	1
2	7
2 to 3	2
3	4
3 to 4	1
4	8
5	3
7	1

died from the pest.[101] The sole exception to the quick death was the unfortunate Wawrzyniec Horoschow, who suffered for his sins for six months while his body wasted away.

Because Jesuits thought the pest was contagious, whenever someone died from the disease they nervously waited to see if anyone else would get it. The pest killed quickly but spread erratically; officials usually insisted upon forty days of quarantine (from the Italian for forty—*quaranta*) for those who had been exposed. Some cases seem to justify official policy, such as that of Brother Giovanni Antonio Olivieri chronicled by Paolo Achille in 1575 and those of two priests at the Jesuit seminary at Brera reported by Giovanni Battista Peruschi in August 1577. The priests became sick thirty-eight days after the death of a Jesuit and died within a few days. The incubation period of most infectious diseases is much shorter than forty days—for plague it is one to six days. So these cases indicate infection from other sources. On occasion Jesuits

---

[101]GERM 134 I: 74, Sunyer to Nadal, Vilnius, January 30, 1572; 152: 122, Stanislaus Rozdrazon to Nadal, Pultusk, October 29, 1571.

gave indications that they considered the quarantine to be excessive; after reporting on the deaths of the priests, Peruschi explained that nothing else had happened in the eight days since they had died and indicated that this was cause for optimism.[102]

In his analysis of pestilential fevers Girolamo Fracastoro asserted, "In some cases buboes or parotitis (tumors near the ears) or other abscesses appear."[103] Nonetheless, for most people, including Jesuits, the most characteristic sign of the pest in all cases rather than just in some was the bubo.[104] If Jesuits were in any doubt about a diagnosis when someone was sick, the appearance of a bubo, even more than the quickness of death, proved the presence of the pest. In fact, Jesuits did not often use the term bubo or its equivalents, for the pest was synonymous with it, as demonstrated by Mateusz Strus' catalogue of the dead at Cluj: pest under the arm and pest in the groin. Jesuits also used "wounds" or "wounded" (*ferito* in Italian and *herido* in Spanish) to indicate the presence of buboes. Paschase Broët was "wounded by the pest (*herido de peste*) behind both ears,"[105] Francesco Centurione was "wounded (*ferito*) in two places, namely, in the throat and under the arm,"[106] and Tiago Carvalho "died from the wounds (*heridas*)... of the pest."[107] Also synonymous with bubo was "the sign of the pest," as indicated by Francisco Sunyer's reports on the incompletely emerged "sign" on Lucas Crassovius and the "signs" on Stanislaus Mielecki. In July 1566 Anton Vinck reported on the sickness of one Jesuit who had a high fever and, what was more ominous, "some sign on his leg beneath the knee."[108] When Milan suffered the first indications of an epidemic in the summer of 1576, Giovanni Battista Peruschi reported on whether the dead and dying had any "signs."[109] The most common location of buboes

---

[102]ITAL 154: 339, to Mercurian, Milan, August 11.

[103]Fracastoro, *De contagione*, 113.

[104]Biraben, *Les hommes*, 2: 43; but see Carmichael, *Plague and Poor*, 20, for a different view.

[105]Lainez, *Lainii monumenta*, 6: 450, Polanco to Madrid, Trent, October 22, 1562.

[106]ITAL 152: 356, Adorno to Mercurian, Parma, December 17, 1576.

[107]LUS 63: 237v, Lião Anriquez to Borgia, Evora, December 17, 1569. Stephen R. Ell, "Three Days in October of 1630: Detailed Examination of Mortality during an Early Modern Plague Epidemic in Venice," *Reviews of Infectious Diseases* 11 (1989), 135, completely misses this special use of *ferito*. He notes the large number of people who died from "wounds" in the parish of San Pietro and speculates that they were involved in a civil disturbance.

[108]GERM 147: 165, to Borgia, Mainz, July 30.

[109]ITAL 152: 43v, to Mercurian, Milan, August 25.

mentioned by Jesuits was the groin, with twenty-four of the forty cases. Five Jesuits had a bubo under the arm, three on the thigh, and one in each of the following locations: behind the ears, lower leg, lower arm, throat, back, feet, and neck, while ten had multiple buboes. As noted in the introduction, the thigh is the most common location in modern cases of plague, closely followed by the groin and the armpit.

A statistical analysis of the symptoms of the pest in Jesuit accounts yields results of questionable utility. Jesuits discussed the symptoms of only 58 of the 372 deaths attributed to the pest and the 29 recoveries, and they did not often present a complete diagnostic picture but merely noted the original or the most notable symptoms. Because the pest was synonymous with bubo, they did not need to mention it when noting that someone had died from the pest. Finally, Jesuits were more likely to report the symptoms of the sick than those of the dead; when a Jesuit died they gave more attention to the edifying details of a good death than to a description of the course of the disease. As indicated by table 5, the most common symptom was the bubo, appearing as it did in 41

TABLE 5: SYMPTOMS OF JESUITS STRICKEN BY THE PEST

Symptom	Number
Bubo	41
Carbuncle	19
Fever	11
Petechia	9
Headache	4
Delirium	3
Abdominal pain	2
Necrosis[a]	2

a. Jesuits did not use this term, but their descriptions indicate the death or decay of body tissues.

of the 58 cases. In addition, Jesuits mentioned single cases of apoplexy, nausea, sleeplessness, difficulty in passing urine, and bleeding from the nose. These symptoms make interesting comparisons with those described by Girolamo Fracastoro and Ambroise Paré, the French physician whose *Liber pestis* was published in 1568. According to Fracastoro, "The following are bad signs: continual delirium, retention of the urine, nose-bleeding that brings no relief, considerable evacuation of the bowels, ... the appearance of spots and abscesses, and presently their sudden subsidence."[110] Paré's list of symptoms included "fever, buboes, carbuncles, purpura [spots], dysentery, delirium, phrenzy, gnawing pains at the stomach, palpitation of the heart, heaviness and weariness of the the limbs, deep sleep, and dulness of all the senses. Some have a burning heat within them, and are cold on the surface, with restlessness, difficulty of breathing, frequent vomiting, dysentery, bleeding from the nose and other parts of the body."[111]

None of the symptoms mentioned by the Jesuits, Fracastoro, and Paré give any indications of the bloody sputum characteristic of pneumonic plague, nor do the accounts reveal anything that would indicate Jesuits were familiar with this variant form of plague. The symptom that comes closest to the bloody sputum was the one case of bleeding from the nose, a symptom also mentioned by Fracastoro and Paré. The bloody nose afflicted the Polish coadjutor Kazimierz, listed by Mateusz Strus in his account of the twenty who died at Cluj in 1586. Kazimierz' other symptoms were carbuncles on the groin, neck, and shin, which would be unusual for a case of pneumonic plague. In February 1562 Gaspar Loarte, the rector at Genoa, reported that a French brother named Pierre was spitting blood; the doctors who examined him asserted that Loarte should send him elsewhere for a change of air as soon as possible because the air of Genoa was "pestiferous for this indisposition."[112] Rather than indicate pneumonic plague, this seems a case of consumption, and in similar cases the prevailing medical opinion was for the sick to have a change of air. In short, pneumonic plague is not evident in Jesuit accounts of epidemic disease.

[110]Fracastoro, *De contagione*, 91.

[111]Quoted from Stephen Paget, *Ambroise Paré and His Times, 1510–1590* (New York: G. P. Putnam's Sons, 1899), 266.

[112]ITAL 121: 137, to Lainez, February 21.

Two cases provide tragic testimony to the delirium and frenzy in the list of symptoms. In 1565 the ex-Jesuit Jonas Adler contracted the pest and became so delirious that he committed suicide.[113] From Vilnius in July 1589 Giovanni Paolo Campana reported that the pest claimed the lives of three students from the parish school next door, one of whom in a fit of madness hurled himself from the window into the garden.[114] The accounts do not contain any cases of suicide by a Jesuit, and the importance that Jesuits attached to a pious death and dying well probably limited comments on delirious deaths. At Milan on Saturday, August 31, 1577, Fabio Giustiniano went to bed with a headache and a swelling in the groin. During the next two days physicians examined him three or four times a day, but they could not decide on a diagnosis, thinking that it might be fear rather than the pest that produced the symptoms. Nonetheless, they provided him with the necessary remedies, and on Monday he gave as many indications of good health as he did of sickness. The heat from the swelling so intensified that evening, however, that the physicians thought it was a case of the pest after all and gave him stronger medicine. Giustiniano suffered greatly throughout the night, but he still managed a pious death, "dying with Jesus in his mouth" on the morning of September 3. In the words of Giuseppe Lamagna, "After he died he became so handsome that he appeared to be smiling, whereas just before his death he had become ·o deformed that we thought he would look like a monster."[115]

The epidemic in northern Italy during 1576 and 1577 provides a number of interesting cases. Francesco Butirone became sick at Milan in December 1576. He had three sores on his thigh that drained so much that everyone considered it amazing; "he was full of evil humors." Butirone recovered.[116] At Brescia in the following July Vincenzo Gambara was "wounded" with nine carbuncles, the vice rector Antonio Marta had four carbuncles and a bubo on both sides of the groin, and Francesco Stefano had three carbuncles and a bubo on the left side of the groin. Gambara and Stefano died, while Marta

[113]Peter Canisius, *Beati Petri Canisii, Societatis Iesu, epistolae et acta*, ed. Otto Braunsberger, 13 vols. (Freiburg im Breisgau: Herder, 1896–1923), 5: 71–72, Borgia to the archbishop of Trier, Johan van der Leyen, Rome, June 20, 1565.

[114]Fondo Gesuitico 645: 98, to Aquaviva, July 31.

[115]ITAL 155: 202, to Sebastião Morais, October 22.

[116]ITAL 153: 100v, Alfonso Sgariglia to Paolo Candi, January 15, included in the letter of Beringucci to Mercurian, Venice, February 6, 1577.

recovered.[117] At Milan again Filippo Contarini discovered that he was sick by the appearance of four buboes on August 27; then petechia appeared six hours before his death on the 31st, but he had none of the other symptoms. His superior, Giovanni Battista Peruschi, complained, "This contagion … comes by treachery and through tricks, without fever, headache, or nausea at the beginning." Six days later Brother Ambrosio, the baker, got up to make the bread and while doing so felt a pain under the arm, where he found a hard spot the size of a nut; he went to bed, developed a fever, and recovered.[118] Ambroise Paré accounted for all these various symptoms, for in his *Liber pestis*, after listing and describing the symptoms, he wrote, "But all these troubles do not always come at once, or to all patients; and some have more of them than others: so that one hardly sees two cases … that are alike."[119]

THE PEST AS A CONTAGIOUS DISEASE

Paré's comments find an echo in the leading plague scholar R. Pollitzer, who cautions scholars on the variability of the plague. Many of the Jesuit descriptions of symptoms likewise indicate that these could be cases resulting from infection by *Y. pestis*, so a tempting conclusion is that these were epidemics of bubonic plague and the continued use of the term pest instead of plague is unnecessary. On the other hand, the Jesuit accounts indicate that the disease or diseases were, as already emphasized, contagious and spread in ways incompatible with the classic model of plague and the conclusions of the Indian Plague Research Commission. The third conclusion of the commission was, "Those attending bubonic plague patients remained singularly free from infection." When a Jesuit became sick, his superior usually placed him in the care of one of the lay brothers (the Jesuits called them temporal coadjutors) and segregated them both in separate accommodations, quite often a room in the college since most epidemics resulted in the suspension of classes. Not all but many of these lay brothers contracted the pest while caring for the sick Jesuit, who in many cases traced his illness to hearing the confessions of the sick.

Brother Giovanni Giovannini took care of Francesco Butirone at Milan in 1576; he contracted the pest but survived,[120] and in the following summer

[117]ITAL 154: 209, Beringucci to Mercurian, Venice, July 13.

[118]ITAL 155: 29v, to Mercurian, September 10.

[119]Quoted from Paget, *Ambroise Paré*, 267.

[120]ITAL 153: 100v, Sgariglia to Candi, January 15, included in the letter of Beringucci to Mercurian, Venice, February 9, 1577.

his superiors sent him to Brescia to perform the same service for the Jesuit community there. According to Pollitzer, people who survive a case of the plague tend to be immune to further infection,[121] but Giovannini's superiors gave no indication that they considered this to be the case; they sent him because his bout with the pest had made him "experienced."[122] Before Giovannini arrived came the news from Paolo Prandi in Brescia that "Giovanni Guidi (that is, Giovanni the cook, whom we call Giovannino or little Giovanni), who was one of those who took care of the pest-stricken," was himself sick; Giovannino died, but Giovannini survived his second encounter with the pest.[123] Three of the pest-stricken at Brescia had themselves contracted the disease after hearing the confessions of the sick. As a result of such incidents, Jesuits pointed to chains of infection or contagion to explain the course of the pest in Jesuit communities. The best example of this occurred at Vienna in 1563, as explained by Diego Lainez: "Our Lord God has taken Marco, a coadjutor, who died from the pest after caring for one of the boarders, who also died from it in one of our vineyards outside Vienna. Another German coadjutor, who cared for Marco, also became sick and died from the same disease, and of those who cared for him a third coadjutor became sick, although God watched over him so that he did not die. A fourth coadjutor is also sick...and we do not know if he survived or not." When the fourth became sick the Jesuits were advised to hire non-Jesuits to care for their pest-stricken.[124]

The fourth conclusion of the commission was, "The contacts of patients who developed bubonic plague after arrival in a hitherto unaffected locality invariably remained well." The perception of Jesuits and others during the sixteenth century was quite the contrary; according to popular belief, the pest often spread by people fleeing infected towns and taking the disease with them. Giovanni Francesco Prandi concisely expressed this belief during the epidemic that spread through northern Italy in 1576: "Those who fled from Venice have infected the world."[125] Jesuits themselves usually fled outbreaks of pest, often seeking refuge at Jesuit colleges in other towns. Oliver Manare,

---

[121]R. Pollitzer, *Plague* (Geneva: World Health Organization, 1954), 137–38.

[122]ITAL 154: 238, Mazzarino to Mercurian, Genoa, July 20, 1577.

[123]ITAL 154: 247v, to Peruschi, July 14, included in the letter from Peruschi to Mercurian, Milan, July 24; 367, Peruschi to Mercurian, Milan, August 19.

[124]Lainez, *Lainii monumenta*, 7: 493, to Madrid, Trent, November 15.

[125]ITAL 155: 150, to [Mercurian], Brescia, October 9.

provincial of the Rhine province in 1588, recognized that this practice was not only dangerous to the other colleges but also disturbing to the political authorities in the other towns; he accordingly ordered all rectors to arrange to have a convenient place of refuge outside their towns.[126] During the epidemic at Avignon in 1577 Jesuits faced accusations that a sick Jesuit from Lyon brought the disease to their college, from whence it spread throughout the city.

The accounts do not contain any other cases of fleeing Jesuits' infecting another college or town, but they do contain cases of fleeing Jesuits' taking the infection with them and of Jesuit colleges becoming infected by the arrival of someone who was already sick. An example of the former occurred when the Jesuits fled the devastating epidemic of pest at Cluj in Romania in 1586; according to Andreas Busau, after arriving at Kolozsmonostor, "on the second or third day...Georg Alman, the sacristan, who perhaps was already infected when he came from the college, began to be sick and on the third or fourth day died from the pest." The pest spread from Alman to other Jesuits, but Busau did not state if it spread to the residents of Kolozsmonostor.[127] Two examples of someone's infecting a college occurred at Vienna. In August 1576 a priest already infected with the pest sought entry to the Jesuit college; he persuaded the janitor to let him in by hiding his condition, and as a result of the incidental contact between the priest and the Jesuit community five died including the janitor.[128] In December of the same year a Hungarian student likewise dissimulated his illness, gained entry to the college, and, "as we think," wrote Emerich Forsler, infected two other students; all three died.[129]

According to the fifth conclusion of the commission, "The great majority of the patients whose history was accurately known had had no contact with previous cases before falling ill." This conclusion is contrary to Jesuit experience. Time and time again Jesuits who attended to the religious needs of those sick and dying from the pest contracted the disease and died, victims of charity, while those Jesuits who avoided contact with the pest-stricken survived. When the pest did enter a Jesuit community and struck those who had segregated themselves there, Jesuits could often point to a Jesuit who had heard the confessions of the sick as the source of the infection. On occasion

[126]GERM 168: 130, to Aquaviva, Mainz, December 17.
[127]*Monumenta Hungariae*, 2: 967, to Peter Skarga, Kővár, August 21.
[128]GERM 137 II: 347, Maggio to Mercurian, Olomouc, October 9.
[129]Ibid., 373v, Brno, December 23; 138 I: 215, Forsler to Mercurian, Vienna, June 12, 1577.

Jesuits who heard the confessions of the sick did not contract the pest, but the tendency of Jesuits to view these cases as a special providence from God illustrates their rarity. When Jesuit confessors remained well at Messina and Monreale in 1575, Giovanni Battista Carminata and Juan Polanco considered it a miracle,[130] and when the same thing occurred at Valencia in 1558 Pedro Parra stated, "We have received a mercy certainly worthy of consideration and recognition of Him who gave it."[131]

One of the best illustrations of the danger that accompanied contact with the ill occurred in 1576 at Milan, where Jesuits became embroiled in a famous dispute with the cardinal archbishop Carlo Borromeo. When Borromeo requested priests to attend the pest-stricken, he was disappointed with the number of Jesuits who assisted and with their refusal to undertake certain tasks considered dangerous. Jesuit superiors were reluctant to commit Jesuits to the service of the sick because, as succinctly explained by the provincial, Francesco Adorno, to send priests to the lazaretto was "to send them to a certain death."[132] The Capuchins, practicing a form of suicide, threw themselves into the lazaretto and soon counted four and eventually a total of ten dead. The cardinal recruited Swiss priests accustomed to caring for the pest-stricken, but one died immediately.[133] The Jesuits Giorgio Farina, Francesco Centurione, and Giovanni Battista Vannini volunteered to serve the sick staying in some huts constructed outside the city; within a few days Farina contracted the pest and died, while Centurione lasted two and a half weeks.[134] Vannini survived the experience, apparently as a result of the precautions he took; he heard confessions at a distance but refused to give communion to the sick. This was not enough for the cardinal, who insisted that they receive communion as well, and as a result he became further annoyed with the Jesuits. The superior of the Casa di San Fidele, Giovanni Battista Peruschi, told the cardinal that it seemed a greater service to God to have a priest hear the confessions of a

[130]ITAL 148: 136–136v, Carminata to Mercurian, July 29; Juan Polanco, *Polanci complementa: Epistolae et commentaria P. Joannis Alphonsi de Polanco e Societate Jesu*, 2 vols. (Madrid: Gabrielis Lopez del Horno, 1916–1917), 2: 370, to Mercurian, October 8.

[131]*Litterae quadrimestres*, 5: 703, to Lainez, June 2.

[132]ITAL 152: 2v, to Mercurian, Genoa, August 17.

[133]ITAL 153: 296v, Giulio Cesare Mazzarino to Mercurian, Genoa, April 17, 1577; 155: 150v, Giovanni Francesco Prandi to Mercurian, Brescia, October 9, 1576.

[134]ITAL 152: 327, 356, Adorno to Mercurian, Parma, December 4 and 17, 1576.

hundred or a thousand people and survive than to have a priest give communion to ten or twenty and die.[135]

The final two conclusions of the commission concern multiple cases of plague in a single household:

> 6. If bubonic cases occurred in a settlement, in the great majority of instances not more than one case occurred per house.

> 7. If multiple cases occurred in any house, they often appeared simultaneously, as if infected from a common source.

The evidence from Jesuit accounts reveals a different pattern. As already indicated, many instances of multiple cases occurred, and Jesuits noted chains of infection as the disease spread from one person to another. In fact, of the 372 deaths of Jesuits attributed to the pest possibly as many as 200, perhaps more, were multiple cases in a single residence, or in other words "in the ... majority of instances ... *more than one case* occurred per house." Some of the more notable and better documented cases include Lisbon, with seventeen deaths between July 22 and September 2, 1569;[136] Vienna, with seven deaths between September 1 and October 9, 1576;[137] Brno, with six deaths between October 15 and November 8, 1584;[138] and Cluj with fifteen deaths between July 19 and August 17, 1586.[139]

Some of these multiple cases could have resulted from simultaneous infection from a single source rather than from chains of infection. It was

---

[135]ITAL 154: 366v, to Mercurian, August 19, 1577; see 286–286v, Vannini to Mercurian, August 2.

[136]LUS 63: 170v, Jorge Sarrano to Borgia, Evora, September 18; 173, Lião Anriquez to Borgia, Evora, September 23; Ignace Dugout, *Victimes de la charité: Catalogue des pères et frères de la Compagnie de Jésus, morts de maladies contagieuses contractées au service des malades* (Paris: M.-R. Leroy, 1907), 9–10; Antonio Franco, *Imagem de virtude em o noviciado da Companhia de Jesus do Real Collegio de Coimbra em Portugal*, 2 vols. (Evora and Coimbra: Na Officina de Universidade and No Real collegio das artes da Companhia de Jesu, 1719), 1: 242.

[137]GERM 137 II: 327, Maggio to Mercurian, Vienna, September 18; 329, 358, Forsler to Mercurian, Vienna, September 21 and October 13.

[138]Alois Kroess, *Geschichte der böhmischen Provinz der Gesellschaft Jesu*, 2 vols. (Vienna: Ambr. Opitz, 1910–1927), 1: 456–58.

[139]According to the letter from Mateusz Strus, quoted in chapter 2, seventeen died between July 17 and August 17, but at least two of those on this list, Georg Alman and Johan Ardulph, died at Kolozsmonostor. Alman could be included here, because those who fled with him believed that he was already sick when he arrived in Kolozsmonostor. See *Monumenta Hungariae*, 2: 1014–15, *Catalogus sociorum in Transylvania peste extinctorum*, September.

possible to determine the number of days between the deaths of Jesuits for sixty-nine of the multiple cases within a single Jesuit residence. On three occasions two Jesuits died on the same day, which is a strong indication of simultaneous infection from a single source. Table 6 shows the number of days for the

TABLE 6: NUMBER OF DAYS BETWEEN DEATHS FROM THE PEST IN A HOUSEHOLD

Number of days between deaths	Number of cases
1	16
2	16
3	3
4	8
5	2
6	3
7	6
8	2
9	3
10	2
11	1
12	1

remainder. Since the incubation period in modern cases of bubonic plague is between one and six days, all the deaths that occurred on the same day and those occurring up to the sixth day and even beyond, depending on the length of time between the appearance of symptoms and death, could indicate simultaneous infection from a single source; that includes the majority of the cases.

However, an analysis of incidents of the above-mentioned multiple cases reveals a different situation. At Brno the deaths occurred over three and a half weeks, at Cluj four weeks, Vienna five and a half weeks, and Lisbon six weeks. The general pattern is one of chains of infection as the pest always went jumping from one person to another.

PLAGUE?

The application of the Jesuit experience to the conclusions of the Plague Research Commission does not exhaust the evidence regarding the perception of the pest as a contagious disease. As already noted, this topic will recur as the contagious nature of the pest affected every aspect of the Jesuit response to the disease. If the Jesuit accounts of the pest were in fact describing outbreaks of bubonic plague, then the sixteenth-century experience of the disease was quite different from modern observation of it. Jesuits perceived a disease that could spread from person to person without requiring the presence of that unholy trinity of culprits, *Y. pestis*, *R. rattus*, and *X. cheopis*. Jesuit accounts describe a disease that was as contagious as pneumonic plague but had symptoms comparable to bubonic plague, and they do not mention a single rat. To enter the dispute between the English rat flea school and the French human flea school, the chains of infections reported by Jesuits provide support for interhuman spread of bubonic plague via *P. irritans* rather than for the classic model of rat—rat flea—human. The problem for the historian is the nature of much of the evidence, based as it is on the interaction between Jesuit perceptions of specific events and prevailing beliefs of the contagious nature of the disease. The belief in the contagiousness of the disease would affect perceptions of it, resulting in a refusal to give serious consideration to contrary experience. On the other hand, some of the evidence, such as the chains of infection, transcends belief and perception and indicates relationships of cause and effect as the disease spread from one person to another. On occasion Jesuits charted chains of infections that even interhuman spread via *P. irritans* would fail to explain. In short, the retrospective diagnosis remains "plague?" rather than "plague."

FOUR

CAUSES AND REMEDIES

JESUITS SUBSCRIBED TO THE Christian notion that God sent disease to punish people for their sins and that penitence was the necessary response to epidemics. God also used epidemics to warn and to educate sinners and to purge the evil and to protect the good. In addition to penitence, the spiritual pharmacopeia available to Catholics included confession, communion, processions, and prayers to protective saints. Jesuits believed, on the other hand, that epidemic disease also had natural causes, such as the corruption of the air and contagion, and unnatural causes, such as intentional poisoning; they argued that the healthy should take precautions and that the sick should seek assistance from medical practitioners. In other words, Jesuits accepted the distinction between primary or religious causes and remedies and secondary causes and remedies.

PRIMARY AND SECONDARY CAUSES AND REMEDIES

In 1577 the Jesuit Antonio Possevino published anonymously a pamphlet entitled *Causes and Remedies of the Pest and of Other Diseases.*[1] The title is misleading, for Possevino argued that sin was the only cause, and penitence would be an adequate summary of his remedies. Ever since the Black Death struck

---

[1] Antonio Possevino, *Cause et rimedii della peste, et d'altre infermità* (Florence: Appresso i Giunti, 1577); I am indebted to J. Patrick Donnelly, S.J., for directing my attention to this pamphlet and to Possevino's authorship. See OPP NN 333: 11, Giacomo Domenichi to Possevino, Rome, February 15, 1597.

Europe in 1347, Christians had viewed outbreaks of pestilence as the just punishment of an angry God for the manifold sins of a wicked people, and in the wake of the scourge of God the Church had promoted penitence as the sole means of placating the divine wrath.[2] Preachers reveled in the opportunity to castigate sinners, citing such Old Testament passages as chapter 9 of Ezekiel, where the Lord spared those who bore the mark of holiness but ordered the slaughter of those who did not: "Slay old men outright, young men and maidens, little children and women, but touch no one upon whom is the mark." These beliefs relate to the Christian doctrine of divine providence that God controls, guides, and directs events according to His purpose. As expressed by Possevino, "Not even a single leaf on a tree moves without the particular knowledge and wish of God."[3]

The doctrine of divine providence was just as evident among Jesuits as among the Protestant reformers, with whom the doctrine is usually associated. Among Protestants, however, the belief in divine providence could produce in its extreme adherents a tendency toward resignation and fatalism; they would ask what benefit could come from human efforts against epidemics in face of the awful omnipotence of the Almighty?[4] Georg Ware, in his account of the epidemic at Prague in 1568, noted that some obviously Protestant Bohemians, "confident in God's predestination," took no precautions against infection. Similarly, among Muslims fatalism in the face of pestilence received support from the following religious tenets: "1. A Muslim should not enter or flee from a plague-stricken land. 2. The plague is a martyrdom and a mercy from God for a Muslim and a punishment for an infidel. 3. There is no infection (contagion)."[5]

---

[2]The belief in epidemics as divine punishment for sins antedates the Black Death and has pre-Christian antecedents; see Jean-Noël Biraben, *Les hommes en France et dans les pays européens et méditerranéens*, 2 vols. (Paris: Mouton, 1975–1976), 2: 7–8.

[3]Possevino, *Cause et rimedii della peste*, 11.

[4]Jean Delumeau, *La peur en occident (XIVe–XVIIe siècles): Une cité assiégée* (Paris: Fayard, 1978), 137; see the discussions in Paul Slack, *The Impact of Plague in Tudor and Stuart England* (London: Routledge and Kegan Paul, 1985), 228–34, Paolo Preto, *Peste e società a Venezia nel 1576* (Vicenza: Neri Pozza Editore, 1978), 63, and A. Lynn Martin, *The Jesuit Mind: The Mentality of an Elite in Early Modern France* (Ithaca: Cornell University Press, 1988), 127–41.

[5]Michael W. Dols, *The Black Death in the Middle East* (Princeton: Princeton University Press, 1977), 109.

Despite their adherence to the doctrine of divine providence, most Christians rejected Turkish fatalism and Protestant predestination and accepted instead the distinction between primary and secondary causes and remedies. Divine providence was the primary cause, but secondary causes included natural phenomena such as celestial influences, corruption of the air, and contagion; God used these agencies to achieve His will. Various forms of religious reform and penitence were the primary remedies, but the most popular secondary remedy was a pill "made of three ingredients called *cito, longe* and *tarde* (swiftly, far, and tardily), namely run swiftly, go far, and return tardily."[6] Primary and secondary causes and remedies were moreover interconnected; some sins, such as gluttony and lust, were unhealthy and disposed the body to receive contagion.[7] On occasion secular and religious authorities became involved in disputes over whether secular or religious remedies should take precedence, but for the most part both sides recognized the need for both types of remedies.[8] Venice was among the leaders in developing public measures such as the quarantine and the *cordon sanitaire* to combat epidemics, but Venetian authorities also believed that the health of the city depended on divine favor and accordingly, when confronting an epidemic, issued decrees condemning immoral behavior and supporting penitence. For example, during the outbreak of the pest in 1576 a decree dated August 9 promoted frequent communion, fasting on Wednesdays, Fridays, and Saturdays, and private prayer, and recommended other, more spectacular displays of devotion, such as barefooted visits to churches.[9] The promotion of both primary and secondary remedies was evident even among the medical profession, which stressed the divine origins of disease and the need for penitence to combat illness. Ambroise Paré, for example, proclaimed in his *Liber pestis,* "Our best

---

[6]Quoted from Carlo M. Cipolla, *Cristofano and the Plague: A Study in the History of Public Health in the Age of Galileo* (London: Collins, 1973), 23.

[7]Slack, *Impact of Plague,* 28–29.

[8]Richard J. Palmer, "The Church, Leprosy and Plague in Medieval and Early Modern Europe," in *The Church and Healing,* ed. W. J. Sheils (Oxford: Basil Blackwell, 1982), 95–99. In a paper entitled "The Origins of the Crisis Procession in the Early Middle Ages," given at a conference in Adelaide on September 27, 1991, John Koenig argued that during the Early Middle Ages the secular authorities took the lead in pressuring religious authorities to permit processions during times of crisis such as epidemics.

[9]Brian Pullan, "Due organizzazioni per il controllo sociale," in *La Memoria della Salute: Venezia e il suo ospedale dal XVI al XX secolo,* ed. Nelli-Elena Vanzan Marchini (Venice: Arsenale, 1985), 13; Antonio Niero, "Pietà ufficiale e pietà popolare in tempo di peste," in *Venezia e la peste, 1348– 1797,* 2d ed. (Venice: Marsilio Editori, 1980), 287; for the decree of August 9 see 138.

antidote against the plague is the conversion and amendment of our lives."[10]
The attitude of the medical profession is not surprising, for even doctors often
recognized that their remedies were ineffective. Nonetheless, those who relied
solely on religious remedies received condemnation; to reject precautions and
cures and rely instead on a miracle was presumptuous, a tempting of God.[11]

Jesuit response to epidemic disease reveals the same distinction between
primary and secondary causes and remedies. Antonio Possevino, for example,
claimed that "the more principal causes" of the pest were different types of sin,
but he also acknowledged that epidemics could arise from the "bad quality of
the humors, or from the corruption of the air, or from contagion."[12] When
Jerónimo Nadal prepared directives for Jesuit colleges confronting an outbreak
of the pest, he began by recommending masses and prayers and then proceeded to practical advice including the fumigation of rooms, the purchase of
medicine, consultation with medical practitioners, the segregation of the sick,
flight to avoid infection, and even the purchase of clothes.[13] In his sermon at
Augsburg on August 29, 1563, Peter Canisius urged people not only to pray and
to do penance in the face of the pest but also to exercise caution.[14] Jesuit comments also reveal an interconnection between primary and secondary causes
and remedies. According to Possevino, primary remedies could produce an
effect on both the primary and secondary causes, for he stated that public processions with the relics of saints could placate the anger of God as well as
purify corrupt air and hence bring health.[15]

[10]Quoted from Stephen Paget, *Ambroise Paré and His Times, 1510–1590* (New York: G. P. Putnam's Sons, 1899), 275. See Alison Klairmont, "The Problem of the Plague: New Challenges to
Healing in Sixteenth-Century France," *Proceedings of the Fifth Annual Meeting of the Western Society for French History* 5 (1977): 120.

[11]Palmer, "Church, Leprosy and Plague," 89.

[12]Possevino, *Cause et rimedii della peste*, 22.

[13]ARSI, OPP NN 159: 493–500, *Ordo per servari poterit tempore pestis* [1562]; see Jerónimo
Nadal, *Epistolae P. Hieronymi Nadal Societatis Iesu ab anno 1546 ad 1577*, 4 vols. (Madrid: Augustini
Avrial and Gabrielis Lopez del Horno, 1898–1905), 2: 138, to Lainez, Innsbruck, November 20, 1562.

[14]Peter Canisius, *Beati Petri Canisii, Societatis Iesu, epistolae et acta*, ed. Otto Braunsberger, 13
vols. (Freiburg im Breisgau: Herder, 1896–1923), 4: 822.

[15]Possevino, *Cause et rimedii della peste*, 63, 65.

PRIMARY CAUSES

Robert Muchembled has noted that in early modern France everyone believed that disease resulted from either divine or diabolical intervention.[16] Jesuits, on the other hand, never blamed the devil for outbreaks of epidemic disease, although they considered him responsible for other misfortunes. Rather than blame the devil, Jesuits praised the Lord for their misfortunes, including epidemics. When General Diego Lainez learned that the pest had killed Paschase Broët in 1562, his response was, "May God Our Lord be thanked for everything," and quoted Paul's letter to the Romans 14:8, "If we live, we live to the Lord, and if we die, we die to the Lord."[17] So frequent are the expressions of gratitude to the Lord, the allusions to the goodness of God, and the attributions of cause to the divinity in the correspondence of some Jesuits that the usage was an obvious rhetorical device. One of the best illustrations of this is the chronicle of death and divine providence at Palermo by Paolo Achille in 1575. One of the worst is Mario Beringucci's use of simile to describe the sporadic outbreaks of the pest in northern Italy in June 1577: "It seems that the Lord wants to hold the bit in our mouths, so that we, like unbridled horses, do not run unreined after our appetites."[18] Beringucci reined in his rhetorical excess when reporting on the deaths of Jesuits at Milan and Brescia in September and exchanged the bridle for a whip: "The Lord still has the whip in his hand, and He has not finished punishing us because we have not finished offending Him."[19] Rhetorical embellishments aside, Jesuits left many indications of their belief that God was the cause of epidemics. Juan Polanco's response to the deaths of several Jesuits at Vienna in 1563 was, "His will be done in life as in death,"[20] and Jesuits sometimes referred to an epidemic as "God's visitation."[21]

---

[16]Robert Muchembled, "Le corps, la culture populaire et la culture des élites en France (XVe-XVIIIe siècle)," in *Leib und Leben in der Geschichte der Neuzeit*, ed. Arthur E. Imhof (Berlin: Duncker und Humblot, 1983), 142.

[17]Diego Lainez, *Lainii monumenta: Epistolae et acta patris Jacobi Lainii secundi praepositi generalis Societatis Jesu*, 8 vols. (Madrid: Gabrielis Lopez del Horno, 1912–1917), 6: 528, to Jean Pelletier, Trent, December 1.

[18]ITAL 154: 58, to Mercurian, Venice, June 1.

[19]ITAL 155: 48, to Mercurian, Venice, September 14.

[20]Nadal, *Epistolae*, 2: 438, to Nadal, Trent, November 7.

[21]For two examples see Ignatius Loyola, *Sancti Ignatii de Loyola, Societatis Jesu fundatoris, epistolae et instructiones*, 11 vols. (Madrid: Gabrielis Lopez del Horno, 1903–1911), 6: 259, to Broët, Rome, January 30, 1554; Lainez, *Lainii monumenta*, 2: 345, to Giovanni Battista Tavona, Rome, August 7, 1557.

Visitation is a neutral word; more forceful are punishment, scourge, and castigation. These three words and variations of them were also more common than visitation and other neutral words in Jesuit accounts of epidemics. Paolo Bisciola used all three in one sentence in his account of the pest at Milan in 1577,[22] and when Pedro Ribadeneira commented in January 1577 on the epidemic of pest affecting Italy, he wrote of his fear that "God wants to punish us for our sins."[23] André Dawant reacted to the news that the pest threatened Chambéry in June 1570 by praying, "May God guard us from the castigation that we deserve,"[24] and Ludovico Corbinelli proclaimed in May 1576, "If Our Lord wants to scourge Italy with the pest we have cause to fear as a result of our sins."[25] Jan Behem abandoned the usual vocabulary for the phrases "the admirable justice of God" and "the clear retribution of sinners" when describing the epidemic at Prague in 1562 and then noted the "mercy of God" in preserving the Jesuits, quoting Psalms 91:7: "A thousand may fall at your side, ten thousand at your right hand; but it will not come near you."[26] On numerous occasions Jesuits did fall victim to the pest, and when Luigi Calligaris died at Messina in November 1575, the rector, Giovanni Battista Carminata, blamed his own sins since God had not answered his prayers for the safe recovery of Calligaris.[27]

Despite their readiness to blame their own and others' sins for an epidemic, Jesuits seldom mentioned particular sins in their accounts. Typical is the comment by Hermann Dorkens, rector of the college at Trier, "So great is the inhumanity of men, so great is the multitude of the unfaithful that it would not be surprising if God withdrew His mercy" and sent the pest.[28] Antonio Possevino did provide a list of sins in his pamphlet, dividing them into five

---

[22]Paolo Bisciola, *Relatione verissima del progresso della peste di Milano: Qual principiò nel mese d'agosto 1576 e seguì sino al mese di maggio 1577* (Ancona: Alessandro Benacci, 1577), 14. An English translation is somewhat awkward: "questi castighi con quali [Dio] ci flagella, e punisse," literally "these castigations with which [God] scourges and punishes us."

[23]Pedro Ribadeneira, *Patris Petri de Ribadeneira Societatis Iesu sacerdotis confessiones, epistolae*, 2 vols. (Madrid: Typis Gabrielis Lopez del Horno, 1920–1923), 1: 751–52, to Cardinal Antonio Carafa, Toledo, January 5.

[24]GAL 83: 74, to Borgia, June 6.

[25]ITAL 151: 123v, to Mercurian, Naples, May 18.

[26]GERM 144: 45, *quadrimestris*, December 28; also GERM 139: 154.

[27]ITAL 149: 76, to [Mercurian], November 1.

[28]Joseph Hansen, ed., *Rheinische Akten zur Geschichte des Jesuitenordens, 1542–1582* (Bonn: H. Berendt, 1896), 517, Dorkens (Thyraeus) to Leonhard Kessel, September 13, 1565.

different categories or causes of the pest: (1) pride, arrogance, ambition, vanity, and blasphemy; (2) heresy; (3) theft, rapine, and usury; (4) luxury and carnality; and (5) dishonest madrigals, disgraceful songs, dirty dancing, indecent familiarity in conversation, sumptuous clothes, immodest books, and nude pictures.[29] When other Jesuits mentioned particular sins, they usually attributed epidemics to Possevino's second cause, heresy. Jesuits considered an epidemic that struck the Protestant community at Graz in 1575 to be "a singular visit by God."[30] An epidemic of pest at Lyon in 1564 gave Emond Auger an opportunity to document another singular act of divine providence: "Whoever does not want to believe that apostasy from the Catholic faith does not result in punishment can easily see it now with his own eyes,...for God moved His hand and delivered such justice to His rebels that few remain here now, and for every dead Catholic more than ten of the [Protestants] died."[31] Everard Mercurian reported that Catholics considered an epidemic of pest accompanied by storms and floods that afflicted England in 1570 to be a result of the pope's excommunication of Queen Elizabeth.[32] A different type of sin brought an epidemic to the inhabitants of Avignon in 1577, for Jean Pionneau partially attributed the epidemic to the city's failure to recognize all the good done by the Jesuits.[33]

Related to the Jesuit view that epidemics were divine punishments for sin was the opinion that God sent epidemics as a warning; the pest had educational and monitory functions. Everard Mercurian speculated that God threatened Tournai with the "physical" pest in August 1564 as a means of healing the inhabitants' "spiritual" pest,[34] and when an epidemic of pest killed "only" fourteen thousand at Milan in 1577, Alfonso Sgariglia thought it a sign that "the Lord wants to threaten but not to punish."[35] Jesuits of course believed that people should heed these warnings by amending their lives, and they complained when this did not happen. Venice and Vienna were the objects of several complaints. At Vienna, Lorenzo Maggio observed in October 1571 that,

---

[29] Possevino, *Cause et rimedii della peste*, 22–29.
[30] GERM 136 I: 124, Johann Reinel to Francisco Antonio, March 2.
[31] GAL 80: 263, to Lainez, September 28; see Martin, *Jesuit Mind*, 134.
[32] GAL 83: 139v, to Borgia, September 18.
[33] GAL 89: 298v, to Coudret, October 7.
[34] GERM 145: 185, to Lainez, August 29.
[35] ITAL 153: 101, to Paolo Candi, January 15.

despite the punishments of God, "one does not see any amendment,"[36] and several months later Emerich Forsler stated that the "very great blindness" of the Viennese prevented them from recognizing "this visit of Our Lord."[37] One report from Venice in December 1576 noted that despite the scourge of God "the same abuses and vices" remained,[38] and in the following year Mario Beringucci expressed his frustrations on discerning "such little amendment of life and such little recognition of the castigation of God."[39] When the epidemic ended in May without further signs of religious renewal, Beringucci seemed disappointed, and he prayed that God would liberate Venice from the "spiritual pest, which was more important than the other, for it infects and kills wretched souls."[40]

When an epidemic of pest struck Cologne in 1552 and 1553, Leonhard Kessel was at first pessimistic that the divine warning would produce the necessary effects: "Oh hardened breast, oh blind eyes, which holy afflictions do not open!"[41] Then the epidemic had its desired result, and Kessel could report with satisfaction on the increase in popular devotion and his hopes for an ample harvest of souls.[42] Jesuits happily reported on similar harvests at Siracusa in 1558, Augsburg in 1564, and Lisbon in 1569,[43] and expressed their pleasure that the divine admonitions resulted in religious fervor and repentance, almost welcoming epidemics as a means of achieving a religious renewal. Dominique Mengin's account of the epidemic of pest at Munich in 1562 is the best example of this: "One can see lately how useful and holy may be this visit. Formerly the people of Munich placed their devotion in the pleasures of this world and the delights of the flesh. Formerly they scorned all piety and had contempt for all religion. Now, in truth, recognizing the power of God, they have transformed their unbridled souls into gentle and religious ones. Indeed, they now embrace the divine sacrament with diligent zeal."[44]

[36]GERM 133 II: 430, to Nadal, October 17.

[37]GERM 134 I: 67v, to Nadal, January 30, 1572.

[38]ITAL 152: 358, Giovanni Battista Buonacorso to Mercurian, Vicenza, December 17.

[39]ITAL 153: 100v, to [Mercurian], February 6, 1577.

[40]Ibid., 51, [May] 18.

[41]Hansen, *Rheinische Akten*, 216, *quadrimestris*, January 10, 1553.

[42]Ibid., 237, July 1, 1553; also in *Litterae quadrimestres ex universis praeter Indiam et Brasiliam locis in quibus aliqui de Societate Jesu versabantur Romam missae*, 7 vols. (Madrid and Rome: Augustinus Avrial, La Editorial Ibérica, and A. Macioce e Pisani, 1894–1932), 2: 347.

[43]*Litterae quadrimestres*, 5: 889, by Michelangelo Labaco, Siracusa, December 1; Canisius, *Beati Petri Canisii*, 4: 808, *quadrimestris* by Wilhelm Elderen, Augsburg, January 13; LUS 63: 224, Jorge Sarrano to Borgia, Evora, December 4.

[44]Nadal, *Epistolae*, 2: 179, Mengin to Nadal, December 9.

On occasion Jesuits also noted that epidemics had a purgative function; God sent the pest to purge the evil and reward the good.[45] When epidemics struck the good, one of God's purposes was, as in the case of Job, to reveal his friends and confound the devil. Guy Roillet attributed the epidemic that struck the Jesuits at Ferrara in 1558 to the fact that "God loves us and wants to punish us."[46] God furthermore sent epidemic disease as a mercy to the faithful; hence, at Trier in 1566 the Lord liberated several Jesuits "from the miseries of this life,"[47] He took three Jesuits "from this vale of tears, Vienna" in 1576,[48] and at Loreto in 1575 eight Jesuits "left this prison."[49] In addition to blaming his own sins for the death of Luigi Calligaris at Messina in 1575, the rector also noted that Calligaris contracted the pest as a result of his work with the pest-stricken, so "Our Lord wanted to reward him for his labors."[50] Not as fortunate was the unrewarded Giovanni Battista Vannini who cared for the stricken Francesco Centurione at Milan in 1576 and survived; Vannini commented, "because I was unworthy of greater grace, the Lord did not want any infection to afflict me."[51]

Despite Vannini's self-effacement, most Jesuits were quick to see the hand of God whenever they survived an epidemic. These were occasions for more rhetorical embellishments. In an obvious reference to the biblical account of Shadrach, Meshach, and Abednego in chapter 3 of Daniel, Peter Canisius proclaimed from Vienna in April 1553, "God...preserves his own especially in the midst of a blazing furnace."[52] Johann Reidt made the allusion more explicit when he wrote from Cologne in January 1565, "God...so paternally guarded his unworthy servants, as He formerly guarded the three in the furnace of Babylon, that not even one person in the college died from the pest or became sick."[53] These are but two of hundreds of occasions when Jesuit accounts of epidemic disease attributed survival to God, singular acts of divine providence, and/or miracles.

---

[45]For two examples see Canisius, *Beati Petri Canisii*, 4: 369, Canisius to Cardinal Stanislaus Hosius, Augsburg, October 29, 1563; ITAL 149: 120, Beringucci to Mercurian, Venice, November 12, 1575.

[46]ITAL 110: 252, 111: 3, to Lainez, December 3, 1557, and January 1, 1558.

[47]Nadal, *Epistolae*, 3: 251, to Borgia, Innsbruck, October 15.

[48]GERM 137 II: 358, Forsler to Mercurian, October 13.

[49]ROM 126b: 94, annual by Benedetto Giustiniano, Rome, January 1, 1576.

[50]ITAL 149: 90, Carminata to Mercurian, November 4.

[51]ITAL 154: 286, to Mercurian, August 2, 1577.

[52]Hansen, *Rheinische Akten*, 222, to Andreas Herl von Bardwick, April 27.

[53]Ibid., 509, *quadrimestris*, January 1.

In their comments on the primary causes of epidemics Jesuits were not unique but followed traditional Christian explanations of fortune and misfortune. To explain epidemic disease the emphasis was on the punishment of sins, but God also warned, educated, purged, revealed, confounded, favored, and protected.[54] Michael W. Dols compares Muslim and Christian attitudes in his book on *The Black Death in the Middle East*: "European writers laid greater emphasis upon the punitive aspect of plague in God's plan than upon the monitory and purgative virtues of the disease found in Muslim society." While it is true that the Christian tradition emphasized the punitive, it also recognized many other, to borrow Dols' phrase, "virtues of the disease," including the monitory and purgative. Dols also argues that the Christian tradition stressed individual sin and punishment while the Muslim tradition emphasized the proper collective behavior of a community.[55] However, Jesuits followed a long Christian tradition of viewing epidemics as collective punishment for collective sin that required collective penitence to placate the anger of God.[56] This is obvious from Jesuit attitudes toward the primary remedies.

PRIMARY REMEDIES

According to Alison Klairmont, a significant difference between Protestant and Catholic response to disease was that Protestants made a distinction between the physical health of the body and the spiritual health of the soul, a distinction that was not as evident among Catholics. As a result of this difference Catholics believed that human efforts could help heal a disease. As explained by Klairmont, the Catholic position meant that "human beings could contribute not only to their physical health but to their spiritual health as well through prayer, good works, processions, and fasts."[57] In Jesuit accounts of epidemic disease human efforts could occur on three different levels, the individual, the collegial, and the collective. Antonio Possevino's remedies focused on the individual: "On hearing of the approach of this visit sent by the hand of God, you should at once put your mind on His Divine Majesty, retire to some

---

[54]See the discussions in Palmer, "Church, Leprosy and Plague," 84, and Preto, *Peste e società a Venezia*, 72.

[55]Dols, *Black Death*, 297, 300.

[56]See Lucinda McCray Beier, *Sufferers and Healers: The Experience of Illness in Seventeenth-Century England* (London: Routledge and Kegan Paul, 1987), 157–59; and Miguel Parets, *A Journal of the Plague Year: The Diary of the Barcelona Tanner Miguel Parets, 1651* ed., James S. Amelang (New York: Oxford University Press, 1991), 13.

[57]Klairmont, "Problem of the Plague," 121–22.

place apart, and put yourself completely and with great hope in His compassionate hands." Possevino then recommended a program of personal renewal that included prayer, charity, confession, communion, spiritual exercises, fasting, and frequent attendance at mass and sermons. He returned to his list of sins by urging people to "liquidate" their "dubious business affairs" and suggesting the burning of offensive books, playing cards, dice, and obscene pictures. Included in the pamphlet was a list of recommended reading that began with the book of Job and contained two works by Possevino's fellow Jesuit, Gaspar Loarte. Finally, when the pest was over, Possevino urged people not only to thank God, the Blessed Virgin, and the saints for delivery but also to persevere in their religious renewal, "waiting in this vale of misery the blessed hope and the coming of the great God."[58]

During the epidemic of pest at Milan in 1576 and 1577 Jesuits promoted a program of religious renewal similar to the one advocated by Possevino. They preached in areas threatened by the pest and, according to their annual letter, "eradicated the abuses of blasphemy, games, dances, and other occasions of sins." They gave communion and heard the confessions of many, some of whom made general confessions of their entire lives.[59] Jesuits reported on similar successes during the epidemic at Cologne in 1553; a virgin rejected a suitor and chose instead Christ as her perpetual spouse.[60] Since the virgin died shortly after making this vow, she avoided the possibility of a moral relapse, but the evidence from the Jesuit sources does not permit an evaluation of the perseverance of an epidemic-inspired religious renewal. Alan D. Dyer and Paul Slack, both commenting on Protestant England, argue that such renewals were short-lived and followed by considerable backsliding.[61] Given human nature, a similar conclusion for Catholic Europe might be appropriate.

According to Catholic theologians, of fundamental importance to the process of healing were the sacraments of communion and especially confession, which could heal spiritual as well as physical infirmities. In 1566 Pope Pius V issued a bull that required medical practitioners to summon a priest for

---

[58]Possevino, *Cause et rimedii della peste,* 49–59.

[59]MED 76: 39v, annual for 1576 and 1577 by Peruschi, March 12, 1578.

[60]Juan Polanco, *Vita Ignatii Loiolae et rerum Societatis Jesu historia,* 6 vols. (Madrid: Typographorum Societatis and Augustinus Avrial, 1894–1898), 3: 267–68, *Chronicon* for 1553.

[61]Alan D. Dyer, "The Influence of Bubonic Plague in England, 1500–1667," *Medical History* 22 (1978): 324; Slack, *Impact of Plague,* 287.

their patients, citing the words of Christ after he had cured people, "Go and sin no more."[62] In his section on the remedies of the pest Possevino stated that people could regain the health of their souls by regaining divine grace through confession of sins.[63] As a result of the views of the theologians, the bulls of popes, and the teachings of others, among Catholics confession was often the first priority when confronted with an epidemic disease, and the best indications of this are the attempts Jesuits made to hear the confessions of the sick, the efforts of public authorities to ensure the availability of priests to hear confessions, and the scramble among the threatened to reach a priest before it was too late. As already noted, Jesuit superiors received requests from municipal authorities to provide confessors, and many Jesuits accepted this task despite the dangers involved. Giovanni Francesco Prandi approved the measures adopted in 1576 at Milan, where "everyone died with the most holy sacraments of confession and communion, for as soon as a case was discovered a priest was sent."[64] Pedro Parra reported with satisfaction from Valencia in 1557 that a rumor of the pest resulted in so many people rushing to confession that the Jesuits could not hear them all.[65]

In 1562 Jerónimo Nadal wrote a set of recommendations for the Jesuit college at Vienna when an epidemic of pest threatened it. These recommendations became official guidelines for other colleges in similar situations. As already noted, Nadal began by encouraging Jesuits to say masses and prayers so that God would spare the town and especially the college; he then suggested that they write to other colleges in the province and to the general at Rome requesting masses and prayers to the same effect. Nadal concluded his short section on spiritual remedies by recommending particular devotion to the two saints regarded as protectors from the pest, Sebastian and Rocco.[66] A similar set of instructions, probably composed during the Italian epidemic of 1575–1577, began with a section entitled "Spiritual Preservatives." The first recom-

---

[62]Palmer, "Church, Leprosy and Plague," 85.

[63]Possevino, *Cause et rimedii della peste,* 50.

[64]ITAL 155: 150v, to [Mercurian], Brescia, October 9.

[65]*Litterae quadrimestres,* 5: 339, August 30.

[66]OPP NN 159: 493, *Ordo per servari poterit tempore pestis.* The entire document is on fols. 493–500; some amendments occur in another hand. See Marcel Fosseyeux, "Les saints protecteurs contre la 'male' mort au Moyen-Age et à la Renaissance," *Bulletin de la Société Française d'Histoire de la Médecine* 19 (1935): 339–49.

mendation in this section likewise counseled prayers and included "mortifications and other devotions in private as well as in public... to placate the anger of God." The second focused on spirituality, that is, the relationship of the individual's soul with God, the third suggested the use of holy water, *agnus dei* (the small wax cake blessed by the pope), religious images, and relics of the saints to protect Jesuit houses, colleges, and churches from infection, and the final recommendation urged Jesuits to prepare themselves to give assistance to the sick.[67] A report from Milan by Alfonso Sgariglia in 1576 indicates that the Jesuits there followed most of these recommendations: "We are all very happy and do not show any fear at all, and we promptly offer ourselves to say prayers and to endure discipline and other mortifications.... Some have offered to risk their lives and to assist others by hearing the confessions of the pest-stricken and helping them die well."[68] The annual letter for 1576 and 1577 reveals what Sgariglia meant by mortifications, for it states that Jesuits went barefoot in winter to the church every day to sing the seven psalms and the litanies.[69]

A concise description of a collective effort to heal disease occurs in Johann Reidt's report on the measures ordered by the archbishop of Cologne to combat an epidemic of pest in the summer of 1564; these included confession and communion, a three-day fast at the end of July, the distribution of alms to the poor, prayers, displays of the holy sacrament and the relics of the saints, and processions.[70] The archbishop's directives covered just about all the collective remedies that people could use to heal themselves. William Creichton reported on the fast undertaken by the inhabitants of Lyon in 1577; after they fasted on bread and water the pest gradually lost its force and disappeared.[71] At Chambéry in 1586 Jesuits advised the senate to order a fast of bread and water for three days a week for six weeks; as at Lyon the fast achieved the desired result.[72] One of the best examples of collective charity during an epidemic occurred at Rome in 1566 when Jesuits organized relief for those affected by the contaminated water, relief made possible by the donations of Roman prelates and

---

[67]OPP NN 159: 513–15, *Istruttione da praticarsi in tempo sospetto di peste*, anonymous and undated, but internal evidence suggests 1576. The author could have been Antonio Possevino.

[68]ITAL 152: 16v, to Mercurian, August 22.

[69]MED 76 I: 41, by Peruschi, March 12, 1578.

[70]Hansen, *Rheinische Akten*, 500, *quadrimestris*, September 1.

[71]GAL 89: 206, to Mercurian, June 7.

[72]Pierre Delattre, ed., *Les établissements des jésuites en France depuis quatre siècles*, 5 vols. (Enghien: Institut Supérieur de Théologie, 1949–1957), 1: 1234.

nobles. Emond Auger became involved in a similar relief effort during an epidemic of pest at Lyon in 1564; he helped distribute food donated by Catholics to some five hundred poor people living along the Rhône River, each morning giving everyone a measure of bread, meat, wine, and plums.[73]

Religious and secular authorities often ordered collective prayers and public masses to avert or to terminate an epidemic of pest.[74] Collective prayer and devotion to the display of the holy sacrament merged in a ritual that lasted for forty hours, in the words of Jean Delumeau, "une sorte de prière *non-stop*."[75] At Lille in 1596 Jesuits exposed the holy sacrament in their chapel on the rue des Malades for forty hours to encourage public prayer in the face of the pest,[76] and Jesuits organized similar rituals in their churches at Reggio in Calabria in 1576 and at Speyer in 1597.[77] Processions, like collective prayer and public masses, were popular means of averting or ending an epidemic and, like the devotion of forty hours, combined several elements including prayer and the display of relics. Jesuits sometimes reported on the processions organized by religious or secular authorities, as did Anton Vinck at Trier in 1564. On occasion Jesuits did not wait for the authorities to act; when the pest struck Augsburg in the summer of 1563 Peter Canisius organized a procession on July 18, but unlike the successful fasts at Lyon and Chambéry it did not put an end to the epidemic for the pest continued for several months.[78] Yet another collective means of healing was for public authorities to make a vow as a means of gaining divine intervention against an epidemic.[79] Jesuits reported on the vow made by the Venetian Senate in 1576 to build a church dedicated to Christ the Redeemer so that the epidemic of pest would cease.[80] In 1582 Emond Auger suggested to the magistrates of Lyon that they vow to undertake a pilgrimage to Our Lady of Loreto to liberate the town from another epidemic of pest.

[73]GAL 80: 263, to Lainez, September 28.

[74]Biraben, *Les hommes*, 2: 64.

[75]Jean Delumeau, *La Peur en Occident (XIVe–XVIIIe siècles): Une cité assiégée* (Paris: Fayard, 1978), 140.

[76]Delattre, *Les établissements*, 2: 1205–6.

[77]ITAL 150: 59, Francesco Mercado to Mercurian, Reggio, January 12; RH INF 48: 58v, annual by Hasius, January 24, 1598.

[78]James Brodrick, *Saint Peter Canisius* (Chicago: Loyola University Press, 1962), 566. For another example see ITAL 152: 170, Pietro Angelo Consoli to Mercurian, Parma, September 28, 1576.

[79]Biraben, *Les hommes*, 2: 70–75.

[80]ITAL 152: 359, Buonacorso to Mercurian, Vicenza, December 17; see Niero, "Pietà ufficiale," 288. The vow resulted in Palladio's magnificent Chiesa del Redentore.

Auger also went on the pilgrimage with two others on behalf of the magistrates.[81] The final act in the collective response to epidemic disease was the thanksgiving when the community was healthy once again by celebrating the *Te Deum Laudamus* and perhaps undertaking solemn processions.[82]

All these remedies reached their culmination at Milan under the guidance of the cardinal archbishop, Carlo Borromeo. Jesuits were interested observers of the spiritual remedies promoted by Borromeo and reported on them with a mixture of approval and bewilderment, and at times even disapproval. Giovanni Battista Buonacorso summarized the cardinal's activities and expressed his approval: "The processions, the sermons, the prayers, and the penitence that he has done and does are amazing and commendable."[83] A bemused Alfonso Sgariglia reported that the cardinal had not stopped finding new ways "to move the spirit to devotion" and had ordered all the priests of his diocese to shave their beards as a "great mortification." Sgariglia nonetheless approved of the cardinal's program to fight the epidemic; "in sum, he plans to use this occasion to reform the entire city."[84] Sgariglia had earlier reported on the concern of many that some of the cardinal's activities, instead of resulting in spiritual healing, might cause the epidemic to spread.[85] On the whole, however, whenever political or religious authorities promoted spiritual healing or primary remedies, Jesuits supported them with fervor and, as the accounts indicate, initiated collective efforts to combat epidemic disease.

According to some historians, the collective response to epidemics demonstrated a tendency toward a more Christocentric piety and a movement away from the protective role of saints and the Virgin Mary.[86] As befitted members of a Society named in honor of Jesus, Jesuits promoted a Christocentric piety even though their accounts of epidemic disease contain no explicit indi-

---

[81]Henri Fouqueray, *Histoire de la Compagnie de Jésus en France des origines à la suppression (1528–1762)*, 5 vols. (Paris: Librairie Alphonse Picard et Fils, 1910–1925), 2: 74–75.

[82]For two examples see ITAL 154: 87–87v, Antonio Micheli to Mercurian, Venice, July 18, 1577; 155: 83, Achille to Mercurian, Palermo, September 22, 1577.

[83]ITAL 152: 358v, to Mercurian, Vicenza, December 17, 1576.

[84]ITAL 153: 101, to Paolo Candi, January 15, 1577.

[85]ITAL 152: 16v, to Mercurian, August 22, 1576. See also Palmer, "Church, Leprosy and Plague," 97–99, and A. Francesco La Cava, *La peste di S. Carlo: Note storicomediche sulla peste del 1576* (Milano: Editore Ulrico Hoepli, 1945), 138.

[86]Niero, "Pietà ufficiale," 289; William A. Christian, *Apparitions in Late Medieval and Renaissance Spain* (Princeton: Princeton University Press, 1981), 220.

cations of their devotion to Christ. Implicit in the Jesuit approach to the primary remedies, however, was an emphasis upon the redemptive qualities of Jesus. This is evident from the focus on supplicatory prayers and masses, confession and communion, and the repentance and penance of the collective responses promoted by Jesuits. When an epidemic of pest threatened Jesuits at Loreto in 1557, General Lainez expressed his hopes that by means of the patron of the college they would remain safe. The patron was the Virgin Mary, which is not surprising given the prominence of her cult at Loreto.[87] However, on occasion Jesuits elsewhere demonstrated devotion to the cult of the Virgin, as Emond Auger did when he suggested that the magistrates at Lyon take a pilgrimage to Our Lady of Loreto, and as the Jesuits of Fribourg in Switzerland did in 1588 to avert the pest.[88] Jesuits in Sicily sought the intervention of Saint Agatha to prevent an epidemic from spreading to Catania in 1576,[89] and Jerónimo Nadal's instructions to colleges confronting the pest recommended devotion to Saints Sebastian and Rocco. So while focusing on Jesus, the Jesuits did not abandon the protective roles of the Virgin and the saints. The obvious conclusion here is that when threatened by an epidemic, particularly of pest, Jesuits were willing to utilize every remedy in the spiritual pharmacopeia available to Catholics.

Secondary Causes

While supernatural causes were the primary causes of epidemics, secondary causes included the natural as well as the unnatural. As already discussed, Jesuits considered contagion to be the most important of the natural causes of the pest, and beliefs concerning the contagious nature of disease affected every aspect of Jesuit response to epidemics, including their analysis of other natural causes. In his *Liber pestis* Ambroise Paré argued that one of the causes of the pest was "the vitiation of the humours of the body" so that they became disposed to take the disease.[90] Although some Jesuits subscribed to the humoral theory of disease, they did not mention it specifically when analyzing why a person contracted the pest. Giuseppe Lamagna came close to it when explaining why Fabio Giustiniano died from the pest at Milan in 1577; Giustiniano's long and tiring studies had disposed his body to the introduction of "that pestilential form."[91] A different approach to infection is evident in a letter from Andreas Rumieievius; he feared that his body absorbed the "pestilential breaths" of the sick who visited him.[92] Both of these different explanations for how the pest attacks an individual indicate a presumption of the contagious nature of disease.

A similar presumption is evident in Jesuit attempts to explain the causes of specific outbreaks. For example, in his account of the epidemic of pest at Milan in 1576 and 1577 Paolo Bisciola began by examining how the disease came to the city. He mentioned four different theories, the first that a woman brought the pest from Marignan where she had visited to care for a sick sister, the second that some people deliberately spread the pest with "cunning ointments," the third that a gentleman fleeing the pest at Mantua brought it to Milan, and the fourth that the people who flocked to the city to honor the governor in tournaments, jousts, and parties "spread the evil seed."[93] Similarly, Jesuits believed that the pest came to Vilnius in 1571 from towns such as Kaunas, with which it had commercial links.[94] The Jesuits at Vilnius did not indicate whether they believed that the infection resulted from infected persons or infected material; comments on the course of the epidemic at Messina between 1575 and 1577 reveal that both could be a source of infection. According to Giovanni Battista Carminata, the pest first entered Messina in June 1575 via some infected material brought by a galley from the Levant.[95] The outbreak abated toward the end of summer but flared again in the autumn, as reported by Juan Polanco, due to some infected persons as well as the belongings of the pest-stricken.[96] Early in the next year Carminata reported, "The situation regarding the pest was recently very good, but now as a result of certain infected goods sold by some rogues it is a bit worse."[97] In the spring of 1577 the epidemic became worse once again, this time also from "some remnants of pestiferous

---

[91]ITAL 155: 201, to Morais, October 22.
[92]GERM 174: 146, Rumieievius to Aquaviva, Kalisch, March 7, 1595.
[93]Bisciola, *Relatione verissima*, 1–2.
[94]GERM 152: 109, Varsevic to Nadal, August 31.
[95]ITAL 148: 3, to Mercurian, June 22.
[96]Polanco, *Complementa*, 2: 367–68, to Mercurian, October 5.
[97]ITAL 150: 197v, to Mercurian, February 22, 1576.

goods."[98] According to a report from Giuseppe Blondo in July, infected goods from Messina were in turn responsible for introducing the pest into six to eight places across the strait in Calabria.[99] Public officials attempted to prevent such goods entering from a pest-infected area, a further indication of the widespread belief that the most important of the natural causes was contagion.

From the time of the Black Death many Europeans had sought the causes of the pestilence in astronomical phenomena such as the conjunction of the planets, eclipses, and comets.[100] In November 1577 Giovanni Francesco Prandi reported on the "extremely happy end" of the pest at Brescia but added, "Three days ago a comet appeared opposite the moon and very close to it; this has frightened this entire wretched city since it is considered an omen."[101] Farther north at Braniewo, Philipp Jakob Widmanstadius reported in December that a comet, perhaps the same one seen at Brescia, had been visible since September and suggested that it was a portent of the epidemic of pest then spreading in Prussia.[102] To consider comets as omens, portents, or divine warnings of an epidemic, however, is not the same as believing them to be causes. Jesuits rarely indicated that they believed astronomical phenomena could produce an effect on an epidemic; Giovanni Battista Peruschi reported from Milan in 1577 that "certain phases of the moon multiplied the cases" of pest,[103] and Gabriel Alonso noted from Lisbon in 1579 that the fear of pestilence in the city had abated, especially since the interlunar period had passed.[104] In short, the evidence suggests that most Jesuits did not accept the role of astronomical phenomena as one of the secondary causes.

The belief that the quality of air could cause disease had a venerable tradition going back to Galen and Hippocrates.[105] In the sixteenth century this belief was evident in two of the most frequent cures suggested by the medical profession—a change of air and, for those far from home, native air. Judging from the frequent references to the quality of air in their accounts, Jesuits

---

[98]ITAL 154: 105, Basso to Mercurian, Naples, June 18.

[99]Ibid., 269v, to Mercurian, Naples, July 27.

[100]Biraben, *Les hommes*, 2: 9–15.

[101]ITAL 155: 281, to Mercurian, November 15.

[102]POL 80: 74v, to Mercurian, December 16.

[103]ITAL 154: 339, to Mercurian, August 11.

[104]LUS 68: 196, to Mercurian, July 26. Amelang, in Parets, *Journal of the Plague*, 24, documents the case of a Jesuit who considered a "special constellation" to be a partial cause of an epidemic in 1652.

[105]Biraben, *Les hommes*, 2: 20.

subscribed to the belief and the cures, and they sought locations with good air for their colleges to maintain their health and sent sick Jesuits to other places to restore their health.[106] Many Jesuits accordingly agreed with Ambroise Paré's contention that the infection and corruption of the air were natural causes of the pest.[107] As already noted, in the midst of epidemics Jesuits made frequent comments on the corruption of the air, infected air, and the contagious nature of the air. If the air was not corrupt or infected, if it was "pure," "untouched," "extremely enjoyable," "very good," or "excellent," then Jesuits had cause for optimism.[108] On the other hand, humid air, air that accompanied storms, and the heating of the air could be dangerous.[109]

In contrast to the numerous comments on the role of air in both epidemic and nonepidemic disease are the few comments on water. Jesuits believed that the pestilence without a name which struck Coimbra in 1558 was somehow connected to a river or a pond and that the epidemic which devastated parts of Rome in 1566 was the result of infected water, but these were isolated incidents. On two occasions Jesuits made enigmatic comments relating water to the pest. In July 1575 Paul Hoffaeus wrote that the Jesuits at Luzern feared an outbreak of pest as a result of a flood.[110] When Jesuits fled the pest at Pultusk in 1572, Peter Skarga claimed that the city would always be pestilential on account of its location near a filthy lake.[111]

The final natural cause that was prominent in Jesuit accounts of epidemic disease is famine. Modern research has discovered that the relationship between nutrition and disease is complex; that levels of nutrition affect both the morbidity and mortality levels of some diseases but do not affect them in

[106]For some examples see ITAL 112: 190, Fulvio Androzzi to Lainez, Florence, June 4, 1558; 121: 187, Adorno to Lainez, Padua, April 30, 1562; and Martin, *Jesuit Mind*, 163–65.

[107]Paget, *Ambroise Paré*, 277.

[108]GERM 139: 198, Jan Behem to Lainez, Prague, May 3, 1563; ITAL 151: 410v, *Avisi cavati da diverse lettere venute da Venetia*, August 6, 1576; 152: 37v, Pietro Angelo Consoli to Mercurian, Parma, August 24, 1576; 153: 314, Mazzarino to Mercurian, Genoa, April 8, 1577; GAL 89: 143, Creichton to Mercurian, Lyon, May 3, 1577.

[109]*Litterae quadrimestres*, 5: 452, by Jérôme Le Bas, Billom, December 19, 1557; GERM 134 I: 84, *Ex literis Maximi*, Brok, February 10, 1572; ITAL 155: 176, Peruschi to Mercurian, Milan, October 16, 1577.

[110]GERM 136 II: 281, to Mercurian, Augsburg, July 11.

[111]Peter Skarga, *Listy Ks Piotra Skargi T. J. z Lat 1566–1610*, ed. Jan Syganski (Cracow: n.p., 1912), 40, to Nadal, Plocia, September 16.

others, such as bubonic plague, while the evidence is inconclusive in yet others.[112] J. Meuvret has noted, however, that in preindustrial France the repeated observation of epidemics following a poor harvest led to the saying, "First dearth and then plague," and he suggests that the causal relationship was the increase in vagabondage in the wake of famine as people in search of food spread epidemic disease.[113] Jesuits similarly made the connection between famine and epidemic disease; table 7 shows the years and countries where famine accompanied epidemic disease according to Jesuit accounts.

Although they made the connection between famine and epidemics, Jesuits did not comment on vagabondage as a cause, and they were vague about the precise causal relationship between the two. Edmond Hay, for example, just stated in November 1573 that although the shortage of food in France was severe, "I am beginning to fear the pest more than the famine,"[114] while Massimo Milanesi, after describing the severe famine's effect on Transylvania in 1586, turned his attention to "the pest, its sister."[115] In another enigmatic comment Peter Canisius noted in December 1586 that the area surrounding Fribourg in Switzerland suffered from famine and pest and then stated that the mathematicians predicted that the pest would be worse the following year.[116] The most detailed attempt to explain the relationship between famine and epidemic disease occurred in a letter dated February 1572, probably written by Massimo Milanesi, from Brok in Poland: "The peasants are already reduced to eating the food that they normally give to pigs, the pigs themselves,... and all types of other animals, even horses. As a result we believe that even if the pest might cease for a while the heating of the air on account of these corruptions and miseries could only result in greater mortality than previously. May God

---

[112]In addition to the sources cited in the introduction, see Andrew B. Appleby, "Epidemics and Famine in the Little Ice Age," in *Climate and History: Studies in Interdisciplinary History*, ed. Robert I. Rotberg and Theodore K. Rabb (Princeton: Princeton University Press, 1981), 74–75; Biraben, *Les hommes*, 2: 147–54.

[113]J. Meuvret, "Demographic Crisis in France from the Sixteenth to the Eighteenth Centuries," in *Population in History: Essays in Historical Demography*, ed. D. V. Glass and D. E. C. Eversley (London: Edward Arnold, 1965), 510–13.

[114]GAL 85: 239v, to Mercurian, Paris, November 14.

[115]*Monumenta antiquae Hungariae*, ed. Ladislaus Lukács, 3 vols. (Rome: Institutum Historicum Societatis Iesu, 1969–1981), 2: 904, to Adam Brock, Cluj, April 29.

[116]Canisius, *Beati Petri Canisii*, 8: 734, *Ad collegii socios de votorum renovatione dicit*, late December.

TABLE 7: THE CONNECTIONS BETWEEN FAMINES AND EPIDEMICS

Year	Country	Type of Epidemic
1557	Spain	pest, *modorra*, catarrh
1571	Germany	Hungarian disease
1571	Poland	pest
1573	France	pest
1575	Portugal	dangerous diseases
1577	Sicily	pest
1578	Poland	pest
1579	Sicily	pest
1585	Germany	epidemic of contagion
1586	France	pest
1586	Spain	pest
1597	Portugal	pestilential epidemic

through His goodness and mercy consent that this not happen."[117] In other words, the different causes were interlocking; famine produced misery that affected the air which in turn led to increased mortality, and the whole was subject to the consent of God.

On occasion people rejected supernatural and natural causes of epidemics and turned instead to unnatural causes by seeking scapegoats to blame for their calamities. At the time of the Black Death many communities focused

---

[117]GERM 134 I: 84, *Ex literis Maximi*, February 10.

their frustrations on the unfortunate Jews in their midst, accusing them of causing the epidemic, usually by poisoning wells. According to Philip Ziegler, the accusations resulted in 350 massacres of Jewish communities.[118] Nothing comparable to such violence occurs in the Jesuit accounts from the sixteenth century, and no Jesuit ever pointed an accusing finger at a Jew, but Jesuits did at times blame Protestants for causing epidemics of pest, and on one occasion the Protestants in turn accused Jesuits of being responsible for their infirmities. As reported by Heinrich Blessem, in 1575 the Protestants at Graz claimed that Jesuits made them sick by means of sorcery, and according to Henricus Vivarius' account of the pest at Ljubljana in 1600, a zealous Lutheran introduced the epidemic, but Vivarius did not indicate whether by means of sorcery or some other method. The other claims that Protestants caused the pest came from France. Oliver Manare and Emond Auger accused the Huguenot community of Lyon of causing the epidemic of pest in 1564 by smearing an ointment on such things as doors, chains, and locks, but Auger abandoned his accusations when the epidemic killed more Huguenots than Catholics.[119] In 1577 William Creichton reported that a rumor was circulating in Lyon that the Huguenots were again responsible for the pest, but he seemed to give it little credence.[120]

In his *Liber pestis* Ambroise Paré did not mention religious dissidents but advised magistrates to "keep an eye on certain thieves, murderers, and poisoners, worse than inhuman, who grease and daub the walls and doors of rich houses with matter discharged from the swellings and carbuncles, and other excretions of them that have the plague, so as to infect the houses, and then break into them and sack and strip them, and even strangle the poor sufferers in their beds."[121] One of the more notorious incidents relating to such spreaders of pestilence, the so-called *untori*, occurred at Milan in 1630 when rumors created panic among the inhabitants. In his account of the epidemic at Milan in 1576–1577 Paolo Bisciola mentioned the rumors that some people were spreading an ointment on such things as doors and walls. However, on this occasion the governor issued a proclamation against the rumormongers and

[118]Philip Ziegler, *The Black Death* (Harmondsworth: Penguin Books, 1970), 110.
[119]GAL 80: 243, Auger to Lainez, July 20; Lainez, *Lainii monumenta*, 8: 112, Manare to Lainez, Paris, July 20.
[120]GAL 89: 117, to Mercurian, April 7.
[121]Quoted from Paget, *Ambroise Paré*, 288–89,

thereby averted public panic.[122] Even so, the Milanese authorities arrested two people for spreading the pest at both Milan and Venice.[123] The Jesuit accounts produce other reports of pest spreaders. In 1577 and again in 1600 stories circulated of attempts to infect Turin, one time by means of an infected bundle of clothes and the other by means of a pestiferous salve.[124] According to Giovanni Battista Atanasio, in 1577 the authorities at Chambéry discovered a plot to spread the pest by using poisoned meat and fruit and arrested more than twenty of the culprits, some of whom freely confessed while others did so under torture. Of course, the pest spreaders could contract the disease as well, so the interrogation uncovered a secret antidote, the details of which Atanasio sent to his superiors: pulverize about twelve dry juniper seeds, mix them with wine, soak two whole burned nuts in this mixture for some time, then drink it early in the morning, and afterwards eat the nuts.[125]

SECONDARY REMEDIES

Several months after informing his superiors of the pest spreaders' antidote, Giovanni Battista Atanasio sent a word of caution—the antidote was unreliable.[126] The set of instructions that were probably composed during the Italian epidemic of 1575–1577 also mentioned the *untori* at Milan and likewise included a recipe for an antidote used by the pest spreaders to protect themselves.[127] The eagerness with which Jesuits collected and disseminated such information is an indication of the failure of the medical profession to deal with epidemic disease; all secondary remedies were, like the pest spreaders' antidote, unreliable. When Giovanni Paolo Organtino was suffering from a type of pest at Ferrara in January 1558, his medicine made him so nauseated that he could scarcely eat.[128] Even less fortunate was Antoine Denys, who died from the medicine he took during an epidemic of dysentery at Billom in October 1577.[129] As a result of such experiences it is not surprising that Alfonso

---

[122]Bisciola, *Relatione verissima*, 1; see also La Cava, *La peste di S. Carlo*, 103.

[123]ITAL 152: 44, Peruschi to Mercurian, August 25, 1576.

[124]MED 76 I: 42, annual by Peruschi, Milan, March 12, 1578; 79: 124, annual for 1600.

[125]GAL 89: 259, to Mercurian, August 27.

[126]Ibid., 379v, December 19.

[127]OPP NN 159: 515, *Istruttione da praticarsi.*

[128]ITAL 111: 45, Roillet to Lainez, January 8.

[129]GAL 89: 297, 297a, Pierre Lohier to Creichton, October 3.

Sgariglia's prescription for the pest was comparable to that pill made of *cito*, *longe*, and *tarde*; "the most effective remedy is to be able to stay away."[130] Nonetheless, Jesuits took the advice of medical doctors during epidemics (as well as for normal illnesses). Jerónimo Nadal's regulations for Jesuit colleges during an outbreak of pest, for example, first recommended that Jesuits follow the advice of doctors in stocking their colleges with antidotes and that they seek the opinion of physicians on the suspension of classes; he then proceeded to more general recommendations: to consult doctors "concerning the total scheme of our living" and to follow their prescriptions whenever someone became sick.[131] Similarly, when Jesuits undertook the relief effort for the victims of the contaminated water at Rome in 1566, they visited the houses of the sick with doctors and followed their prescriptions for each patient. On occasion Jesuits could even report what they considered to be successful treatment of the pest-stricken, as did Oliver Manare in November 1585: "The antidote was so effective that two or even three have recovered." He then added that three died, however.[132]

The practice of medicine in the sixteenth century still took as its authority the ancient doctors, especially Galen, an approach that resulted in an emphasis on the correct balance of the four bodily humors. This emphasis led in turn to three therapeutic programs for epidemic disease as well as for normal illnesses. The first was the development of a healthy body through a proper diet, regular exercise, and the promotion of moderation. The second was the restoration of balance within the body and the strengthening of the body's constitution through proper medication. The third was the expulsion of poisons or toxins through purging, bloodletting, and sweating.[133] All three therapeutic programs are evident in Jesuit accounts of epidemic disease. Many of the practices relating to the first program, the development of a healthy body, are precautionary rather than remedial and in consequence are covered in the next chapter.

The guidelines written for Jesuit colleges contained recommendations concerning the second therapeutic program. Nadal's advice was vague; he

---

[130]ITAL 155: 207, to Mercurian, Milan, October 23, 1577.

[131]OPP NN 159: 493v–494, 495, *Ordo per servari.*

[132]GERM 165: 110v, to Aquaviva, Mainz, November 30.

[133]See Roy Porter, *Disease, Medicine and Society in England, 1550–1860* (London: Macmillan, 1987), 15, for a concise summary.

stated that the colleges should purchase antidotes recommended by doctors and then suggested that the Jesuit responsible for purchasing supplies should use an antidote whenever he came and went.[134] The other guidelines mentioned specific "remedies or preservatives" including juniper, rosemary, sage, rosewater, red vinegar, lemon and citron juice, hyacinth, bezoar, contrayerva, and theriac. These guidelines recommended the use of the preservatives such as rosewater and vinegar to prevent infection by pouring them often on the nostrils, temples, and wrists, while the remedies or antidotes could not only cure the pest-stricken but likewise prevent infection.[135] Theriac was an antidote containing a number of ingredients, more notably viper's flesh and opium, and was one of the most popular remedies for pestilence during the sixteenth century.[136] It was also popular among the Jesuits; they often mentioned medicines and antidotes in their accounts, but the only one they regularly mentioned by name was theriac. The Jesuit who feared the "pestilential breaths" of the sick who visited him requested General Aquaviva to send him theriac,[137] and Lorenzo Maggio called it "the singular remedy against the pest."[138] The use of theriac had recognized problems, however, for Peter Szydlowski believed that the theriac given to a novice suffering from pest and *ignis sacer* aggravated the latter and caused his death.[139]

Jesuit accounts contain few references to the third therapeutic program, the expulsion of poisons or toxins. The most-often-mentioned therapy was bleeding, and Jesuits suffering from a wide variety of diseases and symptoms, including petechia, colds, fever, and headache, had to endure it.[140] A typical treatment for pest during this period was to cut open the bubo or carbuncle, an operation described by Nicolas Lanoy in 1553: "According to the surgeon,

---

[134]OPP NN 159: 494, 497v.

[135]Ibid., 513v–514v. Bezoar is the concretion found in the stomachs and intestines of some animals, especially ruminants, and was formerly regarded as an antidote to poison. Contrayerba is the root of a tropical American plant of the mulberry family and was used as an antidote to snakebite, but it seems odd to find it in use already in the sixteenth century. Perhaps the term originally meant any type of antidote.

[136]Slack, *Impact of Plague*, 30–31.

[137]GERM 174: 146, Rumieievius, Kalisch, March 7, 1595.

[138]GERM 148: 39, to Borgia, Vienna, February 27, 1567.

[139]*Monumenta Hungariae*, 2: 924, to Campana, Oradea, May 21, 1586.

[140]For some examples see ibid., 988, Milanesi to Campana, September 1586; ITAL 111: 349, Fulvio Androzzi to Lainez, Florence, March 19, 1558; LUS 52: 25, *quadrimestris* by Andres Gonçalez, Coimbra, May 1, 1563.

our Wilhelm has had a certain type of pest, and the barber... has cut rotten flesh from this sore many times, as they normally do with carbuncles."[141] Yet another treatment for the pest was to apply some type of medicine to the bubo or carbuncle for the purpose of drawing the poison from the body. Massimo Milanesi, who was a physician, applied this remedy during the epidemic at Alba Iulia in Transylvania. Milanesi used the middle part of an onion and theriac on the carbuncle that appeared on the shin of Paul Woiciechowicz and just theriac on the carbuncle on Urban Elbing's knee. The treatment achieved its immediate goal for both carbuncles ruptured "and a large amount of bloody material came out," but the two died nonetheless.[142] A happier result occurred at Cordoba in 1569 when a Jesuit recovered from the pest that he had contracted at Lisbon; the Jesuits attributed the recovery to diligent care and good air.[143]

Of the various remedies available in the sixteenth century, the primary might seem just as futile as the secondary to the modern mind, but primary remedies at least comforted the spirit while most secondary remedies tormented the body. Jesuit accounts of epidemic disease reveal the horrific suffering that forms the background to the somewhat depersonalized high mortality figures which feature in demographic studies. Nonetheless, Jesuits never lost faith in the primary and secondary remedies available to them. The remedies combined with beliefs in primary and secondary causes reveal a coherent view of epidemic disease. Since divine providence was the primary cause, primary remedies focused on penitence. God used secondary causes to achieve His will and provided humans with secondary remedies to cure illnesses. According to Jesuits, the first response to epidemic disease should be prayer and penitence, but people should not reject the secondary remedies supplied by a merciful God.

---

[141] *Epistolae mixtae ex variis Europae locis ab anno 1537 ad 1556 scriptae nunc primum a patribus Societatis Jesu*, 5 vols. (Madrid: Augustinus Avrial and R. Fortanet, 1898–1901), 3: 143, to Polanco, Vienna, March 9. Wilhelm survived.

[142] *Monumenta Hungariae*, 2: 989–90, to Campana, September 1586.

[143] HISP 141: 253, annual by (Juan) Baptista, January 8, 1570.

———

FIVE

PRIVATE PRECAUTIONS AND PUBLIC REGULATIONS

AT THE APPROACH OF an epidemic of pest those who could took the most effective method of avoiding infection by fleeing to an unaffected place. Most Jesuits did likewise. The policy of the Society of Jesus toward flight developed over time in response to ever-increasing demands on its members, particularly as teachers; the majority should flee to preserve themselves, but some Jesuits should remain behind to fulfill charitable obligations to the sick. Those who did not flee took precautions to avoid contact with all possible sources of infection and, when this proved impossible, used prophylactic or purifying measures. Jesuits also reported on the attempts of municipal authorities to prevent the entry of an epidemic and their efforts to control the epidemic if it did gain a foothold in the town. Although Jesuits often complained of laxity in the enforcement of public regulations to combat and control an epidemic, they themselves often violated these regulations.

FLIGHT

As the pest approached Chambéry in July 1570, the rector of the Jesuit college, André Dawant, sought advice from his superiors on what he should do if the disease entered the city.[1] Most of his contemporaries would have advised him to take that pill made of *cito, longe,* and *tarde;* in other words, flee! Ever since the Black Death people had realized that the most effective private precaution

---

[1]GAL 83: 101v, to Borgia, July 18.

was to leave an infected town and take refuge in another or at a country estate, and in consequence whenever the pest approached an area it precipitated a panic-driven exodus to safety. Only a few individuals would have argued, as Martin Luther did, that people should stay to fulfill their obligations, servants caring for masters, masters caring for servants, neighbors caring for each other, and clergy and magistrates caring for all.[2] A century before Dawant requested advice from his superiors, Cardinal Ammannati-Piccolomini had sought the opinion of Domenico Dominici, bishop of Brescia, on whether people and especially clergy should flee the pest, citing an argument that they should not flee because "it is against charity and...pestilence is a scourge from God which is to be avoided by a change in living and not by a change of place." Dominici's forceful and lengthy response stated that people could indeed flee, just as "the dolphin flees the storm." God might have sent the pest as a scourge, and if He has ordained the death of someone then escape was impossible, but perhaps He ordained the escape of a person by means of flight. The only concession Dominici made to the opposing argument was stating that it was reprehensible for bishops or parish priests to abandon their flocks "if there is no one else to perform their duties equally well."[3]

Jesuit accounts provide ample documentation about people, including magistrates and clergy as well as Jesuits, who fled epidemics of disease. Jesuits quite often reported such flights without comment or condemnation; Pedro Parra, writing from Valencia in August 1557, noted that a "rumor of pest" resulted in the departure of half the town,[4] Johann Reidt stated that the pest which afflicted Cologne in the summer of 1564 was so fierce that it drove many from the city and closed the market,[5] and Emerich Forsler reported from Vienna in January 1572 that between those killed by the pest and those who fled elsewhere, the city appeared to be a desert.[6] More graphic than these accounts was the report from the rector of the Jesuit college at Murcia, Antonio

[2]See the discussion in Paul Slack, *The Impact of Plague in Tudor and Stuart England* (London: Routledge and Kegan Paul, 1985), 41–45.

[3]Dorothy M. Schullian, "A Manuscript of Dominici in the Army Medical Library," *Journal of the History of Medicine and Allied Sciences* 3 (1948): 395–99.

[4]HISP 95: 127, to Lainez, August 11.

[5]Joseph Hansen, ed., *Rheinische Akten zur Geschichte des Jesuitenordens, 1542–1582* (Bonn: H. Berendt, 1896), 500, *quadrimestris*, September 1.

[6]GERM 134 I: 67, to Nadal, January 30.

Hontova, in August 1558: "Such a strange dispersion of the people is difficult to describe, because everyone left on their own, neither neighbor with neighbor nor relative with relative, some to the mountains, some to the countryside, others to their gardens, others for towns and cities, wherever they could take shelter."[7] Several Jesuits noted that the wealthy fled, leaving the poor behind. According to Jorge Sarrano, when the pest struck Lisbon in June of 1569 every person with the means to flee did so,[8] and Iñigo Fonseca reported on the flight from the epidemic of pest that began at Seville in May 1568: "As the disease increased in intensity, so many of the principal people and the merchants began to leave that there did not appear to be a man with a mule remaining in the city but only the people who could not leave as a result of their poverty."[9]

The departure of the wealthy quite often increased the misery of the poor left in pest-stricken towns. As remarked by Francisco Anriquez during the epidemic at Lisbon in 1569, the poor suffered from the lack of alms.[10] Emond Auger encountered a different problem during the epidemic at Lyon in 1564; the leaders abandoned the city, leaving the burden of managing even the most basic requirements, such as the distribution of food, to people not accustomed to the task, including Auger: "I saw [sic] this city cry from hunger, and I went to the bakery (because no one else would do it) to sell bread by the piece."[11] Such abandonment of towns during epidemics and the consequent problems encountered by those without the means to flee might have been responsible for the somewhat bitter comment made by Peter Canisius when the pest afflicted Augsburg in October 1563: "Some nobles and wealthy people have gone to another place because they fear the danger of death; would that they also feared the anger of God!"[12]

Medical practitioners also attracted criticism when they abandoned their patients. Ambrosius Sanctinus ridiculed doctors and surgeons who fled the epidemic of pest at Vienna in 1562 by stating, "I know not whether...the work of the surgeons and doctors was more rare or more dangerous; more rare, I say, because they not only diligently fled from the infected but also

---

[7]HISP 96: 155, to Juan Baptista de Barma.

[8]LUS 63: 170, to Borgia, Evora, September 18.

[9]HISP 109: 109, to Borgia, October 22.

[10]LUS 63: 140, to Borgia, July 18.

[11]GAL 80: 263, to Lainez, September 28.

[12]Peter Canisius, *Beati Petri Canisii, Societatis Iesu, epistolae et acta*, ed. Otto Braunsberger, 13 vols. (Freiburg im Breisgau: Herder, 1896–1923), 4: 350, to Cardinal Stanislaus Hosius, October 7.

avoided the sick when ordered to care for them."[13] Jesuits also reported cases where clergy abandoned their flocks but seldom criticized them for doing so. Emond Auger's comment from Lyon in 1564 was cryptic in its brevity: "All the priests of some churches are dead, others have fled, everything is closed."[14] More critical was Antonio Hontova's comment from Murcia in 1558: "Many parish priests fled and those who remained were so terrified that at first they administered the sacraments with great difficulty."[15] During the widespread epidemic in Portugal in 1581, the flight of parish priests from Evora and Porto meant that Jesuits had to administer the sacraments and bury the dead.[16] Of course, such work was dangerous, and on at least one occasion Jesuits contracted the pest when replacing clergy who had fled; this occurred at Brno in the summer of 1584 when the canons abandoned the church of Saint Peter.[17]

The epidemic at Reggio in Calabria in 1576 created a different problem for the Jesuit community there; according to Francesco Mercado, "the four of us here have little to do because a large part of the city has left for their gardens and farmhouses."[18] When "most of the people of quality" fled the pest at Barcelona in 1557, Juan Gesti complained that the Jesuits had to abandon their classes on cases of conscience and their instruction of Christian doctrine.[19] Magistrates often ordered the closure of schools during outbreaks of pest, but on occasion rumors of approaching epidemics created panic among students and their parents, resulting in their flight and the consequent abandonment of classes. Five hundred students were enrolled at the Jesuit college in Trier when an epidemic erupted in the late summer of 1566; all but fifty fled, and the college remained closed from September 1 to April 30.[20] Similarly, an epidemic at Rodez in the summer of 1572 reduced enrollments from seven hundred to between twenty-five and thirty.[21] During the epidemic at Milan in 1576 Jesuits still managed to occupy themselves when their schools closed, for "some devout, principal persons" requested Jesuits to accompany them to their villas when they fled the

---

[13]GERM 139: 178, *quadrimestris*, April 27, 1563.

[14]GAL 80: 263v, to Lainez, September 28.

[15]HISP 96: 155v–156, to Barma, August.

[16]LUS 53: 34v, annual by Sebastião Morais, January 1, 1582.

[17]GERM 164: 125, Ricardus Zantenus to Aquaviva, March 13, 1585.

[18]ITAL 151: 335, to [Mercurian], July 22.

[19]HISP 96: 247, to Lainez, December 30.

[20]GERM 140: 63v, annual by Adrian Loeff, August 24, 1567; Hansen, *Rheinische Akten*, 550.

[21]GAL 84: 175, Claude Matthieu to Nadal, Tournon, July 8.

pest, while other Jesuits withdrew from the city and heard confessions and preached to the many people who had likewise fled to their villas.[22]

As for the Jesuits themselves, they (or at least most of them) fled serious outbreaks of epidemic disease, and their superiors often gave them orders to do so, so this might explain why Jesuits seldom criticized others for their precipitous flights from the dangers of infection. The Jesuit policy on fleeing epidemics changed over time in response to the development of the Society's mission. In the early days Ignatius Loyola and his followers established a reputation for serving the sick, rushing in to assist when others fled or turned their backs. Loyola incorporated his views on the matter in the *Constitutions* by stipulating that service in hospitals was one of the six testing experiences for novices and by encouraging members to help the sick.[23] However, after the Jesuits established their first college for non-Jesuits at Messina in 1548, while not abandoning the sick, the Society turned its focus onto its educational mission, attempted to cope with many requests to establish more colleges, and encountered the ever-increasing problem of having enough Jesuits to staff them. Although membership increased during the latter half of the sixteenth century, the Society faced a crisis in vocations. It never attracted enough candidates to staff its colleges, and many Jesuits, after spending several years in training to enable them to teach, left the Society.[24] From the Society's point of view it made little sense to spend years giving a Jesuit an education to enable him to teach at a college if he then endangered his life by remaining in a pest-stricken town or by rushing out to serve the infected—better that he flee and preserve himself. On the other hand, the Society remained conscious of its founder's commitment to the sick. So when an epidemic threatened a Jesuit community, the majority fled but some remained behind to guard the buildings and to serve the sick. On occasion no one fled, and on other occasions everyone did, but the predominant pattern was the sensible and the humane one, that is, ensure the safety of the majority but do not forget the obligations to the pest-stricken.

[22]ITAL 152: 165, Adorno to Mercurian, Genoa, September 28; MED 76 I: 40v, annual for 1576 and 1577 by Peruschi, Milan, March 12, 1578.

[23]Ignatius Loyola, *The Constitutions of the Society of Jesus*, ed. George E. Ganss (St. Louis: The Institute of Jesuit Sources, 1970) [66, 650].

[24]See A. Lynn Martin, "Vocational Crises and the Crisis in Vocations among Jesuits in France during the Sixteenth Century," *Catholic Historical Review* 71 (1986): 201–21.

The first case in which Jesuits fled an epidemic involved the Jesuit community at Paris, comprised of young Jesuits completing their education at the university, and their superior Paschase Broët. During the epidemic of pest in 1553 Broët sent some Jesuits to Auvergne and others to villages outside Paris and then decided to join those in Auvergne. He attempted to justify his actions in a letter to Loyola: "Since I was in some danger at Paris as a result of the pest, because it would have been necessary to visit the sick and perhaps the pest-stricken and by this means endanger all the others here, I decided to go."[25] Other Jesuit communities provide other examples of flight in the face of epidemics, and other superiors felt obliged to defend their actions. For example, when Jesuits at Alcalá de Henares fled the pest in 1555, they wrote that they did so on the advice of doctors.[26] The first indication of a change in official Jesuit policies occurred in 1555, when Jerónimo Nadal forbade the Jesuits at Padua and Venice to hear the confessions of the sick because the public health officials would place a quarantine on the Jesuit communities if they did, and Jesuits in consequence would be unable to hear confessions in their churches or to hold classes.[27] In the same year Ignatius Loyola gave Cesare Helmi, the rector at Venice, permission to visit the sick, provided that they were not suffering from the pest.[28] Two years later in 1557 Diego Lainez gave similar instructions to Guy Roillet at Ferrara; he could visit the sick in the hospital as long as they did not have a contagious disease and they were not too numerous.[29]

Another shift in the official policy occurred in 1559, when the death of twenty Jesuits in the province of Aragon prompted Juan Polanco to write on

[25]Paschase Broët, et al, *Epistolae P.P. Paschasii Broeti, Claudii Jaji, Joannis Codurii et Simonis Roderici Societatis Jesu* (Madrid: Gabrielis Lopez del Horno, 1903), 96, to Loyola, November 8; see A. Lynn Martin, *The Jesuit Mind: The Mentality of an Elite in Early Modern France* (Ithaca: Cornell University Press, 1988), 167. Broët's actions at this time are an odd contrast with his actions in 1562, when he refused to flee and gave the impression that he knew how to guard himself from infection.

[26]*Litterae quadrimestres ex universis praeter Indiam et Brasiliam locis in quibus aliqui de Societate Jesu versabantur Romam missae*, 7 vols. (Madrid and Rome: Augustinus Avrial, La Editorial Ibérica, and A. Macioce e Pisani, 1894–1932), 4: 8, by Gil Gonzalez *ex commissione* Manuel Lopez, January 1, 1556.

[27]Jerónimo Nadal, *Epistolae P. Hieronymi Nadal Societatis Iesu ab anno 1546 ad 1577*, 4 vols. (Madrid: Augustini Avrial and Gabrielis Lopez del Horno, 1898–1905), 1: 318, to Loyola, Padua, July 19; see also Juan Polanco, *Vita Ignatii Loiolae et rerum Societatis Jesu historia*, 6 vols. (Madrid: Typographorum Societatis and Augustinus Avrial, 1894–1898), 5: 163, *Chronicon*.

[28]Ignatius Loyola, *Sancti Ignatii de Loyola, Societatis Jesu fundatoris, epistolae et instructiones*, 11 vols. (Madrid: Gabrielis Lopez del Horno, 1903–1911), 10: 368, Rome, December 21.

[29]ITAL 107: 144, Roillet to Lainez, January 29; Diego Lainez, *Lainii monumenta: Epistolae et acta patris Jacobi Lainii secundi praepositi generalis Societatis Jesu*, 8 vols. (Madrid: Gabrielis Lopez del Horno, 1912–1917), 2: 128–29, to Roillet, Rome, February 13.

behalf of Lainez to Francis Borgia, then commissaire of the Society in Spain: "Although everyone must be ready to risk their lives to help the souls of others, superiors ought to decide whether or not to expose them to danger, because sometimes you lose more than you gain in divine service." Polanco went on to explain that because in the colleges education was of greater service to the common good than helping the sick, superiors should not expose everyone in the colleges to the danger of the pest. Instead the teachers and the students should flee while one or two priests and as many lay brothers could remain to help the sick. Polanco next suggested that those whose "complexions" made them more susceptible to infection and those who were "more important for the common good" should leave.[30] Three years after Polanco wrote to Borgia, Jerónimo Nadal incorporated the same advice in his guidelines for colleges confronting an epidemic: "If the pest increases in intensity, the provincial should determine if he can obtain some monastery or castle in which the entire college can shelter, leaving only a preacher, confessors, the sick, a superior, and three or four lay brothers behind."[31]

In 1563 Polanco, again writing on behalf of Lainez, discussed Nadal's guidelines in a letter to Peter Canisius; Jesuits were not obliged to hear the confessions of the sick since that was the task of the parish priests. "Because the sick can save themselves if they are contrite, it does not appear an act of charity to put members of the Society in danger of contracting the pest especially since there are so few of them." Polanco went on to suggest that, although it might seem an act of charity to comfort the infected, it could "impede the greater divine service and the common good."[32] Many years later Polanco's concern for what was "more important for the common good" and "the greater divine service" reached its peak or, depending on one's point of view, its nadir when General Claudio Aquaviva sent instructions to the Jesuit college at Naples in 1592 that instead of caring for Jesuits with a dangerous disease in the Jesuit college, the rector should send them home—so much for Loyola's concern for the sick![33]

---

[30]Francis Borgia, *Sanctus Franciscus Borgia quartus Gandiae dux et Societatis Jesu praepositus generalis*, 5 vols. (Madrid: Augustini Avrial and Gabrielis Lopez del Horno, 1894–1911), 3: 529–30, Rome, July 20.

[31]OPP NN 159: 494v, *Ordo per servari*.

[32]Canisius, *Beati Petri Canisii*, 4: 264, Trent, June 18.

[33]See the response by the provincial, Antonio Lisio, in ITAL 160: 260v, April 20.

Flight thus became the official policy of the Society, moderated as it was by the need to leave a few behind to serve the sick and to guard the buildings. In 1560, a year after Polanco had written to Borgia, the pest threatened the Jesuit community at Barcelona; the provincial, Antonio Cordeses, followed Polanco's instructions by ordering everyone, and especially the rector, to flee except for two priests and two lay brothers who stayed to help the infected.[34] When an epidemic of pest threatened Avignon in 1566, the provincial, Emond Auger, ordered the rector to send everyone to neighboring colleges,[35] and the two sets of guidelines prepared during the Italian epidemic of 1575–1577 recommended that superiors arrange for suitable dwellings in which to take refuge.[36] During the epidemic at Vienna in 1563 the rector, Lorenzo Maggio, received instructions to find a safe place to take refuge, but he refused to do so because of his "zeal to keep the school on its feet." The results were tragic, for two Jesuits contracted the pest and died. So, early in 1564, the superiors closed the school and sent the young scholars and novices to other colleges.[37]

While the official policy was for the majority to flee and a few to remain, that still left Jesuit rectors and provincials with the problem of where to flee. Nadal's guidelines recommended a monastery or castle and prohibited flight to another college,[38] but Jesuits often ignored this. During a widespread epidemic of pest that afflicted much of Germany in 1564, the Jesuits fleeing Innsbruck jostled for places at unaffected colleges with those who had earlier fled from Mainz, and the threatening approach of the pest to the college at Augsburg exacerbated the situation.[39] As previously noted, in 1588 Oliver Manare recognized two problems with this practice: Jesuits fleeing epidemics could infect other colleges, and they could annoy the local magistrates. So he instructed the rectors of Jesuit colleges to arrange refuge elsewhere. Many rectors and provincials did seek shelter away from other Jesuit colleges: in 1566 the Jesuits at Trier managed to take shelter at several monasteries outside the town;[40] Viennese Jesuits took refuge at a Franciscan monastery nine leagues from Vienna in 1570 and again in 1576;[41] when the pest struck Liège in the

---

[34]HISP 97: 383, to Lainez, Murcia, October 8.

[35]GAL 81: 41, to Borgia, Toulouse, March 8, 1566.

[36]OPP NN 159: 491, *Per il tempo della peste*, November 9, 1576; 513, *Istruttione da praticarsi*.

[37]Nadal, *Epistolae*, 2: 485, Lanoy to Nadal, January 27.

[38]OPP NN 159: 494v, 499, *Ordo per servari*.

[39]Canisius, *Beati Petri Canisii*, 4: 668–69, to Lainez, Augsburg, September 23.

[40]GERM 147: 244; and 148: 18v, Vinck to Borgia, Mainz, October 16, 1566, and January 20, 1567.

[41]GERM 133 I: 50v, Forsler to Borgia, January 17, 1571; 137 II: 380, Maggio to Mercurian, Olomouc, October 26, 1576.

summer of 1572 the Jesuits tried to rent a house for several months,[42] but when it came there in the autumn of 1579 they managed to stay in buildings belonging to friends;[43] in the summer of 1576 the Jesuits at Catania took shelter at a vineyard belonging to the college at Palermo;[44] and Jesuits sought refuge from the Venetian epidemic of 1576 in several locations, primarily in country villas belonging to Venetian nobles.[45]

Once superiors solved the problem of finding a satisfactory shelter, they had to confront the problem of which Jesuits fled and which remained behind to serve the sick. Rectors always sent the young novices away during epidemics, and the rector himself often accompanied them, in accordance with Polanco's view that those who were "more important for the common good" should flee.[46] Superiors often tried to ascertain which Jesuits were likely to succumb to an epidemic and used, as Polanco had suggested, "complexions" to determine them. Jesuits used the term "complexion" to mean the combination of the four bodily humors, but they gave few indications of how they used it to decide who stayed and who fled. At Munich in 1562 those with "better complexions" fled,[47] while at Lisbon in 1579 those with "good complexions" stayed.[48] One Jesuit heard the confessions of the sick at Trier in 1567 because he had a "strong complexion,"[49] and Jesuits with "sanguinary complexions" fled Seville in 1568.[50] During the same epidemic at Seville, the provincial sent four old Jesuits to attend the sick, not because they were expendable but because they were less likely than the young to contract the pest.[51] Similarly, in 1563 Nicolas Lanoy claimed that younger Jesuits were "more disposed to catch that disease."[52] Jesuits in Portugal adopted a sensible approach to this problem; during the epidemic at Lisbon in 1569 the provincial ordered the departure of all Jesuits who could not help in the work of serving the sick,[53] and in the

---

[42]GERM 152: 226, Henri Sommal to Nadal, August 7.

[43]GERM 157: 294, Balduin Dawant to Mercurian, October 24.

[44]ITAL 151: 278, Candella to Mercurian, Palermo, July 8.

[45]ITAL 152: 13, Cosso to Mercurian, August 18.

[46]For another example see OPP NN 159: 491, *Per il tempo della peste*, November 9, 1576.

[47]Canisius, *Beati Petri Canisii*, 3: 493, Polanco to Canisius, Trent, October 5.

[48]LUS 68: 248v, Manuel Ruiz to Mercurian, Coimbra, September 10.

[49]GERM 148: 220, Vinck to Borgia, Mainz, September 19.

[50]HISP 108: 254–254v, Avellaneda to Borgia, Granada, June 3.

[51]HISP 141: 223–223v, annual by Melchior de San Juan, January 17, 1569.

[52]Nadal, *Epistolae*, 2: 445, to Nadal, Prague, November 8.

[53]LUS 63: 140, Francisco Anriquez to Borgia, July 18.

following year at Braga all Jesuits who were not necessary for the same type of work fled to other colleges.[54]

Jesuits seldom wrote accounts of their actual flights from a pest-stricken town, and the lack of information perhaps indicates that they left in an orderly manner and encountered nothing worthy enough or horrible enough to include in letters to superiors. Massimo Milanesi's account of the Jesuit flight from Alba Julia in Transylvania during the summer of 1586 reveals more that was horrible than was worthy. Milanesi wrote in September after he had reached the safe shelter of the monastery at Csiksomlyó. The first indication that the pest had entered the college at Alba Julia occurred on June 13, when Stanislaus Javickj became sick with a fever and a headache. On the next day Milanesi and the rector, Mateusz Thomány, visited Javickj; they found the pest on his right groin and immediately sent him to a wooden cottage in the garden, where he died on the 17th. Several Jesuits had already fled to a monastery outside the city, and the others soon joined them after closing the college, leaving one behind to care for the buildings and to serve the sick. Nothing else happened for the next two weeks, but then on July 3 Paul Woiciechowicz became sick while returning to the college in Alba Julia to collect some of the domestic and religious items left behind. Next Urban Elbing, the lay brother who worked as a cook, found a carbuncle on his knee on the 5th, Woiciechowicz died the following morning, that evening Milanesi himself became ill, and Elbing died on the 8th (the person caring for him also died, not from the pest but from inebriation). On the 9th Mateusz Strus began to feel ill. So Milanesi and he returned to Alba Julia, hoping to see a doctor, but the guards at the city gates refused to let them enter. In the meantime a woman who had replaced Elbing as cook contracted the pest and died, Father Peter Erdösi suffered the same fate on July 18, and yet another cook became sick on the 24th. By now the remaining Jesuits realized that God had given them enough warnings, so they decided that two should stay at the monastery and the rest, including Milanesi, who was still suffering the effects of his infection, would flee to Marosvásárhely, which they had heard was still healthy. When they arrived, however, they found it infected and resolved to flee further to the monastery at Csiksomlyó. The four arrived there safely, but only after a difficult journey over harsh mountains and through horrid wilds. As observed in a previous chapter,

[54]LUS 64: 69, Iñigo Tolosa to Borgia, Coimbra, July 16.

Milanese had begun his letter with, "I live, Reverend Father, by the mercy of God"; he ended it with, "I am glad to be alive with my brothers in the Lord."[55]

PRIVATE PRECAUTIONS

In his book on contagion Girolamo Fracastoro concurred with the popular wisdom that "there is no remedy more salutary than flight," but he proceeded to discuss other precautions for those who could not flee. These precautions were of two general types, one concerning the avoidance of persons who might be infected and the other concerning prophylactic measures to prevent infection.[56] Interconnected with the first of these is the belief in the contagious nature of epidemics, particularly of pest, and the earlier discussion of the pest as a contagious disease mentioned many of these precautions. Among Jesuits and others, the belief in contagion and the consequent need to avoid infected persons resulted in what could be considered internal flight, that is, segregation from all contact with the outside. Jerónimo Nadal's guidelines for colleges threatened by the pest put it quite simply: Jesuits should not leave the house and others should not enter.[57] The evidence indicates that Jesuits tried to follow this advice. During the epidemic at Messina in 1576, for example, the rector assured Juan Polanco that the Jesuits did not leave the college except in cases of great need and that those who had to leave or had to have contact with others as a result of their work were staying in separate quarters.[58]

On occasion Jesuits prohibited persons who were possible sources of infection from coming to their colleges or churches. At Saint-Omer in 1575 they forbade the students at the college for the poor from approaching the Jesuit school,[59] and at Venice in the following year the rector, Cesare Helmi, stopped people coming to the Jesuit church for confession when he realized that some of them might be sick.[60] When circumstances made it impossible to prevent others from entering Jesuit residences, Jesuits attempted to minimize the contact. For example, in 1577 the cardinal archbishop of Milan, Carlo

---

[55] *Monumenta antiquae Hungariae,* ed. Ladislaus Lukács, 3 vols. (Rome: Institutum Historicum Societatis Iesu, 1969–1981), 2: 985–93, to Campana.

[56] Girolamo Fracastoro [Hieronymi Fracastorii], *De contagione et contagiosis morbis et curatione, Libri III,* trans. Wilmer Cave Wright (New York: G. P. Putnam's Sons, 1930), 239–41.

[57] OPP NN 159: 497–497v, *Ordo per servari.* Another set of guidelines, *Istruttione da praticarsi* (513v), contains similar advice.

[58] ITAL 151: 89v, Carminata, May 11.

[59] GERM 155: 133v, Jean Harlem to Mercurian, Louvain, August 2.

[60] ITAL 151: 410v, *Avisi cavati da diverse lettere venute da Venetia,* August 6.

Borromeo, insisted that the Jesuits continue to hold classes for non-Jesuits at the seminary despite the presence of the pest; in complying with the cardinal's wishes the Jesuits erected partitions to separate the students, required them to enter through the garden, and forbade them to talk to anyone.[61] Still other measures indicate the precautions taken to preserve the lives of superiors by segregating them from sources of infection. When four Jesuits succumbed to the pest at Nevers in 1584, the provincial, Odon Pigenat, prohibited the rector from entering the college, so he stayed in buildings belonging to friends;[62] and when Mario Beringucci had to consult with the provincial concerning the situation at Venice during the epidemic of 1577, he met him outside the city and shouted at him from a distance.[63]

Two of the guidelines prepared for Jesuit colleges confronting an epidemic paid almost obsessive attention to the procurement of supplies. One recommended the purchase of "grain (and flour if there is not a mill in the house), wine, oil, wood, ham, bacon fat, cheese, spelt, rice, beans, barley (for water and for *orzata* [a barley-flavored syrup]), almonds, raisins, nuts,...anchovies, olives, garlic, onions," and medicine. It also suggested that Jesuits make arrangements for a fresh supply of vegetables, veal, and eggs.[64] One reason for these recommendations was the scarcity of supplies during an epidemic, but such provision would also free Jesuits from the need to leave their residences to purchase food and thereby risk encounters with infected people and goods. In 1572 the rector of the Jesuit college at Braniewo reacted to an outbreak of pest by sending the boarders home, forbidding contact with others, and securing adequate provisions;[65] in 1576 the Jesuits at Milan also tried to obtain supplies.[66] In the same year those at Ferrara exercised even greater foresight, for in addition to furnishing the college with the food necessary for several months to free them from contact with others they also built an oven in the college so they could bake their own bread.[67]

[61]ITAL 153: 296, 314, Mazzarino to Mercurian, Genoa, April 17 and 18.

[62]GAL 90: 240, to Aquaviva, Paris, September 30.

[63]ITAL 153: 315, to Mercurian, April 20.

[64]OPP NN 159: 513v, *Istruttione da praticarsi*; see also 491–491v, *Per il tempo della peste*, November 9, 1576. Jesuits did not live on diets of bread and water!

[65]GERM 134 II: 437, Sunyer to Nadal, near Pultusk, September 11.

[66]ITAL 152: 16v, Sgariglia to Mercurian, August 22.

[67]ITAL 151: 394, Gabriele Bisciola to Mercurian, August 8.

Jesuits who came in contact with the sick, primarily as a result of hearing their confessions and giving them communion, required different types of precautions. One of the guidelines prepared for colleges encountering an epidemic of pest advised Jesuits to avoid the breaths of the sick and included recommendations on prophylactic measures to prevent infection—sponges dipped in rose water, torches of cypress or juniper, and parchment screens soaked in vinegar.[68] Diego Lainez likewise suggested that confessors avoid the breaths of the sick, not put their cap on the bed, and use "much brevity, contenting themselves with only the necessary things."[69] As already noted, Giovanni Battista Vannini attributed his survival among the pest-stricken to his practice of only hearing confessions and refusing to give them communion, but the most common safeguard utilized by Jesuits was distance between themselves and the sick. At Lyon in 1577 Julien Bouclier said mass and preached an exhortation twice a week to the pest-stricken at the hospital "but in a place where he remains free of danger."[70] At Milan in the same year Jesuits heard the confessions of the pest-stricken staying in huts outside the city but without crossing the moat that surrounded them.[71] Such safeguards did not always work; although Jesuits at Brescia exercised great caution when hearing the confessions of the sick through doors and windows, several contracted the pest and died.[72]

Superiors undertook other precautions to protect Jesuits from becoming infected by those who heard confessions or assisted the sick in other ways. Nadal's guidelines stipulated that Jesuits who heard the confessions of the pest-stricken should stay together in a room near the entrance and separate from the rest of the community; they should not have any contact with other Jesuits, and a brother delegated to serve them should place their food on a table so that they could then take it to their room.[73] Portuguese Jesuits at least followed the advice concerning a separate room and the avoidance of contact when epidemics of pest occurred at Braga in 1570 and at Lisbon in 1579.[74] Another set of

---

[68]OPP NN 159: 514v, *Istruttione da praticarsi.*

[69]Lainez, *Lainii monumenta,* 2: 193, 664, to Tavona and Manare, Rome, March 13 and July 24, 1557.

[70]GAL 89: 143, Creichton to Mercurian, May 3.

[71]MED 76 I: 40, annual for 1576 and 1577 by Peruschi, March 12, 1578.

[72]ITAL 154: 178, Beringucci to Mercurian, Stiano, July 5, 1577; 204, Marta to Beringucci, Brescia, September 23, 1577.

[73]OPP NN 159: 493v–494, *Ordo per servari.*

[74]LUS 64: 69, Tolosa to Borgia, Coimbra, July 16, 1570; 68: 248, Ruiz to Mercurian, Coimbra, September 10, 1579.

guidelines was much more stringent than those written by Nadal on the segregation of those who assisted the sick: "They and their provisions must be totally separate from the others, especially in distance, and they must not have any communication at all with them."[75] The evidence suggests that some Jesuit communities tried to follow this advice. During the epidemic at Palermo in 1575, for example, Diego Martinez and Paolo Mantovano heard confessions at the hospital, while Francesco Costantino and Gabriele Puteo confessed those quarantined in their houses; all four lived together in separate quarters.[76] The Jesuits who volunteered to serve the sick in the huts outside Milan stayed near the Porta Romana in a house belonging to the parish.[77]

Another personal precaution was the segregation of the sick so they could not infect the healthy. Nadal's guidelines recommended the immediate removal of a Jesuit with a contagious disease to the garden, but this might have been a specific recommendation for the college at Vienna, which perhaps had a garden equipped with an infirmary.[78] One of the other guidelines just recommended the separation of the pest-stricken.[79] Some Jesuit colleges attempted to prepare an infirmary for their sick, as the rector at Trier, Anton Vinck, did in 1564,[80] while at other colleges superiors tried to segregate the pest-stricken in a separate room, often one of the unused classrooms. Massimo Milanesi, in his account of the epidemic of pest at Alba Julia in 1586, described his efforts to segregate the sick, including himself; some of the sick went to wooden huts constructed in the garden, while Milanesi had to endure the miserable conditions in a "stinking chapel."[81]

Girolamo Fracastoro recommended that those who could not flee and could not avoid situations that might result in infection should use measures to guarantee that the air they breathed was pure; "always keep in your mouth either juniper berries or gentian root or galanga root, or cassia bark, or macer, or the seed of a citron. Also keep touching your nostrils with a small sponge soaked in vinegar and rose water."[82] As noted above, one set of guidelines

[75]OPP NN 159: 514v, *Istruttione da praticarsi.*
[76]ITAL 148: 216–216v, Achille to Mercurian, August 23.
[77]MED 76 I: 39v, annual for 1576 and 1577 by Peruschi, March 12, 1578.
[78]OPP NN 159: 497v, *Ordo per servari.*
[79]Ibid., 514v, *Istruttione da praticarsi.*
[80]GERM 145: 225, to Lainez, October 7.
[81]*Monumenta Hungariae,* 2: 988–90, to Campana, September.
[82]Fracastoro, *De contagione,* 241.

recommended similar measures to protect confessors, as well as frequent fires and "good odors particularly of juniper" to overcome any bad odors. The guidelines also suggested the frequent airing of rooms when good winds came with pure and calm air but the closure of windows when the winds were bad and the days cloudy and humid.[83] On occasion Jesuits noted that they used preservatives or perfumes to protect themselves from contagion. Somewhat vague is the comment from a Jesuit at Brno in January 1572 that the return of the pest forced the community to protect itself once again with preservatives.[84] More revealing is the description by Anton Vinck of precautions undertaken by Jesuits at Trier in 1564: "They take care to use preservatives, such as perfumes in the church and in the house, and also taking them in the mouth."[85] Nadal's guidelines did not mention such perfumes or the airing of rooms, but they did recommend the "fumigation" of buildings,[86] and some accounts mention a similar practice. During an epidemic of pest at Brno in 1583 the Jesuits had their buildings fumigated every morning "to drive away the poison."[87]

Both Fracastoro and one set of guidelines for Jesuits also recommended the cleaning of buildings and the removal of all filth.[88] The best account of such cleaning comes from Ponce Cogordan's description of the epidemic at Paris in 1562: "Before leaving the house, I had it completely cleaned throughout, except the room of Master Paschase and the library, so that all the rooms were clean,...and I had all the furniture moved to the storeroom containing the grain, that is, the highest room in the house."[89] Despite these efforts three Jesuits died in the house, so Cogordan then had to repeat the process, cleaning the house and the furniture and even putting a fresh coat of whitewash on the walls of the rooms.[90] Jesuits adopted similar practices elsewhere; Anton Vinck reported in January 1567 that the place where several Jesuits died at Trier had been cleaned two or three times,[91] and in 1585 the Jesuits at Brno cleaned and

---

[83]OPP NN 159: 513v, *Istruttione da praticarsi*.

[84]GERM 134 I: 62, letter from P. Alexander (possibly Giovanni Battista) dated January 20, included in a letter from Hurtado Perez to Maggio, Olomouc, January 23.

[85]GERM 145: 225, to Lainez, October 7.

[86]OPP NN 159: 494, *Ordo per servari*.

[87]GERM 141: 196, annual for Austria, 1584; see also 158: 288, Sunyer to Mercurian, Braniewo, September 24, 1580.

[88]Fracastoro, *De contagione*, 241; OPP NN 159: 513v, *Istruttione da praticarsi*.

[89]Lainez, *Lainii monumenta*, 6: 421, to Lainez, Noyon, September 29.

[90]Ibid., 711, to Cogordan, Trent, March 11, 1563, in response to Cogordan's letters.

[91]GERM 148: 18v, to Borgia, Mainz, January 20.

whitewashed their residence following an outbreak of pest.[92] Other accounts indicate that after an epidemic fumigation and the "purging" of the air were also necessary before Jesuits could return to a building;[93] and others demonstrate beliefs that no one should live in a house for a certain length of time after someone had died in it—at Paris in 1562 it was one year and at Burgos in 1565 two years.[94] As for clothing, one set of guidelines recommended frequent washing so that Jesuits could change their shirts often,[95] and when Jesuits at Milan realized that they had come into close contact with someone who subsequently contracted the pest, they immediately changed their clothes.[96]

The final precautionary measures relate to the Galenic therapeutic programs mentioned in the previous chapter, in particular the development of a healthy body through a proper diet, regular exercise, and the promotion of moderation. Nadal's guidelines stressed moderation as a means to protect Jesuits from contracting the pest and, presumably, to enable them to survive if infected. He recommended that superiors should employ greater kindness and generosity than normal, ensuring that all forms of exercise—exterior, interior, physical, mental, literary, and spiritual—be moderate.[97] One of the other set of guidelines did not focus on moderation as much as Nadal but did recommend that superiors promote happiness and charity, permit some recreation, and demonstrate concern for everyone's health. "The food should be nutritious, easy to digest, and taken with good herbs such as angelica, sorrel, and the like.... The consumption of wine should be moderate, but the wine should be good and generous, and you should observe the daily regimen suggested by the doctor."[98] The best example of a therapeutic program initiated at a Jesuit college occurred at Messina in the spring of 1592. Because of the large number of illnesses and deaths both within the college and throughout the town, the provincial, Bartolomeo Ricci, after taking medical advice, ordered an additional half hour of sleep, an increase in the time spent in recreation, and a

[92]GERM 164: 121, Ricardus Zantenus to Aquaviva, March 13.

[93]Canisius, *Beati Petri Canisii*, 4: 47, Polanco to Canisius, Trent, February 9, 1563; GERM 168: 49, Manare to Aquaviva, Speyer, November 21, 1587.

[94]HISP 102: 253, Jerónimo Ruiz to Borgia, Salamanca, August 26, 1565.

[95]OPP NN 159: 514, *Istruttione da praticarsi.*

[96]ITAL 155: 202, Lamagna to Morais, October 22, 1577.

[97]OPP NN 159: 495v–496v, *Ordo per servari.*

[98]Ibid., 514, *Istruttione da praticarsi.*

decrease in the time spent in study. "With these precautions and with others regarding the food I hope in the mercy of the Lord that He will deign to keep us healthy."[99]

In summary, as in so many other aspects of their response to epidemic disease, all these precautionary measures practiced by Jesuits were sensible and consistent given their assumptions regarding the contagious nature of disease and the validity of the Galenic therapeutic programs. James C. Riley has argued that until the eighteenth century Europe had a passive, fatalistic response to epidemic as well as nonepidemic disease, but that during the Enlightenment many returned to the Hippocratic belief in the influence of the environment on health and disease. Not content with just accepting these views, eighteenth-century physicians attempted to modify the environment to improve health and conquer disease.[100] In this respect the Jesuits of the sixteenth century were also environmentalists in their efforts to change their circumstances to promote their own well-being. The precautions practiced by Jesuits were also consistent with the policies developed by the Society to protect the majority from the dangers of infection—in Polanco's words, for "the greater divine service"—while still allocating some human resources for the service of the sick.

PUBLIC REGULATIONS

The public health regulations developed by authorities to combat and control epidemics feature prominently in Jesuit accounts, and they also have received considerable attention from historians. Jean-Noël Biraben devotes almost one hundred pages to them in his *Les hommes et la peste*,[101] and Carlo Cipolla has written four books dealing with aspects of the topic.[102] Although public authorities attempted some rudimentary measures to combat the Black Death

[99]ITAL 160: 265, to Aquaviva, April 29.

[100]James C. Riley, *The Eighteenth-Century Campaign to Avoid Disease* (London: Macmillan, 1987).

[101]Jean-Noël Biraben, *Les hommes et la peste en France et dans les pays européens et méditerranéens*, 2 vols. (Paris: Mouton, 1975–1976), 2: 85–181.

[102]Carlo M. Cipolla, *Cristofano and the Plague: A Study in the History of Public Health in the Age of Galileo* (London: Collins, 1973) and idem, *Fighting the Plague in Seventeenth-Century Italy* (Madison: University of Wisconsin Press, 1981), idem, *Public Health and the Medical Profession in the Renaissance* (Cambridge: Cambridge University Press, 1976), and idem, *Faith, Reason, and the Plague in Seventeenth-Century Tuscany* (Ithaca: Cornell University Press, 1979).

and subsequent epidemics in the fourteenth century, major developments occurred in the latter half of the fifteenth century and the first half of the sixteenth, especially in the towns of northern Italy, and then spread to southern Italy and north of the Alps. An important innovation in these towns was the establishment of public health boards that assumed enormous legislative, judicial, and executive powers during epidemics. These boards adopted measures to prevent the entry of an epidemic by restricting the movement of goods and people into the town and, should these measures prove unsuccessful, to limit the spread of the disease by the arrangement of burials, the segregation of the sick either in hospitals or in their homes, the removal, burning, or cleaning of infected goods, and the prohibition of any activities and public gatherings such as sermons that might increase the chances of infection. In all of this the public health officers based their policies on the assumption that they were dealing with a contagious disease. The boards were also responsible for the maintenance of public order and the distribution of relief to the sick and to those whose livelihoods were interrupted by the epidemic. On the whole, Jesuit accounts support the claims that the towns of northern Italy were more progressive than the rest of Europe in developing policies to combat epidemics, but they also document some interesting exceptions to the pattern.

Of the towns in northern Italy, Venice received the most praise for its policies, Milan the most criticism. According to one report from Venice written in July 1576, the authorities were diligent and spared no expense in preventing the pest from spreading, and in consequence "they deserved very great praise, especially for their charity."[103] They removed some of the poor from their cramped and unhealthy houses, sent them to better accommodations, and provided them with food; they likewise attempted to remedy the shortage of cleaners and grave diggers (called *picegamorti* at Venice, *monatti* elsewhere) by offering generous wages and removing edicts of banishment for those willing to take the jobs.[104] At Milan during the epidemic of 1576–1577 all went well at first, and Alfonso Sgariglia praised the officials' efforts to keep the sick segregated outside the city walls and the care taken in purging infected houses by burning the less valuable items and cleaning the rest.[105] By the summer of

---

[103]ITAL 151: 410, *Avisi cavati da diverse lettere venute da Venetia,* July 13 and 16.

[104]Ibid., 410v, August 6.

[105]ITAL 152: 16; 153: 101, to Mercurian and to Candi, August 22, 1576, and January 15, 1577, the latter included in Beringucci's letter of February 2, 1577.

1577, however, as the pest waned somewhat, the authorities loosened their control, and Giovanni Battista Peruschi marveled that the situation had not become worse since the city seemed full of people who did their business and mingled with each other indiscriminately.[106] Peruschi expressed his hopes that the return of the governor, who had fled the epidemic, would result in better order.[107]

The health officials in other towns in northern Italy received good reports for their efforts during the epidemic of 1576–1577. From Forlì, Ridolfo Florio claimed that the officials in the cities of the Romagna exercised great care,[108] and according to Antonio Valentino not even the slightest suspicion of pest existed at Novellara, where the authorities used "great diligence."[109] In the autumn of 1576 all the towns and villages surrounding Brescia were infected with the pest. The officials adopted strict measures to keep it from gaining a foothold in the city by the daily examination of any person who became sick, the prohibition of people leaving or entering the city, the suspension of all business activity, the closure of schools, and a ban on preaching.[110] These efforts were in vain, for the pest entered the city in the summer of 1577 with devastating effects, so the officials then turned to the task of cleaning infected goods, a task made doubly difficult by the death of many and the flight of others.[111] Away from the major centers the authorities were not as diligent in their efforts to combat epidemics, as Antoine Blondet discovered to his horror when traveling from Piedmont into France during an epidemic of pest in 1564; at Avigliano, Chivasso, Rivoli, and other places he found bodies lying in the streets for lack of anyone to bury them.[112]

Jesuits gave favorable but at times mixed reviews of the efforts by health officials in southern Italy and Sicily to control the epidemic of 1575–1577. Neapolitan authorities received commendation for their efforts to prevent the epidemic from spreading from Sicily by sending officials throughout the kingdom as soon as they heard that the pest had entered Messina and by imposing a

---

[106]ITAL 154: 248, to Mercurian, July 24.

[107]Ibid., 367, August 19.

[108]ITAL 152: 184v, to Mercurian, October 3, 1576.

[109]Ibid., 309, to Mercurian, November 26, 1576.

[110]ITAL 155: 150, Giovanni Francesco Prandi to Mercurian, October 9.

[111]Ibid., 204, Marta to Beringucci, September 23.

[112]ITAL 125: 125, to Polanco, Aosta, October.

complete ban on all commerce and travelers from the island.[113] Farther south at Reggio officials attempted to impose a similar ban, but the proximity of Messina made it difficult to enforce, particularly at night; and the rector of the Jesuit college, Francesco Mercado, deplored the lack of order and control.[114] As for the Sicilian towns of Messina and Palermo, in 1575 the health officers introduced the same regulations that were common in the towns on the mainland, and Jesuits praised the efforts, especially those made by the authorities at Messina, to control the epidemic.[115] On the other hand, come 1576 Jesuits began to blame the continued waxing and waning of the epidemic on the poor order maintained by the authorities, again especially at Messina. The exasperated rector of the college, Giovanni Battista Carminata, claimed, "what we need is severity without respect, order with enforcement, and compassion for the needy poor."[116]

Jesuits outside Italy continued the trend of giving favorable reports for some authorities, unfavorable for others. Public health officers on the Iberian Peninsula received commendation for their strictness in enforcing bans and quarantines.[117] In contrast, Jesuits never praised French authorities for their efforts to control epidemics. As already noted, Emond Auger reported that all the people in positions of authority at Lyon fled the outbreak of pest in 1564, leaving essential services in the hands of volunteers, but his comments contain no words of overt criticism. The ease with which Jesuits left pest-infected French towns and traveled to others, moreover, indicates that municipal authorities did not mount effective guards to prevent the entry of infected people, although southern France was more advanced in this respect than the north.[118] The towns of Germany also had a bad record. During the epidemic

[113]Alfonso Salmeron, *Epistolae P. Alphonsi Salmeronis Societatis Iesu*, 2 vols. (Madrid: Typis Gabrielis Lopez del Horno, 1906–1907), 2: 526–27, to Mercurian, Naples, July 9, 1575; ITAL 149: 129, Jerónimo Domenech to Mercurian, Catania, November 18, 1575.

[114]ITAL 149: 158; 151: 335, 340, to Mercurian, November 22, 1575, July 22 and 23, 1576.

[115]For Messina see especially ITAL 148: 3, Carminata to Mercurian, June 22, 1575; and Juan Polanco, *Polanci complementa: Epistolae et commentaria P. Joannis Alphonsi de Polanco e Societate Jesu*, 2 vols. (Madrid: Gabrielis Lopez del Horno, 1916–1917), 2: 368, to Mercurian, October 5, 1575; for Palermo see especially ITAL 150: 158, Achille to Mercurian, February 5, 1576; and Polanco, *Complementa*, 2: 508, to Mercurian, April 2, 1576.

[116]ITAL 151: 89, Carminata to Polanco, Messina, May 11, 1576; see also 12, Domenech to Mercurian, Catania, April 18, 1576, and 104v, Carminata to Mercurian, Messina, May 14, 1576.

[117]See for examples HISP 111: 15–15v, Ambrosio de Castilla to Borgia, Cadiz, June 15, 1569; LUS 68: 232, Gabriel Alonso to Mercurian, Lisbon, August 27, 1579.

[118]Nadal, *Epistolae*, 1: 727–28, to Antonio Araoz, Louvain, July 3, 1562.

of 1553 Leonhard Kessel informed Ignatius Loyola that all the officials, clergy, and nobles at Cologne had fled to their villas.[119] Although authorities elsewhere closed schools at the first sign of an epidemic, Jesuit colleges at Cologne, Trier, and Fulda remained open despite the presence of the pest.[120]

Ambrosius Sanctinus' account of a severe epidemic of pest at Vienna in 1562 reveals that Viennese officials were more comparable to those in northern Italy than to those in Germany. The government appointed a prefect of health to coordinate the precautionary measures, sent medical personnel throughout the city to identify the sick, had white crosses painted on suspected buildings, ordered either the removal of the sick to the hospital or, if their servants agreed to stay with them, their confinement for forty days in their own houses, and arranged for the burial of all the dead in a trench outside the city.[121] Other epidemics at Vienna prompted similarly favorable reports. For example, in October 1582 Hans Rubenstein claimed that "diligent care" removed all suspicion from the city after a few had died from the pest.[122] On the other hand, Viennese officials did not order the closure of all schools as a matter of course during epidemics.[123] Finally, the evidence from eastern Europe indicates that this region was backward in developing measures to control epidemics, although even here the record was mixed. At Pultusk authorities enforced the closure of schools and the barricading of infected areas within the town,[124] but when Philip Jakob Widmanstadius heard of an outbreak of pest in Prussia in 1577, he expressed his fears that it might enter Braniewo, "because the city employs no guards for its gates during an epidemic, and the healthy and the sick are accustomed to mix with each other without discrimination."[125]

The public regulations designed to prevent the entry or the spread of an epidemic affected the Society of Jesus and its work. The various measures to isolate the sick and those exposed to them of course applied to Jesuits. In 1557 Giovanni Battista Tavona visited the hospital at Padua, not realizing that it

[119]*Litterae quadrimestres*, 2: 347, July 1.

[120]GERM 145: 178, Vinck to Lainez, Trier, August 16, 1564; 148: 102, Vinck to Borgia, Trier, May 6, 1567; 136 II: 469, Dorkens to Mercurian, Speyer, November 14, 1575; 138 II: 356v, Dorkens to Mercurian, Fulda, October 15, 1577.

[121]GERM 139: 178–178v, *quadrimestris*, April 27, 1563.

[122]GERM 160: 216, to Elderen, October 22; see also 136 II: 301, Maggio to Mercurian, July 20, 1575.

[123]GERM 137 II: 327, Maggio to Mercurian, September 18, 1576.

[124]GERM 133 II: 387, Milanesi to Maggio, September 21, 1571.

[125]POL 80: 74v, to Mercurian, December 16.

contained victims of the pest. As a result the officials confined all the Jesuits to their house.[126] At Monreale the death of Nicola dei Greci in December 1575 resulted in the quarantine of the school where he had received care but not the college as a whole.[127] In the following year at Catania, however, officials "barricaded" both the college and the house following the death of Giulio Clerici in June.[128] Although the usual location for such confinement was the Jesuit residence, on occasion officials stipulated special quarters. When Ettore Leonelli and Guido Tosco succumbed to the pest at Venice in June 1576, the Jesuit who had cared for them, "Brother Francesco Buono the tailor from Milan," had to spend his quarantine on a barge.[129] The length of confinement was not always the forty days indicated by the term quarantine. At Milan, for example, one group of Jesuits had to endure thirty days of enclosure while another only twenty-two.[130] Niccolò Spinola and Giulio Negrone confronted a different type of confinement. When they traveled to Genoa late in the summer of 1577, the officials insisted that they complete a quarantine outside the city before they could receive permission to enter.[131]

Strict enforcement of the entire range of restrictions could result in the complete cessation of most Jesuit activities. Officials often ordered the closure of all schools for the duration of an epidemic; they did so to cite several examples, at Prague in 1562, at Tournai in 1572, and at Lyon in 1577.[132] While some magistrates requested Jesuit communities to furnish priests for confessions and communion, at Venice in 1575 the authorities threatened the entire community with confinement if any Jesuit visited a "suspected place."[133] In the following year the rector at Venice expressed his frustrations in a letter to General Mercurian: "Our presence here appears to be of little service to God, because we cannot take part in the normal exercises of our ministry in confessions since [the officials] have ordered that no woman can leave her quarter or

---

[126]ITAL 107: 376, to Lainez, March 26.

[127]Polanco, *Complementa*, 2: 439, to Mercurian, Catania, January 3, 1576.

[128]ITAL 151: 278, Candela to Mercurian, Palermo, July 8.

[129]Ibid., 312v, Helmi to Mercurian, July 14.

[130]ITAL 153: 100v, Sgariglia to Candi, January 15, 1577; 155: 202v, Lamagna to Morais, October 22, 1577.

[131]ITAL 155: 41, Giovanni Francesco Vipera to Mercurian, September 13.

[132]GERM 144: 45, *quadrimestris* by Jan Behem, Prague, December 28, 1562; 152: 207, Jean Montaigne to Nadal, Tournai, June 26, 1572; GAL 89: 117, Creichton to Mercurian, Lyon, April 7, 1577.

[133]ITAL 149: 120, Beringucci to Mercurian, November 12.

associate with anyone."[134] The more usual practice was to place a ban on all public gatherings that could increase the chance of contagion, and this included preaching. At Bivona in the summer of 1575 even the rumor of an epidemic resulted in the authorities' prohibiting sermons.[135] At Messina the bans in place during 1575 prompted the rector to make complaints similar to the ones made by his counterpart at Venice: "We wish we could perform some of the ministries of the Society that have been interrupted by this disease, such as teaching, preaching, and others, for in truth...we witness great frigidity here for lack of the word of God."[136]

Aside from affecting the work of the Society, the public regulations could damage its financial situation. Unlike other priests, Jesuits charged no money for their sacerdotal services, so prohibitions on preaching and confessions had no impact on them. Although each college attempted to have a secure source of perpetual income, some towns paid for their colleges through periodic grants. When an epidemic forced the closure of a college, on occasion the municipal authorities refused to pay anything, but meanwhile the Jesuit community still had to provide for its sustenance. This occurred at Messina in 1576. The authorities withheld the stipends paid to the lecturers and the three hundred scudi which they paid to finance the course in philosophy.[137] Compounding the loss of this income was the difficulty in finding food as a result of the restrictions placed on trade, resulting in, according to one report, the great suffering of those at the college.[138]

Public regulations could hurt Jesuit finances in other ways; trading bans could cause a rise in prices, prevent colleges from receiving their income, and exhaust sources of donations. The first two of these happened at Reggio in Calabria; Francesco Mercado complained in 1575 that the bans resulted in much suffering, "especially here in Reggio where everything is supplied from Messina";[139] and in the following year he reported that the bans prevented the college from receiving its income, "which consists of cheeses that come from Sicily."[140] Although the towns of Forlì and Novellara escaped the epidemic of

---

[134]ITAL 151: 312, Helmi, July 14, 1576.
[135]ITAL 148: 210, Sibilla to Mercurian, August 21.
[136]ITAL 149: 364, Carminata to Mercurian, December 17.
[137]Polanco, *Complementa*, 2: 530, to Mercurian, Tremilia, June 30.
[138]ITAL 153: 174, Fazio to Mercurian, Catania, March 3, 1577.
[139]ITAL 148: 178, to Mercurian, August 11.
[140]ITAL 151: 340, to Mercurian, July 23.

1575–1577, the bans on trade with Venice affected the Jesuit communities there because the cessation of commercial activity meant that their benefactors no longer had the means to donate money to them.[141] Another financial loss could occur during an epidemic as a result of the compulsory burning of infected goods. One of the guidelines prepared for the Italian epidemic of 1575–1577 advised superiors to lock away anything valuable, "leaving out only the necessary things so as not to expose everything else to the danger of infection and loss."[142] Even the necessary things could result in loss for a Jesuit community; when Giulio Clerici died at Catania in 1576, the officials burned his bed and clothes.[143]

BREAKING THE BLOCKADE

Implicit in Jerónimo Nadal's guidelines was the need for Jesuits to cooperate with municipal health officials. In particular he argued that Jesuits should care for their sick in such a manner that the officials would have no cause to complain.[144] In his *Causes and Remedies of the Pest* Antonio Possevino also recommended cooperation with the authorities in notifying them of suspected cases and in burning infected goods.[145] On occasion, however, Jesuits were not cooperative. At Pultusk in 1571 Jesuits failed to convince the bishop to revoke the order to close their college,[146] but at Vienna in 1576 they appealed to Archduke Karl, who overrode the decision of the local authorities.[147] One area that demonstrates the potential for conflict between public health officials and their attempts to control the spread of epidemics on the one hand and Jesuits and their attempts to continue their activities on the other hand is correspondence. As outlined in the introduction, the Society's regulations on periodic correspondence produced a steady stream of letters between Rome and the provinces and within each province between officials at various levels. Regulations aside, individual Jesuits often wrote to friends in the Society who worked at other colleges; and Jesuits at every level, from the general to the lay brother working as a cook, were eager to receive news of their fellow members. The

---

[141]Ibid., 406; 152: 55, Florio to Mercurian, Forlì, August 11 and 28, 1576; VEN 105 I: 54, annual by Candi, February 10, 1578.

[142]OPP NN 159: 513–513v, *Istruttione da praticarsi.*

[143]Polanco, *Complementa*, 2: 526, to Mercurian, Carangino, June 15.

[144]OPP NN 159: 498, *Ordo per servari.*

[145]Antonio Possevino, *Cause et rimedii della peste, et d'altre infermità* (Florence: Appresso i Giunti, 1577), 58.

[146]GERM 133 II: 387, Milanesi to Maggio, September 21.

[147]GERM 137 II: 327, Maggio to Mercurian, September 18.

eagerness increased in times of epidemic, as Jesuit communities waited to hear the fate of others.

Public health officials imposed regulations that made such an exchange of correspondence difficult if not impossible during outbreaks of pest. The bans imposed on the entry of people and goods applied to letters, and officials throughout Europe acted on the assumption that a letter could be a source of infection. Jesuits at Evora in Portugal, Olomouc in Czechoslovakia, and Cluj in Transylvania reported difficulties in exchanging letters during epidemics of pest.[148] Elsewhere Jesuits could be more specific in explaining the fate of letters from pest-infected cities. Neapolitan officials burned all the letters coming from Sicily and Calabria in 1575,[149] and the same fate occurred to those coming from Lyon to Chambéry in 1577.[150] According to Francesco Adorno, Genoese authorities first sent all the letters from Milan and other suspected places back to where they had come from, then delayed the forwarding of them in a type of quarantine, and finally burned them.[151] From Bologna in 1576 Francesco Palmio expressed the frustrations he experienced in trying to forward letters from other colleges to Rome; the officials "either send them back here to us, or they do not send them at all, or they open them [to determine their origin], or they burn them."[152] Juan Polanco also complained that officials in southern Italy opened letters to determine if they came from a suspected place (which seems a dangerous practice if indeed the letters were capable of spreading a disease) and explained that such procedures made him reluctant to send confidential information.[153] Another procedure followed in some places was to attempt to disinfect correspondence; Claudio Aquaviva informed General Mercurian from Naples in 1576 that he was forwarding a package of letters from Sicily that had been soaked in vinegar for twenty-four hours.[154]

---

[148]LUS 63: 170v, Sarrano to Borgia, Evora, September 18, 1569; GERM 134 II: 396v, Maggio to [Nadal], Olomouc, August 16, 1572; *Monumenta Hungariae*, 2: 911, Campana to Aquaviva, Cracow, May 10, 1586.

[149]Salmeron, *Epistolae*, 2: 531, to Mercurian, Naples, July 22; ITAL 148: 167, Calligaris to Mercurian, Messina, August 5.

[150]GAL 89: 180, Atanasio to Mercurian, Chambéry, May 21.

[151]ITAL 152: 82, 254, 258, to Mercurian, September 14, November 3 and 6, 1576.

[152]Ibid., 182, to Mercurian, October 3.

[153]Polanco, *Complementa*, 2: 354, to Mercurian, Catania, August 23, 1575.

[154]ITAL 151: 284, July 6. See K. F. Meyer, *Disinfected Mail* (Holton, Kan.: Gossip Printery, 1962), and Jacqueline Brossollet and Andreina Zitelli, "La disinfezione delle lettere," in *Venezia e la peste, 1348–1797*, 2d ed. (Venice: Marsilio Editori, 1980), 155–56. I never encountered any letters at the Jesuit Archives that showed any indications of this treatment.

Letters soaked in vinegar were better than no letters at all (provided they were legible). The effect of the anti-epistolary measures was to disrupt the normal exchange of correspondence between Jesuits, even in those areas that did not have bad public health records. The best examples of the disruption, however, come from the Italian epidemic of 1575–1577, which is perhaps another indication of the relative advancement of public health measures in Italy. As soon as the epidemic began in the summer of 1575, Paolo Achille, the rector at Palermo, began sending the same information in letter after letter in the hope that one of them would reach the general in Rome, but in October the general reported that he had not received any letters for several months.[155] From Reggio, Francesco Mercado wrote in August that he had not heard any news from the Jesuits at Messina for two months, so when officials refused to let a boat from Messina land at Reggio, Mercado went down to the dock and shouted at the Jesuit on board for news.[156]

When the epidemic began in northern Italy, the provincial, Francesco Adorno, was based in Genoa, which like Florence was one of the few major cities to escape the epidemic. At first Adorno could send letters south to Florence and Rome, but he could not always receive them from Jesuit communities in the pest-infected towns of Milan, Venice, Padua, and Brescia; later he could not even send them south because other towns placed a ban on Genoa for continuing to trade with Milan, so he moved to the unaffected towns of Parma and Ferrara.[157] Meanwhile Jesuits in the pest-infected towns had trouble not only sending letters but also receiving them, as indicated by two examples from Venice. In January 1577 Domenico Cosso complained to General Mercurian that the last letter he had received from Rome was dated September 20, in response to his dated August 18,[158] and in February Mario Beringucci claimed that he had written a dozen letters to the provincial without receiving a single reply.[159] If the letters did manage to arrive at their destination, they were quite often late; at Bologna, Francesco Palmio received news from Brescia that he

---

[155]ITAL 148: 46, 151; 149: 26, July 5, August 2, and October 18.

[156]ITAL 149: 178, to Mercurian, August 11.

[157]ITAL 152: 145, 294; 154: 81, to Mercurian, Genoa, Parma, and Ferrara, September 21 and November 20, 1576, June 12, 1577; 152: 303v, Palmio to Mercurian, Bologna, November 24, 1576.

[158]ITAL 153: 52, January 18.

[159]Ibid., 101v, to Mercurian, February 6.

forwarded to Rome even though it had taken three months for the letters to reach him.[160]

As noted in the introduction, the Jesuit Archives contain 350 letters relevant to the outbreak of pest in Italy between 1575 and 1577. To state the obvious, some letters did reach their destination; on occasion the Jesuits managed to beat the blockade. When Paolo Achille explained to Mercurian that he could find neither couriers nor others to take his letters, he went on to assure him that he would do everything he could to send them,[161] and Francesco Adorno made similar assurances.[162] Cosso began his letter to Mercurian by stating that he had written "more than twenty-one times, by means fair and foul." The foul means would be to engage people willing to run the blockade and, of course, to pay them well. On one occasion Mercurian complained of the cost of sending letters to Rome even though they were late.[163] Giuseppe Blondo managed to send his letter from Catanzaro with Capuchin priests on their way to Rome for the Holy Year,[164] Antonio Pignolati sent his correspondence through relatives,[165] and Beringucci sent his through the papal nuncio at Venice.[166] Francesco Filippo made the most complicated arrangements, as he instructed Adorno, "You can send your letters by asking Father Antonio Valentino in Novellara to send them to the commissaire of the court in the package for Count Camillo, Lord of Novellara,... and he will then very securely send them here to Mantua to the secretary of the bishop, whose name is Andrea Antonio, and if you want to write to the [Jesuits] at Verona or to any other place hereabouts this is the best and the most secure way." Filippo also explained that when he traveled from Mantua to Novellara to see Valentino and to give him some letters, the guards refused to let either him or the letters enter the town. Filippo arranged to meet Valentino, however, and secretly passed the letters to him.[167]

---

[160]Ibid., 73, to Mercurian, Bologna, January 26, 1577.
[161]ITAL 148: 46v, Palermo, July 5, 1575.
[162]ITAL 152: 337, Parma, December 10, 1576.
[163]ITAL 70a: 14, to Beringucci, Rome, July 20, 1577.
[164]ITAL 148: 310, to Mercurian, September 11, 1575.
[165]ITAL 153: 151, to Mercurian, Como, February 24, 1577.
[166]ITAL 154: 364, to Mercurian, August 17, 1577.
[167]ITAL 153: 393–393v, Mantua, June 12, 1577.

When Filippo returned to Mantua, he wrote to Adorno complaining about his trip. He had to travel on foot through continuous rain and over terrain of clay, and along the way everyone ridiculed him, saying that the duke of Mantua himself could not gain entry into Novellara. Filippo's uncomfortable journey highlights another area of potential conflict between public health officials and Jesuits, namely travel. As simply put by Iñigo Azevedo from Coimbra in 1569, "it is difficult to go from one place to another because the guards do not permit those who enter or leave pest-infected towns go to others that are healthy."[168] Travelers could obtain bills or patents of health to prove that they had come from a healthy town and thus gain entry to another. In 1561 Jesuits traveling from Augsburg to Italy obtained theirs from the municipal government.[169] Travel without the bills was difficult and dangerous. In 1576 Ridolfo Florio claimed that not even a fly coming from Venice could get into Forlì,[170] and Francesco Adorno reported that those who attempted to travel from Padua to Genoa could face the gallows.[171]

For some groups of people travel was difficult even with the bills of health. Mario Beringucci, when reporting the difficulties he faced in trying to reach Venice in 1577, stated, "Every place has put a ban on clergy and Jews, because they are more likely than others to spread the disease."[172] Other Jesuits noted that the governments of Milan, Bologna, and Ferrara had specifically banned clergy, and in June 1576 Francesco Palmio forwarded to Rome a copy of the decree by the Bolognese authorities: "The Deputies of Health order that the clergy who arrive at the borders of the territory with bills of health … may pass through but without any hope of entering the city."[173] The arrival of ships from infected or suspected places of course could pose as great a threat as travel overland, but it was easier to control. When a Jesuit arrived at Venice in 1566 on a ship from Alexandria, he and his fellow passengers had to spend several days in confinement at the hospital—relatively few since the ship had already spent four months at sea and no one had become sick.[174] Diego de

---

[168]Polanco, *Complementa*, 2: 68, to Polanco, October 8.

[169]Canisius, *Beati Petri Canisii*, 3: 232, Hurtado Perez to Salmeron, September 25.

[170]ITAL 151: 406, to Mercurian, Forlì, August 11.

[171]ITAL 152: 30, to Mercurian, Genoa, August 24, 1576.

[172]ITAL 153: 100, to Mercurian, February 6.

[173]ITAL 151: 183, to Mercurian, June 2; see 52v, Helmi to Mercurian, Venice, April 27, 1576; 66v, Adorno to Mercurian, Milan, May 3, 1576.

[174]Canisius, *Beati Petri Canisii*, 5: 273 n., Helmi to Borgia, September 7.

Sepulveda endured a similar confinement when he arrived at Siracusa in 1576. Because his ship had stopped twenty days previously at Trapani, he had to spend four days under guard at a hermitage located one mile from the town.[175] Other towns were not so hospitable as Venice and Siracusa. In 1576 Juan Polanco received advice that he should not try to pass from Sicily to Reggio, because the government at Reggio was so determined to prevent ships from landing that it was dangerous to attempt it.[176]

The regulations prohibiting the entry of travelers without bills of health and the ban on clergy even with them created difficulties for Jesuits, especially those caught in the middle of an epidemic. When traveling from Spain into France in 1562, Jerónimo Nadal arrived at the town of Tarbes in Aquitaine at 9:00 at night and discovered that he could not enter; neither could he and his companions stay at an inn outside the walls because it was full. They tried again to enter the town and managed to sneak in when the guards opened the gates for some inhabitants who were returning, but once inside they likewise could not find a place to stay until someone took pity on them.[177] In May 1576 Anton Vinck was leading a group of Jesuits from Germany to Rome. They obtained bills of health from Ferrara before proceeding to Forlì, where they still had to spend "a good piece of time" outside the walls before gaining entry and learning that further travel was impossible because the cities of the papal states had banned the entry of clergy. The indignant Vinck expressed his astonishment that clergy had more trouble than did laymen traveling in the lands of the church.[178] Another group of Jesuits from Germany and Flanders arrived at Padua at the same time and received advice from Paolo Candi: "They cannot go from here to Ferrara at all,... [but they could] go to Brescia, where they would arrive without any trouble, and there obtain a bill of health so they could go to Parma, which they might be able to enter. At Parma they could obtain a letter from the duke to go to Modena and Bologna, where they would experience enormous difficulties gaining entry, and as a result I doubt very much that they will be able to proceed; they might have to take the road back to Germany."[179] In 1576 Robert Monreall left Trier at the end of summer for a trip to Rome. As he approached Genoa he discovered that he could not go

[175]ITAL 150: 82, Alfonso de Villalobos to Mercurian, January 17.
[176]ITAL 151: 89v, Carminata to Polanco, Messina, May 11.
[177]Nadal, *Epistolae*, 1: 727–28, to Araoz, Louvain, July 3.
[178]ITAL 151: 74–74v, to Mercurian, Forlì, May 5.
[179]Ibid., 125, to Mercurian, May 18.

further south nor could he return north, so he was stuck for thirty-six days at the town of Carcare outside Genoa.[180]

Just as Jesuits managed to beat the blockade on letters, so also did some manage to circumvent the blockade on travelers. Domenico Cosso, who sent his letters "by means fair and foul," assured Mercurian that he could find a way to travel to Rome despite the restrictions by taking a circuitous route and by serving a quarantine at one of the towns along the route to obtain the necessary papers.[181] Cristoforo Frusiglio managed to travel from Vicenza to Florence in 1576 by making a great detour.[182] Two Jesuits managed to escape the regulations concerning the confinement of passengers arriving from infected ports. Luciano Luciani arrived at Naples in May 1577 aboard a galley from Messina and "with great effort and risk" evaded the guards and disembarked,[183] while Giovanni Giacomo Basso made the same journey in the following month on a galley returning from military service in the eastern Mediterranean.[184] No evidence suggests that the circumvention of either the regulations regarding travel or the restrictions on correspondence resulted in any kind of serious trouble between the public officials and the Society, but it was bound to create tension. Carlo Cipolla has noted the hostility between public health officials and clergy in seventeenth-century Tuscany, as the clergy objected to some of the regulations established to control the spread of epidemics and considered themselves exempt from others.[185] In the sixteenth century some Jesuits believed themselves exempt.

---

[180]ITAL 152: 254, Adorno to Mercurian, Genoa, November 3; GERM 137 II: 408, Monreall to Mercurian, Carcare, November 16.

[181]ITAL 154: 51, Venice, May 31, 1577.

[182]ITAL 151: 87, to Mercurian, Florence, May 11.

[183]ITAL 154: 11v, Blondo to Mercurian, May 18.

[184]Ibid., 104, to Mercurian, June 18.

[185]Cipolla, *Faith, Reason, and the Plague*, 2–3, 6–7.

——

SIX

THE COURSE OF AN EPIDEMIC

OUTBREAKS OF EPIDEMIC DISEASE seldom sprang unannounced on an unsuspecting population; the often slow approach of an epidemic of pest was accompanied by fear and rumor, which could reinforce each other and produce panic among the inhabitants. Once inside the town, the pest at times smoldered fitfully, at other times it struck savagely; but regardless of the rate of spread, the epidemic disrupted normal life and often emptied towns of most of their inhabitants. The cessation of economic activity during epidemics often heightened the miseries of the poor, who could neither flee nor find employment, while the high level of mortality heightened the problems of the municipal authorities, who had to arrange burials. The Jesuit accounts of these epidemics sometimes include figures on mortality, and they also permit an analysis of the seasonality of the pest. This analysis supports the conclusion that the epidemics described by Jesuits might not have been the result of bubonic plague.

BEGINNINGS

On June 22, 1575, the rector of the Jesuit college at Messina, Giovanni Battista Carminata, commenced a letter to General Everard Mercurian by paraphrasing a passage from Job 19:21:

> The hand of God has touched us. We have the pest inside the walls of the town, introduced through some goods purchased from a galley that arrived from the Levant. It has attacked many houses, and we *fear* that it

might become worse. The authorities have ordered us to close the school and stop preaching. Great confusion reigns throughout the city, all business has stopped, many have fled, and others continue to flee as a result of their *fear*. Due to the crowding at the college I have sent many to our vineyard and assigned them a superior. They remain on guard there. From here I provide them with all their needs, and I will go there from time to time. Very many people came to our church today for confession. Father, recommend us and have others recommend us to the Lord![1]

This is the entire letter; short though it is, Carminata mentioned fear twice. Jean Delumeau in *La peur en Occident* describes the collective panic that descended on communities whenever an epidemic of pest approached. Other types of epidemic disease could result in the deaths of thousands, but a few cases of pestilence could create an epidemic of fear that at times had more of an impact on preindustrial towns than did the actual morbidity and mortality of the disease.[2]

The word that Jesuits used again and again when reporting the approach of the pest was fear. Jacob Wujek expressed the feeling with bluntness from Cracow in September 1589: "We feared the pest."[3] From Tournai in August 1564 Everard Mercurian reported on the "suspicions and fear of pest in this city because of the discovery of some pest-stricken families,"[4] Emerich Forsler wrote from Vienna in April 1577 that the pest seemed to sleep but "some signs" created "new fear";[5] and in May 1586 Peter Szydlowski claimed that a reciprocal fear existed between the peasants and the inhabitants of Oradea: the latter feared that the peasants might infect the city with the pest, and the former feared the guards established by the inhabitants to keep them out.[6] During the Italian epidemic in 1576, Jesuits living in the unaffected but threatened cities of Ferrara, Genoa, Rome, and Parma used the same words to describe their own

---

[1]ITAL 148: 3.

[2]Jean Delumeau, *La peur en occident (XIVe–XVIIe siècles): Une cité assiégée* (Paris: Fayard, 1978), 98; see the comments by Richard J. Palmer, "The Church, Leprosy and Plague in Medieval and Early Modern Europe," in *The Church and Healing*, ed. W. J. Sheils (Oxford: Basil Blackwell, 1982), 79 and n. 2.

[3]GERM 168: 203v, to Aquaviva, September 5.

[4]GERM 145: 185, to Lainez, August 29.

[5]GERM 138 I: 169v, to Mercurian, April 1.

[6]*Monumenta antiquae Hungariae*, ed. Ladislaus Lukács, 3 vols. (Rome: Institutum Historicum Societatis Iesu, 1969–1981), 2: 923, to Campana, May 21.

feelings and those of their fellow citizens, "great fear";[7] and throughout Europe Jesuits often noted that conditions of famine, war, or an outbreak of another disease resulted in widespread fear of an epidemic of pest.[8] In addition to the reports of collective fear, Jesuits often described the fear experienced by individuals. When a lay brother assumed the task of caring for a pest-stricken Jesuit priest at Nevers in 1584, he shuddered with fear.[9] Cesare Calvi fled the pest at Venice and took refuge in a villa; his superiors could not speak to him of returning, "because of the great fear and fright he has of falling sick."[10]

Collective fear produced collective response. At Lisbon in 1569 and again in 1579 fear of the pest resulted in a mass flight from the city. In 1569 so great was the fear that "every person who had the means, officials as well as others, began to depopulate the city."[11] "Fear of contagion" caused the dispersion of the Jesuits at Vilnius in 1571,[12] and in 1591 "fear of the pest" twice chased the Jesuits from Cracow.[13] Flight to a safe haven was not always easy, for according to Francesco Adorno "suspicions and fear of the pest" made travel difficult in northern Italy during 1576.[14] Fear also prompted authorities to suspend sermons and close schools,[15] but on occasion Jesuits noted the positive results produced by collective fear. Juan Gesti twice commented on the effects at Barcelona in 1557 and 1558: "Because the fear of death moves people, a very great crowd attends the sermons and confessions," and "the fear of death results in

---

[7]ITAL 151: 394, Bisciola to Mercurian, Ferrara, August 8; 152: 66, 145, Adorno to Mercurian, Genoa, August 31 and September 21; 170, Consoli to Mercurian, Parma, September 28; 70a: 1v, Mercurian to Valentino, Rome, December 15; Jerónimo Nadal, *Epistolae P. Hieronymi Nadal Societatis Iesu ab anno 1546 ad 1577,* 4 vols. (Madrid: Augustini Avrial and Gabrielis Lopez del Horno, 1898–1905), 3: 724, Mercurian to Nadal, Rome, September 22.

[8]For a few examples see Gaspar Loarte, *Antidoto spirituale, contra la peste, dove si contengono alcun avisi, et rimedii spirituali, che possono giovare per la preservatione, et curatione di questo morbo* (Genoa, 1577), 71–72; HISP 114: 261, Juan Suarez to Borgia, Burgos, July 8, 1570; 132: 11, Villalba to Aquaviva, Valladolid, June 2, 1586; GAL 85: 70v, Coudret to Mercurian, Rodez, May 30, 1573; GERM 163: 188v, Campana to Aquaviva, Vilnius, September 16, 1584; 122: 35v, Maggio to Aquaviva, Vienna, June 4, 1594.

[9]GAL 53: 100, annual for the college at Nevers.

[10]ITAL 153: 45, Beringucci to Mercurian, Padua, January 18, 1577.

[11]LUS 63: 170, Sarrano to Borgia, Evora, September 18, 1569; *Documenta Indica*, ed. Joseph Wicki and John Gomes, 18 vols. (Rome: Monumenta Historica Societatis Iesu, 1948–), 11: 626, Sebastiano Sabino to Mercurian, September 30, 1579.

[12]GERM 152: 114, Varsevic to Nadal, October 15.

[13]GERM 169: 254, Ludovico Maselli to Aquaviva, near Cracow, September 9.

[14]ITAL 152: 203, to Mercurian, Genoa, October 12.

[15]For a few examples see LUS 63: 199, Pedro da Fonseca to Borgia, Coimbra, November 1, 1569; GERM 134 I: 169, Rozdrazon to Nadal, Vilnius, April 12, 1572; 138 II: 373, Forsler to Mercurian, Vienna, November 7, 1577; ITAL 149: 349, Achille to Mercurian, Palermo, December 15, 1575.

many confessions, with which many recover [eternal] life, so that one can say that death resuscitates the dead."[16] Giovanni Battista Buonacorso, who was preaching at Vicenza during the epidemic of 1576, expressed his hopes of using "these occasions of terror and fright" to produce some good results.[17] Jesuits seldom understated the fear of the pest; when Massimo Milanesi called pest the sister of famine, he added, "it normally is feared as one of the furies of the inferno, but this time it has been a lamb compared to that fierce lioness," famine.[18]

Another sister of the pest was rumor, which often heightened tensions and caused fear among people anxiously awaiting the arrival of an epidemic. In October 1575 Juan Peña reported that Siracusa was as yet healthy but people feared as a result of the rumors of pest from other towns in Sicily;[19] in August 1576 Pietro Angelo Consoli reported from Parma that the rumors from neighboring towns resulted in "extremely great fear of this pest";[20] and Georg Bader wrote from Mainz in September 1577 that the rumor of pest "terrorized the spirits of many."[21] As often is the case, some of the rumors were true, others were false, and Jesuits argued that some rumors were false when they were in fact true and accepted others that turned out to be false. Alfonso Salmeron claimed in July 1575 that the pest was not as bad at Messina and Palermo as "the rumor sings";[22] he was wrong, as was William Creichton when he reported in March 1577 that the rumor of pest at Lyon was without foundation but maliciously spread by evil men.[23] At times Jesuits did not know what to believe; Jerónimo Domenech used the term "rumor" six times in a brief report on the beginnings of the epidemic in Sicily in 1575,[24] and Giovanni Battista Peruschi expressed the frustrations of a person trying to discover the truth when he

---

[16]HISP 96: 247; Diego Lainez, *Lainii monumenta: Epistolae et acta patris Jacobi Lainii secundi praepositi generalis Societatis Jesu*, 8 vols. (Madrid: Gabrielis Lopez del Horno, 1912–1917), 3: 207, to Lainez, December 30, 1557, and March 21, 1558.

[17]ITAL 152: 358v, to Mercurian, December 17.

[18]*Monumenta Hungariae*, 2: 904, to Adam Brock, Cluj, April 29, 1586. Milanesi would soon change his metaphors.

[19]ITAL 149: 1, to Mercurian, October 1.

[20]ITAL 152: 37v, to Mercurian, August 24.

[21]GERM 138 II: 335, to Mercurian, September 25.

[22]Alfonso Salmeron, *Epistolae P. Alphonsi Salmeronis Societatis Iesu*, 2 vols. (Madrid: Typis Gabrielis Lopez del Horno, 1906–1907), 2: 530, to Mercurian, Naples, July 22.

[23]GAL 89: 98, to Mercurian, March 18.

[24]ITAL 147: 288–288v, to Mercurian, Caltagirone, July 5.

noted in an account of the epidemic at Milan in 1577 that "there are more rumors than the thing itself."[25]

An epidemic seldom caught a population unaware or sprang unannounced with an immediate impact. Instead it slowly approached from surrounding towns and villages, fueling rumors as it came. Lorenzo Maggio, when reporting on the approach of the pest toward Poznan in September 1580, stated, "We observe its dilatory progress."[26] The most dilatory approach occurred at Mainz. In December 1571 Lambert Auer reported that a pestiferous epidemic had shown traces in neighboring areas for almost three years before entering Mainz in the autumn.[27] Even when the pest reached a town, its continued progress could be dilatory. According to Juan Gesti, suspicions of pest circulated for several months at Barcelona in 1557 before receiving confirmation;[28] and in July 1579 Gabriel Alonso wrote that "rumors of pestilence" had been circulating in Lisbon for four months but only fifteen to twenty had died.[29] On occasion an epidemic could suddenly gather force after a slow start; according to Otto Eisenreich's account, the pest entered Augsburg in July 1592 and then erupted at the beginning of September.[30]

On September 21, 1571, Massimo Milanesi wrote an account of the start of an epidemic at Pultusk: "Last Wednesday on the 19th a pest-stricken house was found on the mountain above our Mount Abraham. Five died in this house within two days. Two other houses were discovered in the town; a woman died in one of these, and in the other, there died a furrier, a child, and the wife, and three other children are near death." Nonetheless, the bishop was still willing to wait for further news of the progress of the epidemic before ordering the closure of the Jesuit college.[31] Because of the disruptive consequences of an epidemic on trade with surrounding towns, municipal authorities could be reluctant to declare an outbreak of pest, and at times the medical profession promoted the reluctance by disputing the nature of the disease.[32]

---

[25]ITAL 154: 248, to Mercurian, July 24.

[26]GERM 121 II: 226, to the Bishop of Warmja (Ermeland), September 7.

[27]GERM 133 II: 417, to Nadal, December 12.

[28]HISP 96: 247, to Lainez, December 30.

[29]LUS 68: 186a, 194, to Mercurian, July 12 and 23.

[30]GERM 171: 27, to Aquaviva, January 23, 1593.

[31]GERM 133 II: 387, to Maggio.

[32]Jean-Noël Biraben, *Les hommes et la peste en France et dans les pays européens et méditerranéens*, 2 vols. (Paris: Mouton, 1975–1976), 2: 90–92, 98.

This could have unfortunate consequences. According to Iñigo Fonseca, the pest at Seville in 1568 began to kill many people while the doctors continued to argue whether or not it was the pest;[33] and Jorge Sarrano reported in 1569 that because the principal doctors at Lisbon doubted the presence of the pest, the authorities placed no guards around the infected areas of the city and thereby facilitated the spread of the epidemic.[34] One of the more infamous disputes occurred at Venice in 1576 when two leading physicians from the University of Padua, Girolamo Mercuriale and Girolamo Capodivacca, convinced the senate that the disease then causing a few deaths was not the pest. They argued that the symptoms of carbuncles and buboes were insufficient to demonstrate the presence of the disease but that instead the air had to be infected. To prove their point the two professors, accompanied by two Jesuits, Ettore Leonelli and Guido Tosco, visited the infected houses every morning and examined the patients. The professors were mistaken, Leonelli and Tosco both contracted the pest and died, and after time spent in quarantine Mercuriale and Capodivacca returned to Padua.[35]

IN THE MIDST OF AN EPIDEMIC

Since the Black Death in the mid-fourteenth century, Europeans had likened pestilence to one of the biblical plagues of Egypt, a devouring cloud, a shower of arrows, one of the four horsemen of the Apocalypse, a new deluge, a formidable enemy, and, most often, a fire.[36] Jesuits were usually restrained in the use of imagery in their accounts of epidemics, and they seldom matched the rhetorical excesses of Mario Beringucci's divine horsemanship and Massimo Milanesi's furies of the inferno. Some Jesuits used the imagery of a fire to describe epidemics; Giovanni Battista Carminata wrote from Messina in October 1575, "The fire breaks out now here now there, and we fear that it might ultimately result in a great conflagration";[37] and Giulio Mazzarino, when describing the measures taken by public authorities at Milan in 1577, stated that they were never able "to extinguish this fire" completely.[38] Another image

---

[33]HISP 109: 109, to Borgia, October 22.

[34]LUS 63: 170, to Borgia, Evora, September 18.

[35]Andreina Zitelli and Richard J. Palmer, "Le teorie mediche sulla peste e il contesto veneziano," in *Venezia e la peste, 1348–1797,* 2d ed. (Venice: Marsilio Editori, 1980), 26–27; ITAL 151: 410, *Avisi cavati da diverse lettere venute da Venetia,* June 30.

[36]Delumeau, *La peur en occident,* 103–8.

[37]ITAL 149: 24, to Mercurian, October 17.

[38]ITAL 153: 314, to Mercurian, Genoa, April 8.

of the pest in Jesuit accounts was death; according to Georgio Mercato's account of an epidemic at Palermo in 1558, "Pallid Death struck the huts of the poor and the towers of the kings in a similar manner, followed fleeing men, and cast lots without regard for rank or standing."[39] Other Jesuits compared the pest to an ambush, an as yet unhealed wound, and a cloud covering the entire sky.[40] In his description of an outbreak at Plasencia in 1557, Alfonso Ramiro exhibited a tendency to rhetorical excess when he likened the ferocity of the disease to the ardor of a dog just freed from shackles.[41]

Some epidemics struck with the ferocity of Ramiro's unshackled dog. From Lyon in July 1564, Emond Auger claimed that the pest "was so strong that men died while talking to each other,"[42] and according to Francisco Sunyer the pest that struck Pultusk in the summer of 1572 was so great that men fell dead in the streets.[43] At Paris in 1553 the epidemic continued to gather force even two months after an initial onslaught,[44] at Olomouc in 1571 it spread with ease and caused a great slaughter.[45] It "thrashed" Le Puy, Montpellier, and other French towns in the spring of 1577.[46] The pest infected more than four hundred houses at Tournai in the summer of 1572 and returned three years later, invading fifty-two houses in eight to ten days.[47] When the pest entered Brescia after surrounding it for a year, it struck with a fury that was exceptional. In the words of Antonio Marta:

> The damage to this city has been extremely severe and more than to any other city touched by this pestiferous venom, since many fell sick despite their precautions, and whatever they did to make themselves secure from the danger, including isolation, preservatives, and other similar measures, was not enough. As a result not a single monastery has been untouched,

---

[39] *Litterae quadrimestres ex universis praeter Indiam et Brasiliam locis in quibus aliqui de Societate Jesu versabantur Romam missae,* 7 vols. (Madrid and Rome: Augustinus Avrial, La Editorial Ibérica, and A. Macioce e Pisani, 1894–1932), 5: 845, October 25.

[40] GERM 133 II: 451, Hurtado Perez to Nadal, Olomouc, October 31, 1571; 141: 180v, annual for the college of Molsheim, by François de Costere, Mainz, January 1, 1584; POL 50: 176, annual for professed house at Cracow, 1599.

[41] *Litterae quadrimestres,* 5: 458, December 27.

[42] GAL 80: 234, to Lainez, July 10.

[43] GERM 134 II: 392, to Nadal, near Pultusk, August 16.

[44] *Litterae quadrimestres,* 2: 366, Robert Claysson to Loyola, August 28.

[45] GERM 134 I: 44, Hurtado Perez to Nadal, January 9, 1572.

[46] GAL 89: 139, Auger to Mercurian, Toulouse, May 1.

[47] GERM 152: 242, Balduin Dawant to Nadal, Liège, September 18, 1572; 155: 133v, Harlem to Mercurian, Louvain, August 2, 1575.

nor sex, nor age, nor condition, but all have suffered, from the extinction of many families and almost entire monasteries to the deaths of physicians, surgeons, and many more priests, of whom very few remain alive.[48]

On occasion the spread of the pest could resemble a lumbering turtle rather than an unshackled dog. Jean Montaigne stated that the pest at Tournai in June 1572 "goes meandering little by little,"[49] Jacob Wujek wrote from Poznan in October of the same year, "The pest does not rage but creeps,"[50] and according to Mario Beringucci the epidemic at Venice in March 1577 "always goes nibbling."[51] A similar pattern occurred elsewhere, including Vienna in 1571, Messina in 1575 and 1577, Lyon and Milan in 1577, and Cracow in 1591,[52] but the best documented example comes from Palermo between July 1575 and May 1576. What follows is a chronology of the pest at Palermo during this period from the letters of Paolo Achille, some of which are in chapter 2, and of Juan Polanco:

July 5, 1575: The rumor of the pest continues to increase.

August 2: Over the past two days it seems as if the pest has declined.

August 9: Now increases, now diminishes; eight or ten a day die from it.

August 12: Greatly declined, because they have not taken more than four to the hospital [during the past three days].

August 17: Diminished greatly, for during the past four days they have only taken two to the hospital.

August 23: Varies from week to week, last week it had declined, this week it has increased.... Four or six die every day, although this is not always the case.

[48]ITAL 155: 204, to Beringucci, September 23, 1577.

[49]GERM 152: 207, to Nadal, June 26.

[50]GERM 134 II: 496, to Nadal, October 6.

[51]ITAL 153: 216, to Mercurian, March 17.

[52]GERM 133 II: 476, Forsler to Nadal, Vienna, November 27, 1571; 169: 254, Maselli to Aquaviva, Cracow, September 9, 1591; ITAL 148: 167, Calligaris to Mercurian, Messina, August 5, 1575; 153: 252v, Fazio to Mercurian, Messina, March 28, 1577; 155: 207, Sgariglia to Mercurian, Milan, October 23, 1577; GAL 89: 143, Creichton to Mercurian, Lyon, May 3, 1577.

September 12: Not going very well.... Every day they are taking eight, ten, or twelve to the hospital.

September 19: Varying, now increasing, now diminishing.

October 18: Varies, now increasing, now diminishing; during the past three days it has increased somewhat.

November 1: Has not gone well for the past four days; it always varies, now good, now bad.

November 10: Good for the past four days; during the past week it was very bad.

November 18: Always varies, now increasing, now diminishing. It has increased during the past two days, but last week it was declining.

December 15: Bad during the past several days.

December 27: Much better during the past several days.

February 5, 1576: Very well during the past eight days.

March 10: Not completely [healthy] but much better.

March 12: Very well, although not yet completely finished.

April 2: Well.

April 4: Well, although three days ago they found some cases in a prison.

May 14: The city is very healthy.[53]

Returning to the imagery of fire, such epidemics could smolder for a long time; the pest was present at Vienna from August 1561 until April 1564 except for intermissions during the summer.[54] In September 1568 Adrian Loeff complained of "the continued calamity of pest for three years" at Trier.[55] According to William Good the pest infected Tournai for almost three years, from 1571 to 1574.[56]

---

[53]The letters from Achille are in ITAL 148–51, the others are in Juan Polanco, *Polanci complementa: Epistolae et commentaria P. Joannis Alphonsi de Polanco e Societate Jesu,* 2 vols. (Madrid: Gabrielis Lopez del Horno, 1916–1917), 2: 488–512.

[54]See the appendix and Nadal, *Epistolae,* 2: 497, to Araoz, Rome, February 1, 1564.

[55]GERM 140: 113, annual letter, September 1.

[56]GERM 141: 11, annual for the Belgian province, Louvain, July 15, 1574.

Giovanni Battista Peruschi, after noting that the epidemic at Milan in July 1577 was passing through cycles of diminution and expansion, commented, "The pest does not seem to be as contagious [as previously], because when a case occurs in a family it does not proceed to a second or a third member."[57] As discussed in the introduction, this pattern of contagion within a household and the smoldering nature of many epidemics fit the classic model of bubonic plague with an erratic spread of the disease by infective fleas and the unlikelihood of multiple cases in a single household. Jesuit accounts, however, do document many instances of multiple cases in a single household, including their own communities, as demonstrated earlier, as well as others. In 1562 at Prague the pest killed at least three or four people in every house surrounding the Jesuit college;[58] at Trier in 1564 it attacked the family in the bookshop across the street from the college, taking the mother, two sons, and a daughter;[59] at Paris in 1581 a house adjacent to the college lost four residents;[60] and in 1592 at Augsburg almost everyone in a house near the college died.[61]

On occasion the proximity of the victims created what must have been harrowing conditions. According to Johann Reidt in 1564 the pest "raged wildly" on the college's street in Cologne and so surrounded the college on all sides that the Jesuits could hear their neighbors' suffering.[62] Adrian Loeff made a similar report from Trier in 1568. Infected houses surrounded the college, and in consequence the Jesuits could hear the voices of the dying.[63] Other accounts complained of the smell. According to Giovanni Battista Peruschi, the stench at Brescia in 1577 permeated everything to such an extent that people believed it was the source of contagion.[64] In contrast to all this, Cesare Helmi's complaint of life in Venice in 1576 seems trivial: "We are always enclosed in these lagoons of water, and we do not have a proper place where we can open our eyes a bit."[65] Giovanni Paolo Campana had a vantage point that

[57]ITAL 154: 181, to Mercurian, July 6.
[58]GERM 144: 45, *quadrimestris* by Behem, December 28.
[59]GERM 145: 225, Vinck to Lainez, October 7.
[60]GAL 53: 83v, annual for the French province.
[61]GERM 171: 27, Eisenreich to Aquaviva, January 23, 1593.
[62]Joseph Hansen, ed., *Rheinische Akten zur Geschichte des Jesuitenordens, 1542–1582* (Bonn: H. Berendt, 1896), 508, *quadrimestris*, January 1, 1565.
[63]GERM 140: 113, annual letter, September 1.
[64]ITAL 154: 367, to Mercurian, Milan, August 19.
[65]ITAL 151: 312v, to Mercurian, July 14.

was more salubrious and less harrowing from which to observe the epidemic at Braniewo in 1588; from his balcony in the city he could see the infected houses in the suburbs and the removal of the dead to the cemetery.[66]

The removal of the dead was one of the few activities that took place in most pest-infected towns. The flight of many inhabitants, the isolation of others within their houses either by personal choice to avoid infection from others or by order of the authorities to avoid infecting others, the segregation of the sick at hospitals outside the walls, and the cessation of normal activities combined with the frequent high mortality to produce the impression of abandoned towns. Jesuits reported on the tendency for normal activities to cease during epidemics. At Padua in 1555 an epidemic of pest resulted in the customary flight of many, and those who remained in the town stayed at home and refused to go to work.[67] Giulio Fazio noted that at Messina in May 1576 contacts between people had ceased for the most part as people tried to avoid each other.[68] And in September of the same year, Filippo Trivisano claimed that no one went to work at Milan because no goods could enter or leave the town.[69] Other accounts, such as Emerich Forsler's description of Vienna in 1572,[70] emphasized the depopulation that occurred in the wake of an epidemic. A report from Venice in August 1576 exclaimed, "It was a pitiful spectacle to see the city almost empty of inhabitants [and] all the shops closed,"[71] and in September 1564 Emond Auger described a deserted Lyon: "Who would not weep seeing a city of a hundred thousand inhabitants now reduced to twelve thousand and perhaps not even eight thousand, some dead, others fled. You cannot find three shops open, and if you went through the largest and most populated street, you would not find four people where a little while ago you encountered more than twelve thousand."[72]

Deserted towns such as Lyon were easy prey for thieves, and the breakdown in social order that accompanied a severe epidemic could likewise result in an increase in thefts, especially from abandoned houses. The outbreak of

---

[66]Fondo Gesuitico 645: 98, to Aquaviva, November 19.

[67]Juan Polanco, *Vita Ignatii Loiolae et rerum Societatis Jesu historia*, 6 vols. (Madrid: Typographorum Societatis and Augustinus Avrial, 1894–1898), 5: 157, *Chronicon*, 1555.

[68]ITAL 151: 129, to Mercurian, May 14.

[69]ITAL 152: 87, to Mercurian, September 5.

[70]Cited in chapter 5: GERM 134 I: 67, to Nadal, January 30.

[71]ITAL 151: 411, *Avisi cavati da diverse lettere venute da Venetia*, August 6.

[72]GAL 80: 263v, to Lainez, September 28.

pest at Paris in 1562 that took the lives of the superior Paschase Broët and three others produced another calamity; Ponce Cogordan discovered that four thousand to five thousand francs were missing from the deserted residence. Some neighbors informed Cogordan that they had seen the brother of Louis the porter leaving the house late one night with some packages.[73] In his published account of the epidemic at Milan in 1576 and 1577 Paolo Bisciola described the method of one group of thieves. They worked at night, robbing the houses of those who had fled, and whenever anyone approached they shouted, "Watch out! Keep your distance!" as if to indicate that they were purging the house of infected goods.[74] According to Alfonso Sgariglia, other thieves at Milan entered abandoned houses at night through the roofs, forcing the authorities to establish guards in every quarter.[75]

Filippo Trivisano, while not condoning the thefts, deplored the conditions that drove some people to take to robbery during epidemics, Because of the cessation of economic activity at Milan in 1576, the poor who lived from hand to mouth could not find any work at all, and many in consequence died from hunger while others resorted to thieving.[76] In fact, so bad were the conditions for the poor at Milan that Giovanni Francesco Prandi asserted as a certainty that more were dying from starvation than from the pest.[77] Another consequence of epidemics that created worsening conditions for the poor was the shortage of provisions and resulting rise in prices as the disruption of trade prevented food from entering towns. Peasants in surrounding areas were reluctant to bring their produce to markets. Jesuits commented upon the shortage of food at Cologne in 1552 and Brescia in 1577,[78] and during an epidemic of pest at Dijon in August 1586 Louis Richeome noted "the dearth of all things except misery."[79] As explained in a previous chapter, the flight of the wealthy could also exacerbate the plight of the poor by removing a source of charity. In short, epidemics could often worsen the miserable conditions of the

---

[73]Lainez, *Lainii monumenta*, 6: 428, to Lainez, Noyon, September 29.

[74]Paolo Bisciola, *Relatione verissima del progresso della peste di Milano: Qual principiò nel mese d'agosto 1576 e seguì sino al mese di maggio 1577* (Ancona: Alessandro Benacci, 1577), 12.

[75]ITAL 153: 101, to Candi, January 15, 1577.

[76]ITAL 152: 87, to Mercurian, September 5.

[77]ITAL 155: 150v, to Mercurian, Brescia, October 8.

[78]ITAL 154: 367, Peruschi to Mercurian, Milan, August 19, 1577; Hansen, *Rheinische Akten*, 216, *quadrimestris* by Gerhard Brassica, Cologne, January 10, 1553.

[79]GAL 92: 196, to Aquaviva, August 3.

urban poor, as illustrated by an account from Olomouc in 1599: "Here and there many poor people and travelers, destitute of solace and help, lay sick in the squares, at the gates, and in the corners of the city and suburbs, and in only one workshop... about seventy-three people were lying sick, who partly from the pest and partly from hunger were grievously troubled."[80]

DEATH

An account from Pont-à-Mousson in 1585 reveals a different but just as cruel fate for the poor; when rumors of the pest reached the town, the authorities expelled 340 of the poorest people and left them to suffer from disease and famine.[81] This was not an isolated incident, for authorities in other towns likewise expelled the poor because of the belief that the poor spread the pest, and both contemporary observation and the work of some historians support the claim that the mortality rate among the poor was higher than among the wealthy.[82] Of the reasons advanced for this differential mortality, namely, higher levels of nutrition among the wealthy, the superiority of stone buildings over those of other materials in remaining relatively free from infestation by rodents, and the increased chances of avoiding infection either through flight or by isolation in their houses, the last seems more valid than the other two. At any rate, as noted by Jean-Noël Biraben, the difference was not absolute, for the pest on occasion did attack the privileged ranks of sixteenth-century society,[83] and if few of them died in proportion to others, it could be a function of their small numbers in comparison with the vast majority of limited means. Jesuit accounts provide documentation of mortality among both rich and poor. An epidemic of petechia killed "principal persons" at Siracusa in 1558,[84] and the pest killed members of the nobility at Baden-Baden in 1573, at Venice

---

[80]AUST 132: 364, annual for the Austrian province, 1599.

[81]GAL 62: 38, annual.

[82]Anne G. Carmichael, *Plague and the Poor in Renaissance Florence* (Cambridge: Cambridge University Press, 1986), 106; Carlo M. Cipolla and Dante E. Zanetti, "Peste et mortalité différentielle," *Annales de démographie historique* (1972): 197–202; Jean-Noël Biraben, "Les pauvres et la peste," in *Etudes sur l'histoire de la pauvreté*, ed. Michel Mollat (Paris: La Sorbonne, 1974), 505–18; Brian Pullan, "Plague and Perceptions of the Poor in Early Modern Italy," in *Epidemics and Ideas: Essays on the Historical Perception of Pestilence*, ed. Terence Ranger and Paul Slack (Cambridge: Cambridge University Press, 1992), 101–23.

[83]See Biraben, "Les pauvres et la peste," 506–7.

[84]Lainez, *Lainii monumenta*, 3: 575, Casini to Lainez, September 29.

in 1576 and 1577, and at Mantua in 1577.[85] At Heiligenstadt in 1580 a pestilential disease killed many including "not a few from the order of Senators,"[86] and the pest that struck Fribourg in 1595 "spread longer and more widely in the district of the rich."[87]

As the pest approached Milan in the summer of 1576 Alfonso Sgariglia expressed his fears concerning the damage it could do, "because this city is very crowded with an extremely great multitude of poor."[88] Other Jesuits, while not issuing Sgariglia's grave predictions, noted that the poor died during outbreaks of pest at Barcelona and Valencia in 1558 and Reggio in Calabria in 1576,[89] and in 1566 and again in 1568 Jesuits noticed that the poor were victims of the water-based disease that affected Rome.[90] Epidemics of pest at Seville in 1568 and in the following year provide documentation for high mortality among the poor as well as other groups; according to Iñigo Fonseca in 1568 the highest mortality was among the lower classes, children, and negroes,[91] and in 1569 Diego Avellaneda noted that those who died were children, girls, negroes, and the poor rabble.[92] Iñigo Tolosa also reported that the epidemic of pest at Braga in 1570 killed many children but very few adults,[93] and 75 percent of the victims buried at the Venetian lazaretto in July 1576 were women, while by mid-August twenty-two thousand women, seven thousand men, and six thousand children had fallen victim to the epidemic.[94] Age- and sex-specific mortality is a subject of some dispute among historians; as noted by Stephen R. Ell, "Scholars have placed the greatest mortality variously among children, young adult males, adult females, and elderly males. For each view there is fragmentary evidence extensively extrapolated."[95] The comments from Jesuits add to the fragmentary evidence.

[85]Polanco, *Complementa*, 2: 231, Matthias Zerer to Polanco, Ettlingen, January 24, 1573; ITAL 151: 410v, *Avisi cavati da diverse lettere venute da Venetia*, August 6, 1576; 152: 93v, Adorno to Mercurian, Genoa, September 7, 1576; 154: 27, Palmio to Mercurian, Bologna, May 25, 1577.

[86]GERM 141: 58v, annual for the Rhine province by Costere, Mainz, January 1, 1581.

[87]Peter Canisius, *Beati Petri Canisii, Societatis Iesu, epistolae et acta*, ed. Otto Braunsberger, 13 vols. (Freiburg im Breisgau: Herder, 1896–1923), 8: 392, n. 2, annual, November 25.

[88]ITAL 152: 16, to Mercurian, August 22.

[89]Lainez, *Lainii monumenta*, 8: 433, Gesti to Lainez, Barcelona, January 31; *Litterae quadrimestres*, 5: 702, by Parra, Valencia, June 2; ITAL 152: 315, Mercado to Mercurian, Reggio, November 30.

[90]Polanco, *Complementa*, 2: 50, to the Society, December 31, 1568.

[91]HISP 109: 109, to Borgia, October 22.

[92]HISP 110: 320, to Borgia, May 24.

[93]LUS 64: 69, to Borgia, July 16.

[94]ITAL 151: 410v–411, *Avisi cavati da diverse lettere venute da Venetia*, July 22/26 and August 13, 1576.

[95]Stephen R. Ell, "Three Days in October of 1630: Detailed Examination of Mortality during an Early Modern Plague Epidemic in Venice," *Reviews of Infectious Diseases* 11 (1989), 128.

Jesuits included in their accounts three different types of figures on mortality. The first type was the lethality rate, that is, the percentage of people who succumbed to a disease after contracting it. Jesuits seldom included this information and were usually vague when they did. Anton Vinck reported that the epidemic of pest at Trier in October 1564 was widespread since almost every street had some cases, but few died and many recovered.[96] William Creichton wrote a similar account for an epidemic at Lyon in 1577, but he was a bit more precise; of the 130 people in the hospital, the nun in charge believed only four were in danger of dying.[97] More lethal than these two examples was the outbreak of pest at Braga in 1570. According to Iñigo Tolosa half of the 150 who contracted the disease died,[98] but a lethality rate of 50 percent is still less than the 60 percent to 90 percent cited by modern authorities on the bubonic plague.

The second type of figure was the number of deaths per day or, less often, per week or several days. While many Jesuits provided precise figures, others were content to note that few or many were dying. To cite two examples at the opposite extremes, Lorenzo Maggio claimed that the pest afflicting Poland in December 1571 was "doing unheard of things in killing people,"[99] while Johannes Nicolaus wrote from Vienna in May 1584 that the pest "scarcely causes the death of one poor person every five or six days."[100] Table 8 shows daily (except where noted) mortality figures in pest-stricken towns taken from Jesuit accounts. Some of the figures are suspect, especially those for Cairo and Constantinople, and when reporting on the latest figures from Venice in December 1576, Giovanni Battista Buonacorso expressed his doubts about their reliability because the Venetian authorities might have been understating the extent of the epidemic to convince people that it was safe to return.[101]

To put the figures from table 8 in perspective, Augsburg in the sixteenth century had a population of forty to fifty thousand. Between 1501 and 1592 the average annual mortality during normal years was 1,592 (sic), a mortality rate of about 30 to 40 per thousand. During years of epidemics the average annual mortality more than doubled to 3,554, a mortality rate of about 70 to 90. In

---

[96]GERM 145: 230, to Lainez, October 12.
[97]GAL 89: 143, to Mercurian, May 3.
[98]LUS 64: 69, to Borgia, Coimbra, July 16.
[99]GERM 133 II: 503v, to Nadal, Vienna, December 31.
[100]GERM 162: 284, to Aquaviva, May 24.
[101]ITAL 152: 358, Buonacorso to Mercurian, Vicenza, December 17.

normal years about thirty inhabitants died each week; in years of epidemics almost seventy.[102] As shown in table 8, in November 1563 Augsburg had almost 50 deaths a week during an epidemic of pest; if these were deaths attributable to the epidemic, and if another 30 inhabitants died as they would in a "normal" week, then the total would be almost 80. Fifty deaths per week would of course be 7 per day, so some of the figures represent very high rates of mortality even for large cities such as Venice and Milan. On occasion Jesuits commented on the excessive daily mortality in view of the few people left in pest-stricken towns as a result of flight and death; both Padua in August 1576 and Brescia in July 1577 had only about ten thousand inhabitants and yet had daily mortality rates of 40 to 50 and 100 respectively.[103]

The third type of mortality figure included in Jesuit accounts was the total number killed by an epidemic, as indicated in table 9. As with the figures for daily mortality, some of these are obvious exaggerations, the most obvious example being Venice, but a few match the estimates of modern authorities. According to A. Francesco La Cava, the mortality at Milan during 1576–1577 was 18,000,[104] while Karl Julius Beloch uses the precise figure of 17,329.[105] The figure of 35,000 for Brescia in 1577 is too high; Beloch's precise figure is 19,396, and La Cava and Paolo Preto agree on 20,000.[106] According to O. J. Benedictow, 1,533 died at Chambéry in 1586.[107] The sixteenth-century epidemics do not match the ferocity of the Black Death, and some epidemics of the seventeenth century had higher mortality figures, but some of the "minor" outbreaks of the sixteenth century were notable for their demographic consequences. According to the contemporary records of mortality during the epidemic at Venice in 1576 and 1577, the pest claimed 46,721 lives. The population of Venice in 1575 was

[102]My calculations of the statistics in Roger Mols, *Introduction à la démographie historique des villes d'Europe du XIVe au XVIIIe siècle*, 3 vols. (Louvain: Publications Universitaires de Louvain, 1954–1956), 3: 176.

[103]ITAL 151: 411, *Avisi cavati da diverse lettere venute da Venetia*, August 6, 1576; 154: 204, Mazzarino to Mercurian, Genoa, July 13, 1577.

[104]A. Francesco La Cava, *La peste di S. Carlo: Note storico-mediche sulla peste del 1576* (Milano: Editore Ulrico Hoepli, 1945), 89–90.

[105]Karl Julius Beloch, *Bevölkerungs-geschichte Italiens*, 3 vols. (Berlin: Walter de Gruyter, 1937–1940), 1: 68.

[106]Ibid., 3: 123; La Cava, *La peste di S. Carlo*, 30; and Paolo Preto, *Peste e società a Venezia nel 1576* (Vicenza: Neri Pozza Editore, 1978), 112.

[107]Ole Jøregen Benedictow, "Morbidity in Historical Plague Epidemics," *Population Studies* 41 (1987), 417.

about 180,000, so about 25 percent of the population died from the pest.[108] The statistics for Brescia verify Antonio Marta's report on the severity of the epidemic there, for half of the total population of forty thousand perished. While Marta emphasized the horrors at Brescia, Alfonso Sgariglia minimized those at Milan by claiming that the total of fourteen thousand deaths was for a city the size of Milan (with some one hundred thousand inhabitants) "a nothing."[109]

Even if fourteen thousand deaths constituted "a nothing," Milanese authorities still faced the mammoth task of burying the corpses. During an epidemic people abandoned the normal rituals surrounding funerals and burials, rituals that were as important for the living as they were for the souls of the deceased, and accepted procedures that in normal times they considered scandalous and sacrilegious.[110] The removal of the dead was a high priority for the municipal authorities because of the belief that corpses could contaminate the air and hence further spread the disease. According to the anonymous account of the water-based epidemic at Rome in 1566, the stench from the unburied bodies inside houses was enough to infect the air. On this occasion the authorities overcame the considerable difficulties in arranging burials by appealing to a religious confraternity called the Company of Death, whose members arrived with the necessary coffins.[111] Already mentioned in the previous chapter were Antoine Blondet's horrifying discovery of dead bodies in the streets of Rivoli, Avigliana, and Chivasso for lack of anyone to bury them and the Venetian authorities' efforts to find enough workers to remove the corpses and dig the graves. Giovanni Francesco Prandi reported that at Milan in 1576 people were throwing bodies from the windows into the streets.[112] On occasion Jesuits emphasized the problems created by the high mortality; at Venice in August 1576 authorities had trouble finding enough boats to transport the corpses,[113] and a year later at Brescia so many died that more than thirty carts were insufficient to remove the dead.[114] An ignominious burial

---

[108]Preto, *Peste e società*, 111–12.
[109]ITAL 153: 101, to Candi, January 15, 1577.
[110]See the discussion in Delumeau, *La peur en occident*, 115–16.
[111]ROM 126a: 238, untitled.
[112]ITAL 155: 150v, to [Mercurian], Brescia, October 9.
[113]ITAL 152: 13, Cosso to Mercurian, August 18.
[114]ITAL 154: 367, Peruschi to Mercurian, Milan, August 19.

TABLE 8: DAILY MORTALITY IN PEST-STRICKEN TOWNS

Town	Date	Mortality
Vienna	December 1561	20–30
Cairo	April 1562	2,000
Nürnberg	November 1562	500 in three days
Augsburg	November 1563	almost 50 a week
Zaragoza	summer 1564	116–120
Cologne	October 1564	"more than 200 at the most"
Seville	early July 1568	20–30
Lisbon	August 1569	600
Pultusk	December 1571	26 a week
Venice	June 1576	17–24
	July 1576	120 in the city, another 500–600 in the lazaretto
Padua	August 1576	40–50
Milan	September 1576	300 on the worst days
Venice	December 1576	4–7
Brescia	July 1577	100
	August 1577	3,000 in five days
Prague	August 1582	200
Oradea	January 1586	100–120
Constantinople	September 1592	5,000

TABLE 9: TOTAL MORTALITY IN PEST-STRICKEN TOWNS

Town	Date	Mortality
Paris	1553	50,000
Cologne	1553	25,000
Cologne	1564	12,000
Lyon	1564	over 30,000 in the city, 12,000 in environs
Seville	1568	2500
Lisbon	1569	30,000
Pultusk	1571	2,000
Monreale	1575	2,000
Messina	1576	18,000
Milan	1576–1577	14,000
Venice	1576–1577	140,000
Inzago	1577	700
Avignon	1577	1500
Brescia	1577	35,000
Lisbon	1579	400
Nevers	1584	4,000
Chambéry	1586	2,000
Cracow	1589	12,000
Poznan	1589	over 2,000
Pultusk	1589	over 1,000
Constantinople	1592	70,000
Cambrai	1596	almost 10,000
Saint-Omer	1596–1597	at least 9,000

awaited the victims. From Vienna in 1563 Ambrosius Sanctinus deplored the fate of the dead, who were taken in a shabby cart outside the walls and thrown into a trench;[115] and at Milan in 1576 the naked bodies of the dead lay in mass graves near the lazaretto.[116]

The bodies of Jesuits who succumbed to the pest probably had the same fate as others, burial without ceremony in a mass grave. Jesuits seldom noted the treatment accorded to the corpses of their pest-stricken brethren, and when they did mention that the corpse went to a mass grave, they did so without further comment.[117] On two occasions, at Gandia in 1559 and at Seville in 1569, Jesuits secretly buried in their churches brethren who had died from the pest,[118] and on two occasions at Milan in 1576 and 1577 Jesuits who had succumbed as a result of their service to the sick were buried in churches but openly and with the apparent approval of the municipal government.[119] Whether the burials were open or secret, in mass graves or in churches, the predominant impression left by an epidemic, especially an epidemic of pest, was death, so much so that the limited use Jesuits made of "pallid Death" in their imagery is surprising. Jesuits expressed the pervasive sense of death in other ways without resorting to allegory and metaphor. Giovanni Battista Buonacorso complained during the epidemic of 1576 that Jesuits at Vicenza had difficulty putting their minds on study when everything in the surrounding area was full of the images of death.[120] Hubert Vandaleene's comment made while residing at the residence of the king of Poland in May 1591 emphasizes that epidemics were not the only conveyers of death in the sixteenth century: "We were so afflicted by pest, war, and poverty that I seemed to be confronted with uninterrupted death."[121]

[115]GERM 139: 178v, *quadrimestris*, April 27.

[116]ITAL 155: 150v, Prandi to [Mercurian], Brescia, October 9.

[117]Polanco, *Complementa*, 2: 526, to Mercurian, Carangino, June 15, 1576; ITAL 152: 13, Cosso to Mercurian, Venice, August 18, 1576; 154: 105, Basso to Mercurian, Naples, June 18, 1577; for an exception see *Monumenta Hungariae*, 2: 925, Szydlowski to Campana, Oradea, May 21, 1586.

[118]Antonio Astrain, *Historia de la Compañia de Jesús en la Asistencia de España*, 7 vols. (Madrid: Sucesores de Rivadeneyra, 1902–1925), 2: 527; HISP, 110: 319v, Avellaneda to Borgia, Seville, May 24, 1569.

[119]ITAL 152: 327, Adorno to Mercurian, Parma, December 4, 1576; 155: 202, Lamagna to Morais, Milan, October 22, 1577.

[120]ITAL 152: 358v, to Mercurian, December 17.

[121]OPP NN 332: 138, to Campana, *Ex domo Regis Poloniae*, May 31.

In his study of western attitudes toward death, *The Hour of Our Death*, Philippe Ariès argues that in the sixteenth century, Jesuits devalued the traditional emphasis that Christian thought and practice had placed on the importance of a good death—the last ordeal of the faithful.[122] Jesuit accounts of deaths from epidemic disease do not support Ariès' argument; Jesuits often indicated that a good death was an important sign of a person's faith, and Jesuits delighted in the bad deaths of their enemies. During the epidemic at Lyon in 1564, Emond Auger contrasted the deaths of the Calvinists and the Catholics. The former "died for the most part mad, with horrendous invocations of the devil, to whom they once again freely offered themselves; the viscera of some burst open, and many ran amuck. The Catholics on the contrary consoled each other and died voluntarily."[123] While not often giving details of the physical aspects of death or diagnosis of the cause, Jesuits thought it important to include in their accounts of the deaths of their brethren edifying details on the successful completion of their last ordeal. Hence, Gerard Grammeye died at Maastricht in August 1577, "demonstrating much patience, strength, and charity during his illness";[124] at Paris in September 1584 Jacques de Lattre "rendered his soul to God with hands joined [and] did not stop praying until the end";[125] and when Paul Woiciechowicz died at Alba Iulia in July 1586, he was "well composed and contrite."[126] Because delirious and insensate deaths were the worst, Jesuits made a point of noting the good deaths of those who overcame such conditions. Giulio Fazio described the happy death of one such Jesuit at Genoa in 1572: "Although he was in perpetual delirium and frenzy for many days, a few hours before his death it pleased the divine goodness to restore his judgment so that he could better prepare himself for death and receive all the sacraments with great devotion."[127] Philippe Faber was so "out of his mind" as he lay dying at Mantua in February 1558 that it threatened to create a scandal. A friend of the Society asked him to recite Psalm 70, and Faber indicated that he did not want to do so. Faber returned to his senses on

---

[122]Philippe Ariès, *The Hour of Our Death* (Harmondsworth: Penguin Books, 1983), 297–312; see A. Lynn Martin, *The Jesuit Mind: The Mentality of an Elite in Early Modern France* (Ithaca: Cornell University Press, 1988), 177–79.

[123]GAL 80: 263, to Lainez, September 28; see Martin, *Jesuit Mind*, 97; for another example see OPP NN 339: 90v, annual for the mission to Sweden by Ardulph, Stockholm, October 1, 1581.

[124]GERM 156: 184, Harlem to Mercurian, Louvain, September 24.

[125]GAL 91: 240, Pigenat to Aquaviva, September 30.

[126]*Monumenta Hungariae*, 2: 990, Milanesi to Campana, September.

[127]ITAL 143: 260, to Nadal, April 25.

February 26, the day that he died, and as David Wolf read other Psalms to him, he lifted his eyes to heaven.[128]

THE END

While epidemics could begin either with a fierce onslaught or, to borrow the terms used by Jesuits, by meandering, creeping, and nibbling, the end of an epidemic was often an anticlimax not often mentioned in Jesuit accounts. Towns often issued public declarations of their liberation from an epidemic and celebrated the end with public processions in thanksgiving, but Jesuit accounts contain just a few references to them. In July 1577 Mario Beringucci expressed his hopes that the authorities at Padua would soon publish the liberation,[129] and Antonio Micheli described the solemn procession held at Venice in the same month.[130] One reason for the lack of celebratory comments in the accounts might be the pattern of alternating diminution and expansion of epidemics of the pest as documented in the chronology of the epidemic at Palermo in 1575 and 1576. A period of low or even no mortality might suddenly give way to a recrudescence. As a result Jesuits could only note that the epidemic was in decline, hoping and praying for its definite end. As expressed by Alfonso Sgariglia from Milan in December 1577, "the suspicious cases are declining in such a way that we hope that the city will soon be completely free."[131] Sometimes Jesuits proclaimed the end of an epidemic by announcing their return to a town and the reopening of their college. To cite one example, in October 1566 the Jesuits returned to Trier and began preparations to open their college within a week.[132] The Jesuits at Vienna recognized the best way to be certain that an epidemic was over. When they observed that the Imperial Chamber and Regiment returned to the city in January 1571, they knew that it was safe.[133]

Another way of determining the end to an epidemic was to note the approach of winter. Jesuits often expressed their belief that cold weather halted an epidemic of pest and that during winter all diseases were less dangerous and contagious. Writing from Ferrara in January 1557, Guy Roillet asserted that Jesuits could visit the sick in the hospitals, "because in this weather it is not as

---

[128]Lainez, *Lainii monumenta*, 3: 163–64, Wolf to Lainez, March 1.
[129]ITAL 154: 178, to Mercurian, Stiano, July 5.
[130]Ibid., 87–87v, to Mercurian, July 18.
[131]ITAL 155: 356v, to Mercurian, December 11.
[132]GERM 147: 250, Vinck to Borgia, Mainz, October 21.
[133]GERM 133 I: 50, Forsler to Borgia, January 17.

dangerous as it is during hot weather."[134] As for epidemics of pest, Jesuits throughout Europe predicted that the advent of winter would bring an end to the disease. From Rome in November 1553, Ignatius Loyola wrote that the epidemic at Cologne would be less severe with the approach of winter,[135] Gil Gonzalez predicted that the rumors of pest circulating at Valladolid in November 1569 would cease as a result of the cold weather,[136] and during the epidemic at Messina in 1575 Vincenzo Romena claimed, "I do not see any danger of infection during this winter."[137] Jesuits also expressed their hopes (rather than predictions) that cold weather would put an end to epidemics. When the pest closed the Jesuit college at Vienna in 1572, Lorenzo Maggio wrote, "We hope that everything will return to normal within a few days because it has been very cold,"[138] and the return of the pest to Vienna four years later resulted in a similar comment from Maggio: "We hope in God that the cold of winter will extirpate it."[139] In addition to predicting and hoping, Jesuits observed that the cold of winter resulted in the decline of the pest, often in the month of January. In January 1573 Dominique Mengin reported that the epidemic at Munich "has already ceased on account of this extremely cold weather,"[140] and Oliver Manare wrote from Vienna in January 1583, "As for the pest in Austria, thanks to God scarcely one person dies daily as a result of the cold."[141] Despite the predictions, hopes, and observations, on occasion epidemics of pest did continue throughout the winter. When reporting on the epidemic at Barcelona in March 1558, Juan Gesti observed, "Many people fear and take it as a bad sign that it did not cease in spite of the great cold that we had this winter."[142]

Mario Beringucci wrote from a pest-infected Venice in February 1577, "We have much fear of the coming spring, because the cold weather has passed without being able to extinguish this disease completely."[143] Just as the approach of winter led to hopes for the decline of an epidemic, so the

---

[134]ITAL 107: 144, to Lainez, January 29.

[135]Ignatius Loyola, *Sancti Ignatii de Loyola, Societatis Jesu fundatoris, epistolae et instructiones*, 11 vols. (Madrid: Gabrielis Lopez del Horno, 1903–1911), 5: 746, to Kessel, Rome, November 28.

[136]HISP 112: 122v, to Borgia, November 10.

[137]ITAL 149: 224, Romena to Polanco, December 8.

[138]GERM 134 II: 520v, to Polanco, November 4.

[139]GERM 137 II: 373v, to Mercurian, Brno, December 23, 1576.

[140]GERM 152: 278, to Polanco, Freising, January 6.

[141]GERM 161: 33, to Aquaviva, January 29.

[142]Lainez, *Lainii monumenta*, 3: 268, to Lainez, March 21.

[143]ITAL 153: 100v, to Mercurian, February 6; see also his letter of January 18: 45v.

approach of warm weather heightened fears of a new outbreak. Not just epidemics but all diseases increased in vehemence during summer. For example, Fulvio Androzzi complained that the mud in the cellar of the Jesuit house at Florence would infect everyone during the summer.[144] Jesuits in the countries of Italy, Spain, and Portugal with Mediterranean climates feared the recrudescence of pest in the spring. In January 1570 Lião Anriquez wrote that although the epidemic at Lisbon had declined somewhat, "the doctors believe that come spring the disease will revive with vehemence,"[145] and when forwarding news from the Jesuits at Venice and Padua in April 1577, Francesco Adorno told General Mercurian, "They only fear the end of May."[146] In Italy people had cause for optimism if the months of July and August passed without incident,[147] while further north, summer and especially autumn held greater fears, and Jesuits often noted that the vintage season in September and October was dangerous in Germany and Austria.[148]

Statistics compiled from the chronology of epidemics in Jesuit accounts and the deaths of Jesuits from the pest support the predictions, hopes, fears, and observations of the seasonality of epidemics. As demonstrated in graph 1, quantifying the number of times Jesuits mentioned that the pest was present in a particular month (presented as a percentage of the total) reveals that the incidence of epidemics was lowest in March and reached a peak in September. Graph 1 also reveals a similar pattern in the seasonality of Jesuit mortality, but with a peak in August. The mortality percentages demonstrate that epidemics were more virulent in the summer months since the percentages of deaths in July, August, and September are greater than the percentages of incidence for the same months. Although graph 1 demonstrates the effects of seasonal change on the incidence and virulence of epidemics of pest, it fails to distinguish between the different climatic regions of Europe. Graphs 2, 3, and 4 show the incidence and mortality percentages in the three major climatic regions of the Mediterranean (data for the countries of Portugal, Spain, Italy, Slovenia,

---

[144]ITAL 112: 190, to Lainez, June 4; see also Francis Borgia, *Sanctus Franciscus Borgia quartus Gandiae dux et Societatis Jesu praepositus generalis*, 5 vols. (Madrid: Augustini Avrial and Gabrielis Lopez del Horno, 1894–1911), 2: 289, to Bartolomé Bustamante, Madrid, March 31, 1557; LUS 64: 223, Lourenço Mexia to Borgia, Bragança, December 22, 1571.

[145]LUS 64: 13, 23, to Borgia, Evora, January 21 and February 28.

[146]ITAL 153: 307v, Ferrara, April 19.

[147]ITAL 152: 51, Gabriele Bisciola to Mercurian, Ferrara, August 28, 1576; 154: 249, Sgariglia to Mercurian, Milan, July 24, 1577.

[148]For a few examples see Canisius, *Beati Petri Canisii*, 4: 854, sermon at Augsburg, September 12, 1563; GERM 136 II: 376, 397v, Maggio to Mercurian, Graz, September 23 and 30, 1575.

GRAPH 1: SEASONALITY OF EPIDEMICS

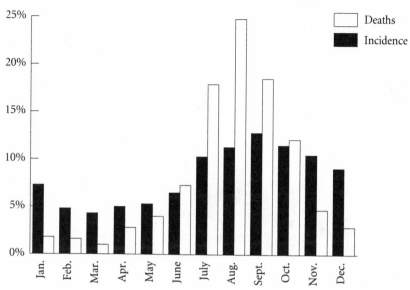

Albania, Macedonia, Greece, Turkey, and Egypt), the Northwest (France, Belgium, Netherlands, and England) and Central and Eastern Europe (Germany, Switzerland, Austria, Hungary, Romania, Czechoslovakia, Poland, Lithuania, Moldavia, Russia, and Sweden). In the Mediterranean epidemics reached their peaks in the months of June, July, and August (with 36 percent of the incidence and 62 percent of the mortality) and declined in the months of January, February, and March (17 percent of the incidence and 3 percent of the mortality). In northwestern Europe the peak and the trough were one month later, July, August, and September (46 percent of the incidence and 77 percent of the mortality) and February, March, and April (9 percent of the incidence and 2 percent of the mortality). In central and eastern Europe the peak in incidence was another two months later, September, October, and November (42 percent), but mortality peaked one month before this in August, September, and October (61 percent), while the trough occurred in March, April, and May (10 percent of the incidence and 6 percent of the mortality).

Historians do not disagree as much on the seasonality of pestilence as they do on age- and sex-specific mortality, for they are in general agreement

GRAPH 2: SEASONALITY OF EPIDEMICS: MEDITERRANEAN EUROPE

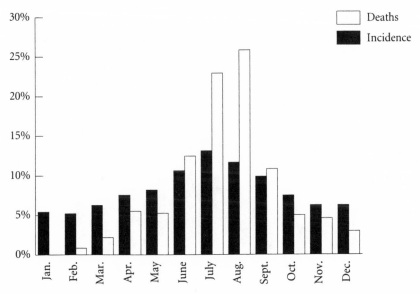

that epidemics increased in warm weather and declined in winter. Historians do differ somewhat, however, depending on the particular region and period they are studying. Jean-Noël Biraben, whose studies have no chronological or geographical limits, is content to state that epidemics rose with the heat and declined with the cold, but he does stress the relationship between humid and particularly rainy weather and increased activity.[149] According to Ann G. Carmichael's study of Florence, during the fourteenth century the greatest mortality occurred from May to September, but the minor epidemics of the fifteenth century extended the peaks into October and November.[150] The study of fifteenth- and sixteenth-century Florence by Alan S. Morrison, Julius Kirshner, and Anthony Molho likewise emphasizes the peaks of summer and autumn,

[149]Biraben, *Les hommes*, 1: 134–37. D. J. Schove, "Chronology and Historical Geography of Famine, Plague and Other Pandemics," *Proceedings of the XXIII International Congress of the History of Medicine 2–9 September 1972* (London: Wellcome Institute of the History of Medicine, 1974), 1270–71, argues that during the sixteenth century the plague was absent during wet and cold years, but his argument suffers from the fact that some of the years he cites as almost free of the plague, 1569, 1579, and 1588, had a high incidence of epidemics.

[150]Carmichael, *Plague and the Poor*, 63–67.

GRAPH 3: SEASONALITY OF EPIDEMICS: NORTHWESTERN EUROPE

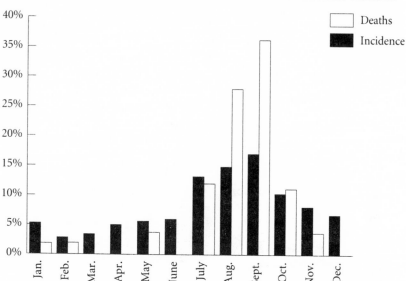

but they are unwise to generalize as they do from their examination of one city: "There can now be no doubt that serious epidemics in early modern Europe were primarily summer and autumn events."[151] Stephen R. Ell found that the Venetian epidemic of 1630–1631 had the highest mortality between October and December.[152] Turning from Italy to England, Robert S. Gottfried's evidence demonstrates that for the fifteenth century mortality from epidemics began to increase in the autumn but often peaked in the winter,[153] while J. F. D. Shrewsbury's statistics from the sixteenth and seventeenth centuries emphasize the period between July and September.[154] Edward A. Eckert's study of the seasonality of the Swiss epidemic of 1628–1630 discovered a

[151]Alan S. Morrison, Julius Kirshner, and Anthony Molho, "Epidemics in Renaissance Florence," *American Journal of Public Health* 75 (1985): 532, 535.

[152]Stephen R. Ell, "The Venetian Plague of 1630–1631: A Preliminary Epidemiologic Analysis," *Janus* 73 (1986–1990), 88, 94.

[153]Robert S. Gottfried, *Epidemic Disease in Fifteenth-Century England: The Medical Response and the Demographic Consequences* (New Brunswick: Rutgers University Press, 1978), 108–16.

[154]As cited in Edward A. Eckert, "Seasonality of Plague in Early Modern Europe: Swiss Epidemic of 1628–1630," *Reviews of Infectious Diseases* 2 (1980): 956.

GRAPH 4: SEASONALITY OF EPIDEMICS: CENTRAL AND
EASTERN EUROPE

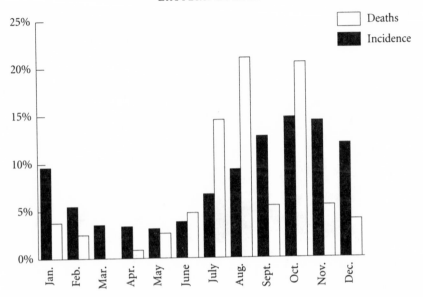

concentration in autumn and early winter.[155] Finally, Boris and Helga Velimirovic argue that the epidemic of 1653–1656 at Vienna resulted in excess mortality during the months of September, October, and November; and, just as Jesuits linked epidemics to the vintage, the Velimirovics note that contemporaries believed in a seasonal pattern due to the spread of the disease from Hungary through the seasonal migration of workers to harvest the grapes.[156]

All of these historians proceed on the assumption that they are dealing with epidemics of bubonic plague, and many in consequence try to fit what is known about the epidemiology of plague with the seasonality of the epidemics. Gottfried, for example, states, "*X. cheopis* seems to flourish between 68° and 78° F and the occurrence of bubonic plague in England is almost always in late summer and early fall."[157] However, as noted above, Gottfried's own evidence indicates that mortality from "plague" epidemics in England increased

[155]Ibid., 955.
[156]Boris and Helga Velimirovic, "Plague in Vienna," *Reviews of Infectious Diseases* 11 (1989), 818.
[157]Gottfried, *Epidemic Disease*, 62.

in autumn and often reached a peak in winter, when the temperature would have been much lower than 68° F. An examination of the effects of climate on *X. cheopis* by Dan C. Cavanaugh and James E. Williams indicates that the flea larvae require a relative humidity above 65 percent. Excessive precipitation, on the other hand, harms the adults. Neither the larvae nor adults can survive cold temperatures, and temperatures above 27.5° C make it less likely for the flea to become "blocked" and hence capable of spreading the disease.[158] Hence, epidemics of bubonic plague would be unlikely in the hot, dry summers of Mediterranean Europe and in the cool autumns of the north. The seasonality of epidemic disease in preindustrial Europe is a complex issue requiring further study, but the seasonality of the epidemics of pest in Jesuit accounts of the sixteenth century does not always fit the epidemiology of bubonic plague.[159]

[158]Dan C. Cavanaugh and James E. Williams, "Plague: Some Ecological Interrelationships," in *Fleas: Proceedings of the International Conference on Fleas*, ed. R. Traub and H. Starcke (Rotterdam: A. A. Balkema, 1980), 247–49.

[159]Graham I. Twigg, "The Black Death in England: An Epidemiological Dilemma," in *Maladies et société (XIIe-XVIIIe siècles): Actes du colloque de Bielefeld, novembre 1986*, ed. Neithard Bulst and Robert Delort (Paris: Editions du CNRS, 1989), 77–81, 95–97, arrives at a similar conclusion.

R P PETRVS CANISIVS. SOCIETATIS IESV

P. Aubry excu!

SEVEN

IN THE SERVICE OF THE SICK AND THE SOCIETY

THE OFFICIAL POLICY OF the Society of Jesus when confronted with an epidemic was the humane and sensible one of preserving the majority of its members by sending them elsewhere but recognizing its obligations to the sick by leaving some members to provide them with spiritual and physical assistance. This policy was responsible for the famous dispute with the cardinal archbishop of Milan, Carlo Borromeo, who was disappointed in the number of Jesuits who served the sick and the type of service they provided them during the epidemic of 1576–1577. As a result of this dispute, the Society's reputation has suffered in comparison with that of the Capuchins, but many Jesuits died in the service of the sick and hence were victims of charity. Because of the difficulties encountered in staffing its colleges, the Society could ill afford the loss of these men. Outbreaks of epidemic disease could also create problems for Jesuit finances, discipline, and administration, but the death of members was by far the greatest calamity.

SERVING THE SICK

Juan Polanco's distinctions regarding what was "more important for the common good" and "the greater divine service" and Jerónimo Nadal's guidelines for Jesuit colleges in pest-infected towns resulted in the policy that the majority fled epidemics while a few remained to guard the buildings and to care for the sick. In December 1562 Polanco discussed Nadal's guidelines in a letter to Peter Canisius: "The shortage of members that we have in Germany obliges us to conserve them as best we can for the divine service and the common good. Although we ought to prefer the good of another's soul to our own life, we should not expose the life of an effective servant for the consolation of one person, because if the servant lives he could help many souls." [1] On several occasions a few Jesuits demonstrated greater concern for their own lives than for the good of another's soul. At Reggio in Calabria in July 1576 Francesco Mercado complained that when the authorities asked for Jesuits to hear the confessions of the sick at a hospital outside the city, he had to refuse, "because I have not found any inclination in these priests to do this, except for one who is already hearing confessions throughout the city." [2] During the following year at Brescia the vice rector heard the confessions of the pest-stricken, despite the policy forbidding Jesuits in positions of authority to undertake such tasks and despite letters from the vice provincial ordering him not to do so. The vice rector, Antonio Marta, excused himself by stating that he felt obliged to serve the sick when none of the other priests demonstrated any willingness whatsoever to perform such a task; on the contrary, they expressed their opposition to it. [3]

The evidence indicates that those Jesuits who refused to serve the sick were in the minority. Most Jesuits would have agreed with the views expressed by Philippe Faber when "a certain type of fever" was killing many at Modena in January 1558. Although friends urged the Jesuits to avoid the sick and thereby preserve themselves, Faber argued the opposite, claiming that Jesuits could not deny what little assistance God had granted them to give when the sick came begging for a priest to hear their confessions. [4] More frequent than the reports of Jesuit refusals to assist the sick were those of Jesuits' requests that superiors let them perform such service. Anton Vinck wrote from Trier in 1564 that some Jesuits, especially novices, begged him for permission to serve those stricken with the pest. [5] At Lisbon during the epidemic of 1569, most Jesuits offered to risk their lives "in the service of Our Lord for the spiritual and physical well-being of others," [6] while at Zaragoza in 1564 and at Messina in 1578 the Jesuits

[1] Peter Canisius, *Beati Petri Canisii, Societatis Iesu, epistolae et acta*, ed. Otto Braunsberger, 13 vols. (Freiburg im Breisgau: Herder, 1896–1923), 3: 547–48, Trent, December 1.

[2] ITAL 151: 340, to Mercurian, July 23.

[3] ITAL 154: 178, Beringucci to Mercurian, Stiano, July 5, 1577.

[4] ITAL 111: 78, to Lainez, January 14.

[5] GERM 145: 230, to Lainez, October 12.

[6] LUS 63: 170, Jorge Sarrano to Borgia, Evora, September 18.

were unanimous in expressing the same sentiments.[7] Many Jesuits at Cologne in 1597 begged their superior for his permission by throwing themselves on the ground.[8] In conclusion, although the official policy was the humane and sensible one of sending the majority away and leaving the care of the sick in the hands of a few, and although some Jesuits refused to risk their lives, the general impression produced by the correspondence is one of stoic and at times enthusiastic acceptance of the risks involved, while some superiors had to beat off the zealous entreaties of many. According to Jean-Noël Biraben, most clergy accepted their responsibilities to serve the sick, while on rare occasions epidemics so terrorized some priests that they refused to approach the pest-stricken. So members of the Society of Jesus were comparable to other clergy in their response to epidemic disease.[9]

A complete account of the Jesuit record in the service of the sick would be long. It would also be repetitive as time after time Jesuits heard the confessions of the sick in the Jesuit churches, as they did at Valencia in 1557;[10] in the homes of the sick, as they did at Trier in 1564;[11] or in public hospitals, as they did at Monterey in 1561.[12] At Siracusa in 1557 Jesuits received requests to visit the sick both day and night,[13] and the Jesuit community at Palermo had trouble finding time to eat during the epidemic of 1558 as a result of the continuous appeals to hear confessions.[14] During the epidemic of pest that struck Transylvania in 1585, Valentinus Ladó heard 128 confessions in a few days at Suplac.[15] The goals of all these efforts were to console the sick as they faced death, to assist them to die well, and to save souls. As succinctly expressed by Juan Baptista de Barma concerning an epidemic at Granada in 1559, "It was necessary for us to undertake the administration of the sacraments, because many were dying without them."[16] In other words, Jesuits considered it their duty to help

---

[7]HISP 101: 317, Thoribio to Lainez, September 3, 1564; SIC 182: 228v, annual for 1578.

[8]RH INF 48: 52v, annual by Joannes Hasius, January 24, 1598.

[9]Jean-Noël Biraben, *Les hommes et la peste en France et dans les pays européens et méditerranéens*, 2 vols. (Paris: Mouton, 1975–1976), 2: 136.

[10]*Litterae quadrimestres ex universis praeter Indiam et Brasiliam locis in quibus aliqui de Societate Jesu versabantur Romam missae*, 7 vols. (Madrid and Rome: Augustinus Avrial, La Editorial Ibérica, and A. Macioce e Pisani, 1894–1932), 5: 491, by Parra, January 6, 1558.

[11]GERM 145: 225, Vinck to Lainez, October 7.

[12]*Litterae quadrimestres*, 7: 555, by Juan de Valderrabano, September 10.

[13]Ibid., 5: 388, by Casini, September 27.

[14]Ibid., 845, by Mercato, October 25.

[15]*Monumenta antiquae Hungariae*, ed. Ladislaus Lukács, 3 vols. (Rome: Institutum Historicum Societatis Iesu, 1969–1981), 2: 864, annual for Poland.

[16]Diego Lainez, *Lainii monumenta: Epistolae et acta patris Jacobi Lainii secundi praepositi generalis Societatis Jesu*, 8 vols. (Madrid: Gabrielis Lopez del Horno, 1912–1917), 4: 317, to Lainez, Valencia, May 1.

the sick die a Christian death by administering the sacraments of especially confession, less often communion, and occasionally extreme unction, and this was always the focus of Jesuit efforts. Jesuits sometimes assisted authorities in other ways, such as in preparing the dead for burial and burying them.[17]

While the focus was on spiritual assistance to the sick, on occasion Jesuits became involved in efforts to provide assistance for the body. Some historians, myself included, have argued that the concern expressed by Catholic reformers for the sick and the poor focused on spiritual welfare to the exclusion of the physical, and my blunt conclusion from an examination of the record of Jesuits in France was, "A Jesuit would rather save a starving man's soul than feed him."[18] While Jesuits did express greater concern for spiritual welfare than for the physical, my blunt conclusion is misleading because it does not appreciate the many efforts of Jesuits to provide physical relief for the sick during epidemics. The best example of such an effort occurred at Rome in 1566, and Emond Auger's work at Lyon in 1564 is another previously cited example. One method of relieving the sufferings of the sick was to seek alms on their behalf from the wealthy, as Jesuits did at Murcia in 1558 and at Olomouc in 1599.[19] During an epidemic at Ferrara in 1558 the Jesuits gave "capons, chickens, and other things for the sick" to those who came to their church.[20] At Messina in 1575 they went from house to house distributing bread to six thousand poor people,[21] and when the authorities at Pont-à-Mousson expelled 340 of the poor during the epidemic of 1585, the Jesuits passed out bread and wine to them twice a week for the space of two months.[22] When an epidemic affected more than a thousand people at Ferrara in 1569, Andrea Padovano reported, "since no one was available to care for them, we performed the office of Martha, also providing them many times with the necessities of life."[23] At Bragança in the same year, two Jesuits served the sick at the

---

[17] *Litterae quadrimestres*, 5: 579, by Giovanni Paolo Mirabello, Ferrara, March 21, 1558; LUS 52: 34v, annual for Portugal by Sebastião Morais, January 1, 1582.

[18] A. Lynn Martin, *The Jesuit Mind: The Mentality of an Elite in Early Modern France* (Ithaca: Cornell University Press, 1988), 216; see Brian Pullan, "Catholics and Poor in Early Modern Europe," *Transactions of the Royal Historical Society*, 5th ser., 26 (1976): 29–30; Wilma J. Pugh, "Social Welfare and the Edict of Nantes: Lyon and Nîmes," *French Historical Studies* 8 (1974): 358–59.

[19] *Litterae quadrimestres*, 5: 765, by Hontova, Murcia, August 27; AUST 132: 364, annual for Austria.

[20] ITAL 111: 45, Roillet to Lainez, January 8.

[21] ITAL 148: 136, Carminata to Mercurian, July 29.

[22] GAL 62: 38, annual letter.

[23] VEN 100: 209–209v, annual, December 22.

hospital of Saint Martha, "applying medicine to the souls as well as to the body."[24] In conclusion, the application of medicine to the souls might have been the first priority, but Jesuits did not neglect the bodies of the sick.

On occasion religious and secular authorities placed restrictions on Jesuit service of the sick. As discussed in chapter 5, health officials often banned public gatherings such as sermons to prevent the spread of the epidemic, and sometimes Jesuit communities either endured the confinement of quarantine or the threat of it as a result of their work among the pestiferous. Three incidents reveal other ways in which the wishes or commands of religious and political leaders could affect Jesuit assistance to the suffering. The first occurred at Braga during the epidemic of 1570 when the archbishop requested the Jesuits to stay away from the hospital established outside the town but instead to concentrate their efforts on those afflicted who remained in their homes.[25] The second occurred at Monreale in 1575. As reported by Juan Polanco, the authorities ordered the Jesuits there to avoid all contact with the sick and thereby preserve themselves and their church for the assistance and consolation of the entire town.[26] The final incident happened at Bourges in 1582. After two Jesuits had died as a result of their service to the sick and others had become seriously ill, the municipal magistrates forbade the Jesuit community to continue with these efforts so that the Jesuit college would not lose any more teachers.[27]

More frequent than limits placed on Jesuit assistance to the sick were requests for such service. The Cardinal of Ferrara, for example, gave the Jesuit community at Tivoli the task of helping the sick during an epidemic in 1568.[28] Similarly, during an outbreak of petechia at Brescia in 1570, the officials sought Jesuit assistance at the hospital of the incurables, where many dying women were not receiving sacraments owing to the deaths of three chaplains.[29] As a result of the frequent bans on preaching and other religious observances and

---

[24]LUS 64: 16, annual by Eduard de Sande, January 24, 1570.

[25]Ibid., 69, Tolosa to Borgia, Coimbra, July 16.

[26]Juan Polanco, *Polanci complementa: Epistolae et commentaria P. Joannis Alphonsi de Polanco e Societate Jesu*, 2 vols. (Madrid: Gabrielis Lopez del Horno, 1916–1917), 2: 368, to Mercurian, Messina, October 5.

[27]Pierre Delattre, ed., *Les établissements des jésuites en France depuis quatre siècles*, 5 vols. (Enghien: Institut Supérieur de Théologie, 1949–1957), 1: 872.

[28]Polanco, *Complementa*, 2: 55, to the Society, Rome, December 31.

[29]ITAL 139: 135, Peruschi to Borgia, August 2.

the complete cessation of normal rituals associated with funerals and burials during epidemics, civil authorities wanted to ensure that at least some of the religious rites and sacraments continued as a means to comfort and console the panic-stricken citizens. Jesuit communities in consequence received requests from political authorities to provide priests for this purpose. To cite three examples, in 1575 the governor at Messina requested the Jesuits to send priests to the lazaretto outside the town,[30] the requests of the authorities at Genoa in 1579 led to the deaths of three Jesuits in the service of the sick,[31] and the appeal for help from the magistrates of Saint-Omer in 1596 resulted in seventeen volunteers.[32] Such requests and appeals were not always successful; at Maastricht in the summer of 1598 the Jesuits rejected efforts by the magistrates "to requisition" them to serve the pest-stricken.[33] In addition to the requests from political authorities, bishops and other religious leaders could make their own appeals. During the severe outbreak of pest at Brescia in 1577, the bishop applied pressure on the Jesuits to provide priests to hear the confessions of the sick, pressure that almost resulted in the death of the vice rector when he could find no one else willing to do it.[34]

THE DISPUTE WITH CARLO BORROMEO

As noted in an earlier chapter, the cardinal archbishop of Milan, Carlo Borromeo, likewise put pressure on the Jesuits to supply priests to serve the sick during the epidemic of pest at Milan during 1576 and 1577, an epidemic now sometimes known as *la peste di San Carlo* as a result of the cardinal's pastoral care of the sick. *La guerra di San Carlo* would be an appropriate title for the dispute between Borromeo and the Jesuit superiors, especially from the point of view of the five superiors involved, the provincial of Lombardy, Francesco Adorno; the rector of the Collegio di Brera at Milan, Alfonso Sgariglia; the superior of the Casa di San Fidele at Milan, Giovanni Battista Peruschi; the rector of the seminary at Milan, Filippo Trivisano; and the general of the Society at Rome, Everard Mercurian. The first indication of the dispute in the

---

[30]ITAL 148: 167v, Calligaris to Mercurian, August 5.

[31]MED 76 I: 57, annual for Milan by Peruschi, Milan, February 1, 1580.

[32]Delattre, *Les établissements*, 4: 815.

[33]Alfred Poncelet, *Histoire de la Compagnie de Jésus dans les anciens Pays-Bas*, 2 vols. (Brussels: M. Lamertin, 1927–1928), 2: 462, n. 2.

[34]ITAL 155: 204v, Marta to Beringucci, September 23.

Jesuit correspondence is a letter dated August 17, 1576, from Adorno in Genoa to Mercurian: "The Lord Cardinal is trying to obtain priests to hear the confessions of the sick, and for this purpose he has assaulted ours, who have excused themselves awaiting my order. I did not want to resolve anything at all.... I leave everything to your judgment; please write me what they should do and how they should respond to the Lord Cardinal." In the meantime Adorno informed the superiors in Milan that they should not send any priests to suspected places that could then endanger other Jesuits when they returned to their place of residence, that they should not send any at all to the lazaretto because this would be sending them to a certain death, and that the cardinal should establish a separate residence for any Jesuits "whom God inspires to offer themselves for this holy work of assisting the sick." [35]

Sgariglia wrote a brief account of the cardinal's requests on August 22, Peruschi reported in greater detail on the 25th, while Trivisano waited until September 5. The cardinal had called a meeting of all the superiors of religious houses in Milan and asked them first for their assistance in prayers, masses, and processions and then for volunteers to assist the sick if the situation required it. In particular he pressed the Jesuit superiors for volunteers, but Peruschi, Sgariglia, and Trivisano replied that they required the permission of the provincial and the general. Peruschi then complied with Borromeo's request by seeking volunteers and forwarding a list of them with some of their written statements to Mercurian. One of the statements was by Giulio Coccapani: "I offer myself in this occasion of pest to give my life to the glory of His Divine Majesty and to the assistance of souls." [36] Peruschi asked Mercurian to look at the list and advise him "who should go and who should not go, and who would be more apt and less damaging," but he begged Mercurian to put himself at the top of the list. In his letter to Mercurian, Trivisano reported on a subsequent conversation with Borromeo. The cardinal expressed his disappointment that none of the Jesuit superiors had come forth with any volunteers; Trivisano responded that they had to get the approval of their provincials and generals. In turn Borromeo replied that he did not want to be subject to the wishes of the provincials and the generals, and he informed Trivisano that he was going to ask the pope to order the Jesuits to do whatever the cardinal

---

[35]ITAL 152: 2v–3.
[36]Ibid., 15, to Peruschi, August 22.

wanted them to do in this matter. Also included in Trivisano's letter was another list of volunteers.[37]

Mercurian responded to Adorno's letter of August 17 on September 7, probably before he had received any of the letters from the Milanese superiors. He gave Adorno the authority to permit volunteers to assist the pest-stricken but suggested that the teachers and scholars at the Collegio di Brera be exempt from such service.[38] Adorno accordingly ordered that the Jesuits from the college should stop hearing the confessions of the sick but gave his permission to those from the Casa di San Fidele. As a result some priests from San Fidele visited the sick in the city, taking a white rod with them on their peregrinations to warn people that they were suspect; and Giorgio Farina, Maurizio Ghini, and Francesco Centurione volunteered to serve the pest-stricken who had been sent to the huts constructed outside the city. When the cardinal chose Ghini to hear the confessions of all the priests serving the sick, Giovanni Battista Vannini took his place. Farina and Centurione succumbed to the pest almost immediately, but Vannini survived, and Giovanni Battista Domini volunteered to take the place of Farina.[39] As a result Borromeo could scarcely find fault with the Society and its superiors in this affair, and the dispute seemed resolved.

La guerra di San Carlo erupted again in July of 1577. Peruschi wrote to Mercurian on the 6th, informing him that Milan was returning to normal as the number of victims declined, but that the Jesuits of San Fidele continued with the dangerous work of their ministry to the sick. "For the rest the situation here is calm and somewhat good. The major trouble is with the cardinal, who does not understand or like the manner and the spirit of the Society." Peruschi proceeded to explain at length the reasons for the cardinal's dissatisfaction. The Jesuits proceeded according to the doctrines established by the Doctors of the Church and according to the procedures of the Society, but the cardinal believed that these procedures were too liberal and damaged ecclesiastical discipline. In short, he did not want those doctrines and procedures which interfered with, in Peruschi's words, "a certain idea of perfection that he has formed in his mind, and he wants to draw everyone to it by force." In particular, Borromeo claimed that priests should administer all the sacraments

[37]Ibid., 16v–17, Sgariglia; 43–43v, Peruschi; 86–86v, Trivisano.

[38]The letter is partially edited in Giuseppe Boero, Risposta a Vincenzo Gioberti sopra le lettere di S. Carlo Borromeo (Rome: Marini e Marini, 1849), 113.

[39]ITAL 152: 165v, 203v, 327, 356, Adorno to Mercurian, Genoa, September 28 and October 12, Parma, December 4 and 17.

and perform all the normal offices and ministries for the pest-stricken, and he was disappointed with Vannini's insistence on just hearing confessions and his failure to give communion.[40] The Jesuits, after consulting their theologians, claimed (quite rightly) that the normal ministry was unnecessary and that the cardinal's position was contrary to doctrine. Bernardino Viottino, who taught theology at the seminary, explained to the cardinal that the dangerous task of giving communion to the pest-stricken was not necessary, to which Borromeo replied that he did not want this doctrine. Viottino responded, "Monsignor, we teach the doctrine that we have from the Holy Doctors and nothing else." Borromeo shot back, "You are not a bishop, and to say that we should do that is none of your business; I do not like this doctrine and I do not want it." Borromeo was so angered by this exchange that he threatened to expel Viottino from his diocese and to replace Trivisano with another superior.

The cardinal had hoped that he could point to the activities of the Jesuits as an example to all the other priests, but he was disappointed with the number of Jesuits who had served the sick and the manner in which they did it. To circumvent the refusal of superiors to permit Jesuits to volunteer for such service, he obtained a brief from Rome giving him the power to free members of religious orders from their vows of obedience so that they could serve the sick. He also suspected that the Jesuits had communicated their opinions to the rest of the clergy, some of whom fled while the rest created an uproar and claimed that they were not obliged to serve the sick in the manner prescribed by the cardinal. Although Jesuit service to the sick formed the bulk of the cardinal's complaints, Peruschi's letter to Mercurian mentioned other matters of contention. Early in 1577 Borromeo and the Jesuit superiors had become involved in another dispute when the cardinal wished to renew classes, suspended as a result of the epidemic, for the seminarians at the Collegio di Brera and the Jesuits objected because of the dangers of infection.[41] Finally, Borromeo suspected Pedro Parra, who was confessor to the Spanish governor of Milan and his family, of using his position to subvert the cardinal's authority.[42]

For the rest of 1577 Borromeo's anger toward the Society alternately rose and fell, but mostly it rose. Late in July Peruschi informed Mercurian that the

---

[40]See ITAL 154: 286–286v for a letter from Vannini to Mercurian, Milan, August 2, 1577, justifying his actions.

[41]For this dispute see the letter from Mercurian to Adorno, Rome, March 7, 1577; ITAL 70a: 4.

[42]ITAL 154: 181–182v.

cardinal had become much calmer, "although he remains dissatisfied with our doctrine and our manner, and if he could manage the seminary without the help of the Society he would gladly do so." [43] By mid-August he was angry again. As reported by Peruschi, "The cardinal was in a very great rage these past days and showed much dissatisfaction, and he said very irritating things to me." The reason for this outburst was the Society's slowness in recommencing classes for seminarians at the Collegio di Brera after the deaths of two priests who attended classes there. Borromeo used the occasion to review and renew all the past disputes and to issue threats—because he had founded the college he could "unfound" it.[44] During September the superiors at Milan kept Adorno informed of Borromeo's intentions to recommence the classes even though the pest had become worse. Adorno forwarded this information to Mercurian and advised him that since the cardinal would become angry if the Jesuits opposed his wishes, perhaps the pope could write to him suggesting that he defer the classes until the epidemic had ceased. Adorno also reported that the cardinal insisted on the removal of Trivisano from his position as superior of the seminary, "because he remained very much dissatisfied with him in this time of the pest." [45] Meanwhile, back in Milan, Peruschi had given up. He informed Mercurian in mid-October, "As for observing the things ordered by the Cardinal, we cannot do anything but submit." An indication of the immense animosity between Borromeo and the Jesuits was his attempt to obtain special briefs from the pope, one permitting Jesuits and other religious to leave their orders without license of their superiors, and the other prohibiting any clergy from entering the Society of Jesus while attending classes at the seminary in Milan or for four years following.[46]

Come December the epidemic was almost over, and Adorno could report to Mercurian that the war was over as well: "As for the Lord Cardinal Borromeo, Father Peruschi wrote that he is now satisfied with me,... and I believe that he will generally remain satisfied with the Society, although perhaps not with some particular points." [47] Adorno's optimism notwithstanding, A. D. Wright's assessment of the relationship between the cardinal and the

---

[43]ITAL 154: 247v, July 24.

[44]Ibid., 339, 366–67, August 11 and 19; see also Peruschi's letter of September 10; ITAL 155: 29–30.

[45]ITAL 155: 115–115v, Genoa, October 4, 1577.

[46]Ibid., 175–175v, October 14.

[47]Ibid., 353, Ferrara, December 11.

Society is too sanguine: "Borromeo's relations with the Jesuits at Milan remained indeed correct rather than conspicuously warm." [48] To put the dispute in context, a few years before, in 1570, Borromeo had obtained a brief from Pope Pius V prohibiting clerics attending the seminary from joining the Society, and two years later in 1579 he would demand the removal of a Jesuit preacher, Giulio Cesare Mazzarino. Borromeo's confrontation with the Society during the epidemic was but part of his long-term goal of placing all the clergy of his diocese under his control. [49]

Borromeo died in 1584 and was canonized in 1612, an unusually short length of time (by comparison Ignatius Loyola died in 1556 and was canonized in 1622). His canonization was primarily due to his pastoral work among the sick during *la peste di San Carlo*, and he joined Sebastian and Rocco as popular saints invoked for protection during times of pestilence. The situation has its ironies. The first irony is that a person who rejected the doctrine of the Church when it did not suit his purposes or when he did not like it, and who subverted the discipline in religious orders and the authority of religious superiors when they interfered with his schemes, then became a saint of the Church. The second irony is that the group which promoted the cult of San Carlo during epidemics of pest was the Society of Jesus. [50] The final irony is that *la guerra di San Carlo* resulted from the Milanese superiors' insistence on the approval of the provincial or the general before committing any Jesuits to serve the sick and from the Jesuit refusal to administer all the sacraments to the sick. Yet elsewhere Jesuit superiors committed Jesuits without such approval, and also elsewhere Jesuits administered all the sacraments. The inflexibility and stubbornness of both sides were responsible for the dispute.

---

[48] A. D. Wright, "The Borromean Ideal and the Spanish Church," in *San Carlo Borromeo: Catholic Reform and Ecclesiastical Politics in the Second Half of the Sixteenth Century*, ed. John M. Headley and John B. Tomaro (Washington: Folger Books, 1988), 191.

[49] Adriano Prosperi, "Clerics and Laymen in the Work of Carlo Borromeo," in *San Carlo Borromeo: Catholic Reform and Ecclesiastical Politics in the Second Half of the Sixteenth Century*, ed. John M. Headley and John B. Tomaro (Washington: Folger Books, 1988), 125, 128.

[50] Stefania Mason Rinaldi, "Le immagini della peste nella cultura figurativa veneziana," in *Venezia e la peste, 1348–1797*, 2d ed. (Venice: Marsilio Editori, 1980), 221.

VICTIMS OF CHARITY

The final toll of Jesuits dead from the pest at Milan during the epidemic of 1576–1577 was six, at least two of whom succumbed after their work among the pest-stricken. Several contracted the disease but recovered, and others who served the sick survived unscathed. The Capuchins lost ten of their brethren, all after service in the lazaretto. Jean Delumeau has speculated about the different public opinion regarding the two religious orders: "If the Capuchins, who were with the Jesuits the principal agents of the Catholic Reform, never experienced a hostility comparable to that suffered by members of the Society of Jesus, this resulted from their self-sacrifice during epidemics of pestilence." [51] Delumeau's assessment is unfair, perhaps influenced by the dispute at Milan, which has been incorrectly interpreted by historians. Vincenzo Gioberti, for example, claimed that the Jesuits at Milan withdrew from the service of the sick because they loved life too much. [52] While the Society's record does not match that of the Capuchins, which bordered on reckless disregard for the consequences, Jesuits in the service of the sick succumbed in large numbers during the sixteenth century. Of the 494 Jesuits who died from epidemic disease, at least 92 were victims of charity, that is, they became infected and died after attending the religious needs of the sick, and at least another 22 died after becoming infected by those who served the sick. The vast majority of the 92 succumbed during epidemics of pest. To return to irony, if the disease these Jesuits confronted was the bubonic plague, spread as it is by *R. rattus* and *X. cheopis* and not by contagion or interhuman contact, then they were not victims of charity after all. They were just as likely to contract the disease as were the Jesuits who stayed behind in their colleges and residences; only flight would have saved them. One could quibble and turn the argument full circle, for if flight would have saved them and they stayed to serve the sick, then indeed they were victims of charity.

As illustrated by the situation at Milan, some Jesuits who served the sick survived the experience. At Alcalá de Henares in 1557, a series of deadly diseases killed many inhabitants but only one Jesuit, a brother named Lorenço Padilla,

---

[51] Jean Delumeau, *La peur en occident (XIVe–XVIIe siècles): Une cité assiégée* (Paris: Fayard, 1978), 128.

[52] See Boero, *Risposta a Vincenzo Gioberti*, 112–13.

even though all the Jesuits had cared for the sick.[53] In June of 1558 Pedro Parra reported from Valencia that the Jesuits had been hearing the confessions of the pest-stricken and giving them care every day for an entire year, but the only ones who had become sick were two brothers and the gardener, and they had not been involved in these activities.[54] The Jesuits at Vienna produced a similar record, but here the epidemic lasted for two years, from 1562 to 1564.[55] The epidemic that affected more than ten thousand at Ferrara in 1569 did not touch a single Jesuit despite their performing "the office of Martha," [56] and the priests who served the pestiferous at Luzern in 1595 and Chambéry in 1596 remained unaffected.[57] On other occasions Jesuits contracted the disease but survived. During the epidemic at Seville in 1568, Juan Gracia administered the sacraments of confession, communion, and extreme unction when other priests were not available. He was "wounded by the pest" in the lower arm, and the fever was so intense and the wound so close to his heart that others believed that he would die within three days, but he recovered.[58] The petechia that killed three chaplains at the hospital in Brescia during 1570 also almost killed two Jesuits who had replaced them.[59]

Jesuits in the service of the sick similarly recovered from the "great infestation of the air almost like half a pest" at Loreto in 1557 and the pest at Brescia in 1577, but the same epidemics also produced victims of charity, Michelangelo da Fabriano and Francesco Stefano.[60] Rather than document all ninety-two victims, some examples should suffice. Philippe Faber, who rejected the advice of friends to avoid the sick during the epidemic at Modena in 1558, died on February 26 after becoming sick at the hospital.[61] During an epidemic of pest at Burgos in 1565, the rector, Gaspar de Acebedo, heard the confession of the sick and then brought the infection to the Jesuit residence. He and three others

---

[53]*Litterae quadrimestres*, 5: 503, by Andrés Capilla, January 11, 1558.

[54]Ibid., 703, June 2, 1558.

[55]Jerónimo Nadal, *Epistolae P. Hieronymi Nadal Societatis Iesu ab anno 1546 ad 1577*, 4 vols. (Madrid: Augustini Avrial and Gabrielis Lopez del Horno, 1898–1905), 2: 497, 502, to Aroaz, Rome, February 1, 1564.

[56]VEN 100: 209, annual by Padovano, December 22.

[57]GERM SUP 65: 111, annual for Luzern, December 15; LUGD 28: 142v, annual for Lyon.

[58]HISP 108: 278, Avellaneda to Borgia, Granada, June 28.

[59]ITAL 139: 135, Peruschi to Borgia, August 2.

[60]*Litterae quadrimestres*, 5: 398–99, by Riera, October 5, 1557; ITAL 109: 68, Manare to Lainez, July 16, 1557; ITAL 154: 209, Beringucci to Mercurian, Venice, July 13, 1577.

[61]Lainez, *Lainii monumenta*, 3: 163–64, Wolf to Lainez, March 1.

died.[62] At Seville in May 1568, Alonso Velasco heard the confession of a student, placing his hands over the sore; in turn Velasco was "wounded" on the hand and the arm, and a tumor developed in his groin—he died on the 19th.[63] Luigi Nugnez heard the confessions of those suspected of having the pest at Messina in 1576 and died after an illness of fifteen days.[64] The Polish Jesuit Peter Szydlowski died on June 19, 1586, at Oradea in Transylvania. He became sick after baptizing and confessing the pest-stricken. His superiors especially lamented his death because he had just been ordained and had already learned enough Hungarian to help with the Jesuit mission among the Hungarians.[65]

THE EFFECTS ON THE SOCIETY OF JESUS

In 1575 the Society of Jesus had 3,905 members, a figure which represents a rapid growth since its foundation in 1540. However, these Jesuits were responsible for the administration and instruction in 210 educational institutions—colleges, seminaries, and universities—thus averaging only nineteen members per institution. Many of these institutions had large enrollments. For example, the college at Paris had 3,500 students. Not all of the 3,905 Jesuits would have been sufficiently advanced to take their places in the classroom and on other missions, for many were novices and others were still undergoing training. In short, the Society had a staff shortage, and it could ill afford the loss of members such as Peter Szydlowski.[66] Juan Polanco's letter to Peter Canisius specifically mentioned the shortage of members in Germany as the reason for restricting Jesuit service of the sick. Indicative of the situation was the decision made by Ignatius Loyola when an epidemic of pest struck Padua in September 1555; because of the closure of the school at Padua the teachers could transfer to Venice and ease the shortage there.[67] This was a rare occasion when an epidemic helped resolve a staffing problem. Another occasion occurred at Venice in 1570 when the Jesuits helped care for sick soldiers recently returned from the Levant and then became sick themselves with "a very serious and contagious

[62]Polanco, *Complementa*, 2: 649, *Commentariola.*

[63]HISP 108: 254, Avellaneda to Lainez, Granada, June 3.

[64]ITAL 151: 368, Carminata to Mercurian, July 30.

[65]*Monumenta Hungariae*, 2: 940, Fanfoni to Aquaviva, Cluj, June.

[66]See A. Lynn Martin, "Vocational Crises and the Crisis in Vocations among Jesuits in France during the Sixteenth Century," *Catholic Historical Review* 71 (1986): 209–10.

[67]Ignatius Loyola, *Sancti Ignatii de Loyola, Societatis Jesu fundatoris, epistolae et instructiones*, 11 vols. (Madrid: Gabrielis Lopez del Horno, 1903–1911), 9: 654, to Helmi, Rome, September 28.

infirmity." One young man assisted the Jesuits in caring for all the sick and was so impressed that he joined the Society.[68]

The normal situation was for epidemic disease to aggravate the shortage of personnel. In the wake of the pest at Paris in 1562 that killed four Jesuits, General Diego Lainez gave Ponce Cogordan permission to move Jesuits from other places in France to Paris,[69] and he also arranged for other provinces to send Jesuits to Aragon after an epidemic there killed six in 1564.[70] This practice eased a problem in one place by creating another elsewhere. The worst personnel crisis occurred as a result of twenty-six deaths in Transylvania in 1586. The depleted mission faced increasing competition from Protestants, and rumors circulated that they were posed to take possession of the deserted college and church at Cluj.[71] Antonio Possevino forwarded these and other rumors to General Claudio Aquaviva in September and urged him to send replacements at once, "without waiting for winter to impede their travel or for the heretical ministers to regain entry in our places." [72] Aquaviva responded by asking the provincial of Rome to determine if any Jesuits were willing to go to Transylvania, especially those who spoke Slavic languages,[73] but the Transylvanian mission did not recover from the blow. On occasion, rather than the number killed, it was the type of Jesuit who succumbed that created problems for superiors. The death of Stephan Rimel at Graz in July 1572 meant that Lorenzo Maggio had the difficult task of finding a good German preacher,[74] and at Venice the death of three priests resulted in a shortage of capable confessors in 1577.[75] Aside from the difficulties caused by the deaths of Jesuits, epidemics could create temporary difficulties. During the epidemic of pest in 1575 and 1576, Jesuit superiors could not send the badly needed "good teacher of rhetoric" to Sicily, and the epidemic made it difficult for bishops to ordain priests.[76]

Lorenzo Maggio confessed that the death of Stephan Rimel and the difficulties in finding a replacement made him "quite often sigh and shrug the

[68]ITAL 138: 73, Micheli to [Borgia], March 3.

[69]Lainez, *Lainii monumenta*, 6: 711, Trent, March 11, 1563.

[70]Ibid., 8: 252, to Araoz, Rome, October 17.

[71]*Monumenta Hungariae*, 2: 969, Busau to Skarga, Kövár, August 21, 1586.

[72]Ibid., 995, Rome.

[73]Ibid., 998–99, to Fabio di Fabi, Naples, October.

[74]GERM 134 II: 350v, Maggio to Nadal, Olomouc, July 30.

[75]ITAL 154: 365, Beringucci to Mercurian, August 17.

[76]Polanco, *Complementa*, 2: 405, 528–29, Mercurian to Polanco, Rome, November 19, 1575; Polanco to Mercurian, Tremilia, June 30, 1576.

shoulders." Jesuits seldom expressed their emotional reactions to the deaths and problems that resulted from epidemics, but the psychological burden must be considered among the effects that accompanied outbreaks, especially of the pest. Giulio Fazio was at Siracusa when he learned of the deaths of Ippolito di Alberto at Palermo and Angelo Sibilla at Messina in June 1577. He wrote to Mercurian, "You can imagine what anxiety and apprehension I experienced when I heard on the same day, quite unexpectedly, of such news from two major colleges of this province, both afflicted by the pest, and of the deaths of two notable members." [77] In the following month Mario Beringucci seemed overwhelmed by the news of the sickness of Jesuits at Brescia, including the vice rector, Antonio Marta.[78] Marta's replacement, Giovanni Francesco Prandi, in turn was upset by the additional responsibilities. "In such calamitous times...I have encountered only troubles and afflictions from all sides." [79] Giovanni Paolo Campana did not report on the stress he felt as a result of the epidemic in his province of Poland, an epidemic that closed the colleges, dispersed the Jesuit communities, and killed several of his subordinates; but another Jesuit, Paul Boxa, informed General Aquaviva in January 1589 that the situation so tormented Campana's spirit that he had many sleepless nights.[80]

The most famous Jesuit victim of charity was Luigi (Aloysius) Gonzaga, son of the lord of Castiglione, who died at Rome on June 21, 1591, aged twenty-three, after a long illness contracted while caring for the sick at a hospital. A contemporary diarist, rather than note the distress of the Jesuits, reported on the emotions of the people: "The crowd at his funeral was great, and great was its desire to have some of his relics, so much so that they had great difficulty in saving his holy body from the eagerness of the devout." [81] To use twentieth-century terms, Gonzaga's death was good public relations for the Jesuits, especially since he was eventually canonized in 1726. As a new religious order, the Society of Jesus was concerned about its image and reputation, and as much as it could ill afford the loss of members, victims of charity together with martyrs for the faith enhanced the status of the Society. When General Diego Lainez

---

[77] ITAL 154: 95v, June 15.
[78] Ibid., 209, to Mercurian, Venice, July 13.
[79] ITAL 155: 281, to Mercurian, Brescia, November 15.
[80] GERM 168: 132, Braniewo, January 8.
[81] Quoted from Riccardo G. Villoslada, *Storia del Collegio Romano, dal suo inizio (1551) alla soppressione della Compagnia di Gesù (1773)* (Rome: Apud sedes Universitatis Gregorianae, 1954), 121.

informed the Jesuits in France that some of their brethren had been martyred in Africa, he stated, "By the grace of God things are going from good to better with us." [82]

Service of the sick also earned the Society a good reputation, and some Jesuits admitted that the reason they undertook such dangerous work was to save the Society from calumny. From Vilnius in October 1571, Stanislaus Varsevic reported that although most Jesuits had fled, he and several others remained to comfort the sick so that the Protestants would not have occasion to slander them and the Catholics would not have occasion to doubt their charity.[83] According to Emerich Forsler, some Jesuits heard the confessions of the sick during an epidemic of pest at Vienna in 1577, "because to refuse those calling for us would create a scandal." [84] Jesuits often informed their superiors that their service of the sick resulted in favorable opinion for the Society. When many people fleeing the epidemic at Lisbon in 1569 began to die near Evora, the Jesuit community sent two priests and two brothers to give them physical and spiritual aid. The sick "received them as angels come from heaven," and, in the words of Jorge Sarrano, "not only in this city but in all the others people [said] a thousand good things and [showered] us with a thousand blessings."[85] Jesuit service of the sick likewise enhanced the Society's reputation at Siracusa in 1558, Pultusk in 1572, and Vienna in 1585;[86] and Juan Polanco informed Peter Canisius in 1564 of the consequence of Emond Auger's work during the epidemic of pest at Lyon: "The very sweet aroma of the Society has spread throughout the entire kingdom." [87]

On occasion rumor threatened the sweet aroma of the Society. The most notable example of this occurred during the epidemic at Avignon in 1577, when a rumor circulated that the Jesuits were responsible for the disease because they had sheltered a pest-stricken colleague from Lyon. At Bivona in

---

[82]Quoted from James Brodrick, *The Progress of the Jesuits (1556–1579)* (London: Longmans, Green, 1946), 209 n. For a discussion of the Society's concern with its reputation see Martin, *Jesuit Mind*, 121–22.

[83]GERM 152: 114, to Nadal, October 15.

[84]GERM 138 II: 373, to Mercurian, November 7.

[85]LUS 63: 171 to Borgia, September 18; see also Sarrano's letter to Borgia of December 4 (224) and Lião Anriquez's letter to Borgia of December 17 (237v).

[86]Lainez, *Lainii monumenta*, 3: 575, Casini to Lainez, Siracusa, September 29; POL 65: 28, *Compendium Historiae Collegii Pultoviensis;* GERM 141: 267, annual for Vienna.

[87]Canisius, *Beati Petri Canisii,* 4: 716–17, Rome, November 7.

1556 rumors circulated that all the Jesuits at the college had the pest,[88] and at Palermo in 1577 Jesuits had to contend with a rumor that half of them had succumbed to the same disease.[89] The Society opposed such rumors because they prevented students from attending its colleges and people from coming to its churches. When Jesuits administered the sacraments to the sick during an epidemic at Valencia in 1557, Pedro Parra reported, "many people did not approach us as a result of the great fear they had for this infirmity." [90] In 1564 the Jesuits at Venice hid the fact that some of them had contracted a contagious disease so as not to frighten away the devout.[91] Had the devout discovered the truth, it might have damaged the Society's reputation more than any of the rumors.

THE VISITATION OF JUAN POLANCO

When the epidemic of pest erupted in Sicily in June 1575, it caught Juan Polanco making an official visitation of the Society's colleges and residences on the island. Not only did the disease interrupt Polanco's visit, but it also created other problems (as well as some opportunities) for the Society, problems (and opportunities) that were not unique to Sicily nor to this epidemic. Polanco's most immediate and obvious problem was travel. When the epidemic began he was at Caltagirone, from which he could not travel to Siracusa, so he went to Catania because travel was still possible from there to Siracusa.[92] Thus began a saga lasting sixteen months as Polanco traveled around Sicily, at times avoiding Jesuit communities in towns afflicted with the pest, at times visiting such communities, all the time looking for an opportunity to cross to the Jesuit college at Reggio on the mainland and then go to Naples before returning to Rome.[93] At one time or another he or others on his behalf sought special permission to cross to Reggio from the captain and archbishop at Reggio, the duke of Terranova, the marquis of Santa, the viceroy in Naples, and don Pedro González de Mendoça, the son of the viceroy. As Polanco explained in a letter to Mercurian from Catania in October 1575, because Palermo, Monreale,

---

[88]*Litterae quadrimestres*, 4: 617, by Romena, December 27.

[89]ITAL 154: 105, Basso to Mercurian, Naples, June 18.

[90]HISP 95: 213, to Lainez, December 2.

[91]ITAL 124: 224v, Lucio Croce to Lainez, May 20.

[92]Polanco, *Complementa*, 2: 348, to Mercurian, Catania, July 27.

[93]See the copious correspondence, ibid., 351–568.

Bivona, and Messina had the pest, "After leaving one of these we cannot enter another [city] except after many days, as happened here despite the friendship of the [authorities]."[94] Even so, he traveled from Catania to Siracusa, back to Catania, then to Messina, back to Catania (because he hoped he could then get to Reggio), Caltagirone, Palermo (in March 1576), Carangino, and Siracusa (in August), before finally reaching Reggio in late September and Naples in October.

During his visit Polanco had to contend with the illnesses and deaths of Jesuits, the resulting shortages of staff, the closure of colleges, the quarantine of some Jesuit communities and the dispersion of others, the financial difficulties experienced by some colleges as a result of the pest, the difficulty in maintaining discipline and adherence to the Society's regulations, and trouble communicating with other Jesuit communities in Sicily and with General Mercurian in Rome. At first in August 1575 the provincial of Sicily, Jerónimo Domenech, assured General Mercurian that Polanco's visit was a success despite the epidemic, but come November he was forced to admit that the presence of the pest in Palermo, Monreale, Bivona, and Messina made it impossible to accomplish everything that was necessary.[95] Polanco himself recognized the difficulty in enforcing "the regulations, the constitutions, and our manner of proceeding" in the midst of the epidemic.[96] Other Jesuit visitors faced similar difficulties at other places during other epidemics, the most notable being the itinerant Jerónimo Nadal, whose visits encountered outbreaks of disease in 1555, 1562, 1566, and 1568.[97]

The financial situation of most Jesuit institutions was precarious at the best of times, and epidemics made it worse. During 1570, for example, the college at Vienna incurred an additional six hundred florins in expenses as a result of the pest.[98] As discussed in chapter 5, public regulations could reduce the incomes, raise the costs, and otherwise play havoc with the budgets of Jesuit institutions. Juan Polanco discovered that public regulations aside, the college at Messina could not collect what it was owed as a result of "the trou-

---

[94]Ibid., 384, October 30.

[95]ITAL 148: 245; 149: 129, Catania, August 29 and November 18.

[96]Polanco, *Complementa*, 2: 414, 455, to Mercurian, Catania, November 25, 1575, and January 21, 1576.

[97]Loyola, *Epistolae*, 9: 442, to Nadal, Rome, August 10, 1555; Lainez, *Lainii monumenta*, 6: 468, to Hoffaeus, Trent, October 31, 1562; Nadal, *Epistolae*, 2: 131, Lainez to Nadal, Trent, November 14, 1562; 3: 322, Borgia to Nadal, Rome, December 3, 1566; 4: 621, to Borgia, Verdun, July 25, 1568.

[98]GERM 133 I: 17, Adalbert Bauzek to Borgia, January 4, 1571.

bles of the times" and in turn could not pay its own debts, and he attempted to solve the severe economic difficulties of the college by transferring Jesuits elsewhere.[99] Epidemics could affect the financial situation of Jesuit colleges in many different ways beyond the obvious expense of preventive medicine and medical treatment. At Barcelona in 1558 and at Lisbon in 1569 Jesuits discovered that the flight of many, and mainly the wealthy, resulted not only in decreased alms for the poor but also in decreased donations to the Society,[100] and at Lisbon relief for the poor took the money that might have otherwise gone to the Jesuit colleges.[101] On occasion colleges suffered financially when they had to feed Jesuits fleeing from epidemics in other towns. This happened to the colleges at Munich in 1564, at Mainz in 1568, and at Montilla in 1569.[102] In 1571 the college at Pultusk lost three hundred florins of income because a terrible epidemic of pest made it impossible to harvest the fields.[103] The final way epidemics could hurt the finances of the Society was through theft. In addition to the loss of 4,000 to 5,000 *francs* from the abandoned Jesuit residence at Paris in 1562, during an epidemic at Pont-à-Mousson in 1585 many furnishings disappeared from the college.[104]

On rare occasions epidemics could help the finances of a Jesuit community. Jesuit service of the sick at Siracusa in 1558 so impressed some people that they made donations to the Society.[105] In 1575 a wealthy friend left his estate to the Jesuit college at Maastricht after succumbing to the pest.[106] And in the same year, even the hard-pressed college at Messina gained an additional two hundred scudi in income as a result of the epidemic.[107] The college at Monreale

[99]Polanco, *Complementa*, 2: 446, 511, to Mercurian, Catania and Palermo, January 17 and April 2, 1576.
[100]Lainez, *Lainii monumenta*, 3: 208, Gesti to Lainez, Barcelona, March 21, 1558; LUS 63: 220, Lião Anriquez to Borgia, Evora, December 4, 1569.
[101]LUS 63: 179, Anriquez to Borgia, Coimbra, October 7.
[102]Canisius, *Beati Petri Canisii*, 4: 699, Polanco to Canisius, Rome, October 20, 1564; GERM 149: 59, Vinck to Borgia, Mainz, March 7; Francis Borgia, *Sanctus Franciscus Borgia quartus Gandiae dux et Societatis Jesu praepositus generalis*, 5 vols. (Madrid: Augustini Avrial and Gabrielis Lopez del Horno, 1894–1911), 5: 134, Juan de Vergara to Borgia, Montilla, July 24.
[103]GERM 133 II: 345, Antonio Francesco to Maggio, September 4.
[104]Auguste Carayon, ed., *Documents inédits concernant la Compagnie de Jésus*, vol. 5=*L'Université de Pont-à-Mousson* (Poitiers: Henri Oudin, 1870), 202.
[105]*Litterae quadrimestres*, 5: 890, by Labaco, December 1.
[106]GERM 155: 81v, Balduin Dawant to Mercurian, Louvain, April 20.
[107]ITAL 149: 224, Romena to Polanco, Messina, December 8.

also received bequests in 1575, some of which obliged the Jesuits to say masses for the souls of the benefactors. This was contrary to the Society's regulations, but the needs of the college were so great as a result of the epidemic that the rector asked Polanco if he could make an exception in this case.[108] In addition to the possibility of gaining bequests and donations, epidemics could present Jesuit superiors with opportunities to improve untenable situations. In 1575 Juan Polanco used the refusal of the authorities at Messina to pay for the college during the epidemic as an excuse to transfer the studies of philosophy and theology to Catania, which was the location of the university.[109] Superiors in France acted in a similar manner; they used an outbreak of pest at Verdun in 1569 as an excuse to close the unsuccessful college,[110] and they thought that the epidemic at Avignon in 1577 was a good occasion to attempt to obtain more money from the magistrates to finance the college there. All these donations, bequests, and opportunities failed, however, to overcome the severe financial difficulties that resulted from epidemic disease.

In addition to creating havoc with the budgets of Jesuit communities, epidemics disrupted classes and routines and on occasion discipline. Polanco reported on the disruption of the Jesuit novitiate, which he transferred to Catania in 1575 to escape the pest at Messina. Disorder reigned in Catania; "there was accommodation for only twenty-five or thirty people, nothing to eat, no school except for the humanities, [and no] money."[111] Less tangible than food and money were the psychological effects of epidemics. According to Heinrich Blessem, the college at Prague continued to suffer for a year from the distraction and weakness caused by the epidemic of 1582–1583.[112] Jesuit superiors attempted to minimize disorder and distraction. One of the guidelines for colleges affected by the pest encouraged the maintenance of happiness, charity, and recreation but also recommended the promotion of regular routines and exercises.[113] When Nadal visited the college at Vienna during the epidemic of 1562, according to Abrosius Sanctinus, he abolished "the harsh dis-

---

[108]Ibid., 215, Ippolito Voglia to Mercurian, Monreale, December 6; Polanco, *Complementa*, 2: 422, to Mercurian, Catania, December 20.

[109]Polanco, *Complementa*, 2: 368–69, to Mercurian, October 5, 1565.

[110]GAL 82: 102, André Dawant to Manare, Paris, July 30; 119v, 137, Manare to Borgia, Lyon, August 15 and 31.

[111]Polanco, *Complementa*, 2: 445, to Mercurian, January 17, 1576.

[112]GERM 162: 47v, to Aquaviva, Graz, January 10, 1584.

[113]OPP NN 159: 514, *Istruttione da praticarsi*.

cipline, which included very frequent flagellation and fasting. In its place he prescribed very frequent prayer and confession and communion twice a week." Sanctinus observed that this regimen succeeded in reducing the fears and melancholy of the Jesuits.[114] Instead of flagellation and fasting, Polanco discovered that the Jesuits at Messina had used the epidemic as an excuse to stop singing the mass and vespers, and those at Palermo had done the same with vespers. Polanco was inclined to permit the practice to continue, especially for the Jesuits at Messina, "because in truth they do not know how to sing well." [115] Polanco twice assured Mercurian that despite the presence of the pest and the subsequent closure of colleges and cessation of other activities, the Jesuits were not wasting their time but were continuing to study through private lessons.[116] Other Jesuits sent similar assurances to their superiors. To cite two examples, even though the epidemic of pest at Trier in 1564 had endured for almost half the year, Anton Vinck claimed, "In all this time we have continued with our normal exercises in the churches and in the schools," [117] and according to the annual letter from Vienna in 1571 the "fearful pestilence" that lasted for nine months "was endured with such patience that neither the domestic study of letters and piety nor the public ministry ceased." [118]

In December 1562 Francisco Sunyer assured Juan Polanco that in spite of the widespread epidemic of pest in his province, "all these colleges remain very quiet through a singular grace of the Lord, and there is not the least difficulty in any of them." Judging from the lack of comments in the accounts, Sunyer's experience was typical, but on at least two occasions epidemics produced disciplinary problems. The first occurred at the Jesuit college in Padua. When the vice provincial, Mario Beringucci, visited it in August 1577, he discovered, as he informed General Mercurian, that "the affairs of that college are very loose, and regular discipline is very negligent; this results in part from a failure to maintain a regimen during the entire time of the pest." [119] In a subsequent letter, however, Beringucci asserted that the negligence occurred in matters that were not very important.[120]

---

[114]Nadal, *Epistolae*, 2: 621, *quadrimestris*, April 27, 1563.

[115]Polanco, *Complementa*, 2: 372, 451, to Mercurian, Messina, and Catania, October 6, 1575, and January 17, 1576.

[116]Ibid., 388, 499, Catania and Palermo, October 30, 1575, and March 21, 1576.

[117]GERM 145: 266, to Lainez, December 14.

[118]GERM 133 II: 399v, September 30, 1571.

[119]ITAL 154: 364, Venice, August 17.

[120]Ibid., 390, August 24.

The other disciplinary problem occurred at Venice and was more drawn out and more complicated than the minor difficulty at Padua. It began in July 1576 when Cesare Helmi tried to send eight Jesuits to the safety of a hostel belonging to the college at Padua. Most of these Jesuits refused to go to the hostel because they feared it was not safe enough, and when Helmi tried to find a villa where they could all be together and so maintain their religious life, some wanted to flee by themselves. Another Jesuit, Flaminio Ricchieri, told Helmi that he was afraid of dying from the pest and that if he or any others wanted to flee Helmi could not stop them.[121] Although the documentation is incomplete, apparently many Jesuits fled and found accommodation wherever they could, most of them in villas near Verona. After Helmi died, his replacement, Domenico Cosso, tried in December to get these Jesuits to return to Venice to help serve the sick. Some including Ricchieri returned, others did not.[122] When Mario Beringucci arrived in mid-January, he found a house that "has had spiritual and corporal tribulations, especially after the death of good Father Cesare, because some have had doubts concerning the legitimacy of Father Domenico Cosso's authority." [123] As it turned out, most of the antagonism was between Cosso and Ricchieri, who accused him of usurping Helmi's position. The affair dragged on for many months. In August, Mercurian requested a detailed report from Beringucci, who responded on September 14. Although his comments were cautious and his criticisms implicit, Beringucci supported Ricchieri's view concerning Cosso, took the side of Ricchieri in the resulting disputes with Cosso, and made excuses for Ricchieri's flight.[124] Ricchieri died a Jesuit in 1603; Cosso either left the Society or was dismissed from it—the records do not state which—in October 1578, which might be an indication that Cosso was at fault.

According to one study, 35 percent of the Jesuits either left the Society or were dismissed from it,[125] so Cosso's departure was not extraordinary. What is extraordinary is the few disciplinary problems encountered by Jesuit superiors in the wake of epidemic disease. In "normal" times the Society's record was far

---

[121]ITAL 151: 312, 314, Helmi to Mercurian, July 14; see also 155: 47v, Beringucci to Mercurian, Venice, September 14, 1577.

[122]ITAL 152: 358, Buonacorso to Mercurian, Vicenza, December 17.

[123]ITAL 153: 100, to [Mercurian], Venice, February 6, 1577.

[124]ITAL 155: 47–48, Beringucci to Mercurian, Venice.

[125]See Martin, "Vocational Crises," 205.

worse. Although no evidence supports the contention, perhaps the disciplinary problems receded during epidemics because Jesuit communities provided religious, physical, and psychological security in spite of the increased dangers of contracting the disease through service of the sick. Far worse than the disciplinary problems were the financial difficulties suffered by Jesuit communities as a result of epidemic disease, difficulties that exacerbated their already precarious financial situation. Over time, however, most communities would have recovered. No evidence suggests that any Jesuit institution disappeared as a result of a budgetary crisis initiated by an epidemic. As already mentioned on several occasions, the real losses for the Society of Jesus were Jesuits, whether they were victims of charity or simple victims of disease.

———

EIGHT

C_ONCLUSI_ON

THE FREQUENT JESUIT ENCOUNTERS with epidemic disease in the sixteenth century, the deaths of brethren and others, the financial difficulties, and the interruption of their work in colleges and churches did not result in widespread despair, anger, or pessimism. To be sure, many Jesuits shared in the widespread fear of pestilence, some were appalled by the slaughter, and a few suffered emotional trauma. During the religious wars in France, some Jesuits exhibited impatience with the interruptions created by the interminable conflict. The fighting interfered with Jesuit efforts to educate the young, save souls, and convert heretics.[1] Implicit in the Jesuit reaction to disease was the same impatience; the epidemics interrupted and interfered with the Jesuits' educational and religious programs. During some outbreaks Jesuit communities attempted to maintain their normal activities, even refusing to close their schools, and at the first signs of the end to an epidemic they were likewise keen to recommence any work that had been interrupted. The Society of Jesus was an activist religious order, and Ignatius Loyola wanted his followers to lead an active life of Christian service. The Jesuit response to epidemic disease reinforces this aspect of the Society's character.

A psychological prerequisite for an active life is a sense of optimism—a belief that action produces results. In contrast to religious movements such as

---

[1] See A. Lynn Martin, *The Jesuit Mind: The Mentality of an Elite in Early Modern France* (Ithaca: Cornell University Press, 1988), 91.

Calvinism and Jansenism that took their inspiration from Saint Augustine, Jesuits had an optimistic rather than a pessimistic view of divine providence. Jesuits, as did Calvinists and Jansenists, believed that God sent pestilence as a punishment for sin; God was the primary cause of disease, and penitence was the primary remedy: "Go and sin no more!" Jesuits, however, did not view divine providence in just this negative sense, for they considered that punishment for sin was only one of the reasons why God sent epidemics. Pestilence had educational and monitory functions, and God used it to reveal his friends and confound his enemies. No evidence suggests that Jesuits ever lost their faith in divine providence as a result of epidemic disease If the pest spared a community or slaughtered thousands, if a Jesuit succumbed while serving the sick or recovered, Jesuits continued to sing the praises of the Lord.

What is more surprising is that Jesuits likewise retained their faith in the medical profession and its preservatives and remedies. One reason for their continued faith is related to their optimistic view of divine providence: A merciful God supplied people with secondary remedies to cure their physical infirmities. Hence, Jesuit superiors recommended that communities consult with medical practitioners, follow their advice, and take their medicines, even though this exacerbated the financial difficulties that resulted from epidemics. The confidence could have been shaken—though no evidence suggests that it was—as a result of the cases, some of which were notorious, when doctors could not agree on a diagnosis of an individual or an entire epidemic. On occasion some Jesuits enthusiastically reported on medical remedies that seemed to work. Since the accounts indicate that twenty-nine Jesuits recovered from the pest, on at least twenty-nine occasions a sixteenth-century medical practitioner could accept the credit for saving the life of a Jesuit, even if the Jesuits themselves were in the first instance ready to give the credit to a beneficent divinity. By the sixteenth century most of the medical profession had accepted the popular opinion of pestilence as a contagious disease, and as a consequence doctors were prescribing flight or segregation as the best means of protection. Jesuits followed this advice as best they could. Some stayed to serve the sick and guard the buildings while the majority fled to neighboring colleges, villas, or towns.

I have called the Jesuit policy humane and sensible, sensible because it preserved the lives of the majority including the young, who were the Society's future, and including the superiors, who were the rudders of the young

Society, humane because it did not neglect the Society's special responsibility to the sick and the poor. The Society's record was not as good as that of the Capuchins, so one could denigrate the Jesuit efforts in the service of the sick. Carlo Borromeo denigrated Jesuit efforts, perhaps a bit unfairly, and in *la guerra di San Carlo* my sympathies tend toward the Society, even though it was not blameless in the dispute. Many Jesuits who served the sick took sensible precautions, primarily by keeping a healthy distance between themselves and the sick whenever possible, while Capuchins rushed in mindless of the consequences. Be that as it may, Jesuits could proudly point to at least ninety-two victims of charity. Because the documentation is incomplete as a result of the disappearance of so much of the correspondence from the Jesuit Archives, the total number of victims could be much higher, as could the total number of Jesuits who succumbed to epidemic disease in the sixteenth century.

The deaths of its members created obvious staffing problems for the Society. During his first thirteen years as general, from 1581 to 1594, Claudio Aquaviva had to reject 150 proposals to establish new Jesuit educational institutions for lack of sufficient staff. In 1569 General Francis Borgia had stipulated that the number of staff required to operate a college was thirty,[2] so by that criterion alone the deaths of 494 Jesuits through epidemic disease meant sixteen fewer colleges. In spite of Borgia's regulation, in 1575 the Society had 3,905 members who operated 210 institutions, an average of nineteen Jesuits for each institution, so that the 494 could have operated twenty-six colleges. Since the 494 deaths are documented in Jesuit accounts and since so much of the correspondence is no longer extant, these figures could be much higher, perhaps thousands of Jesuits dead and a hundred potential colleges. The correspondence documents one case of someone's joining the Society as a result of gaining a favorable impression of Jesuit service of the sick. Others might have done likewise. When asked why they had joined, four Polish Jesuits pointed to a close brush with pestilence.[3] In other words, the fear of death led some to embrace a religious life. So epidemic disease also helped staff Jesuit colleges; I doubt that the numbers were sufficient to compensate for the deaths. Another effect that epidemic disease had on the Society was in the area of preventive medicine.

---

[2]See Martin, *Jesuit Mind*, 20 n., 53.

[3]Unpublished manuscript by T. V. Cohen, citing *Universae Societatis Iesu vocationum liber autobiographicus.*

Jesuits adopted the Galenic therapeutic program of a proper diet and regular exercise, promoted moderation in physical, mental, and spiritual endeavors, sought healthy locations for their colleges and residences, and supported personal cleanliness. Rather than fatalistically accept their environment, Jesuits sought to modify it to preserve their health and prevent incursions by epidemics through the promotion of a positive program of preventive medicine.

Antonio Niero and William A. Christian have argued that one effect of pestilence was a turn away from the cults of Mary and the saints and toward a Christocentric piety. Jesuit piety was always Christocentric, but in the midst of epidemics Jesuits also turned to the Virgin Mary and to the saints, especially those regarded as protectors from pestilence, Sebastian and Rocco, and in the seventeenth century they would turn to San Carlo Borromeo. Instead of interpreting this as a move away from Christocentric piety, I view it as a manifestation of the special circumstances that existed during epidemics when Jesuits and others utilized every remedy available to them in the spiritual pharmacopeia. In addition to the cults of Mary and the saints, Jesuits and other Catholics turned of course to petitionary prayer and fasts as well as processions, pilgrimages, and the sacraments of confession and communion—remedies not available to Protestants. In summary, Jesuits could face epidemics with equanimity and perhaps even bravery, confident in divine providence, in the medical profession, in their therapeutic program and preventive medicine, and in the spiritual remedies available to them; and if this was not enough, they could flee.

Jesuits tried to spread their views on divine providence and spiritual remedies throughout Catholic Europe, for these views derived from the doctrines of the Catholic Church, whose champion was the Society of Jesus. Wherever they went, Jesuits promoted religious remedies such as fasts, processions, and pilgrimages. The most obvious example of this effort was Antonio Possevino's pamphlet, *The Causes and Remedies of the Pest and of Other Diseases.* According to Possevino the one cause was sin, and the one remedy was penitence, which would give little help to readers seeking practical help; but his program of personal renewal provided comfort to those confronting the terrors of an epidemic. Some Jesuits noted that a serious epidemic was an ideal occasion to achieve a religious reformation and renewal, and many applauded the positive effects that pestilence had on the religious life and morals of a city; but the evidence does not permit an evaluation of the endurance of such renewals. In addition to promoting their views on divine providence, Jesuits incorporated many aspects of their therapeutic program and preventive medicine in the regimen at their colleges; the goal was a sound mind in a healthy body.[4]

Many Jesuits who served in missions or taught in colleges north of the Alps were Italian, and many who were not Italian had completed their novitiate in Italy or received some of their education there. So they had an opportunity to observe the public health regulations initiated by the cities of northern Italy and to promote their adoption north of the Alps, especially since Jesuits often became advisers to religious and political leaders. Many Jesuits on missions in northern Europe deplored the efforts of magistrates to contain epidemics, but their correspondence provides no evidence of their attempts to influence policies. I suspect that they did so. Wherever Jesuits went they courted the favor of local rulers, both secular and religious, as the best means of advancing their religious and educational programs. Hence they followed the advice contained in Loyola's *Constitutions* "to retain the benevolence … of the temporal rulers and noble and powerful persons whose favor or disfavor does much toward opening or closing the gate to the service of God."[5] Many Jesuits attempted to circumvent the regulations established by local authorities to control outbreaks of epidemic disease, especially those concerned with the exchange of correspondence. Although the evidence does not permit a definite assessment, on occasion Jesuit circumvention of the regulations probably resulted in the diminution or the loss of the benevolence of some temporal rulers. Jesuits were such devoted letter writers, however, that they would have no doubt justified their actions by adopting Juan Polanco's casuistry: "Sometimes you lose more than you gain in divine service."

Returning to J.-P. Goubert's advice contained in the introduction, is a retrospective diagnosis of any epidemic encountered by Jesuits in the sixteenth century likely, probable, or irrefutable? The most probable is that of epidemic influenza during the years 1557, 1562–1563, and 1580. The patterns of high morbidity and low mortality combine with the descriptions of the usual symptoms of influenza to make a diagnosis that is more than likely but not quite irrefutable. Epidemics of typhus are in the likely category, but the accounts produce

---

[4]On this point see Philippe Ariès, *Centuries of Childhood: A Social History of Family Life* (New York: Vintage Books, 1965), 88–89.

[5]Ignatius Loyola, *The Constitutions of the Society of Jesus*, ed. George E. Ganss (St. Louis: Institute of Jesuit Sources, 1970), [824].

very little evidence of Jesuit encounters with smallpox and nothing on measles. Throughout this book I have refused to concede that Jesuits encountered epidemics of bubonic plague in the sixteenth century. Jesuit accounts contain descriptions of symptoms comparable to bubonic plague—buboes in areas associated with the lymph glands, that is, the groin, thigh, and armpit, carbuncles on the extremities, and fevers. They also indicate a mortality rate comparable to bubonic plague, and, as in modern cases of the plague, death came quickly after the appearance of symptoms. Some epidemics also spread in an erratic manner, creeping, nibbling, and meandering in the manner of modern epidemics of plague. On rare occasions the accounts also provide evidence of a comparable incubation period of from one to six days. On the other hand, when the accounts provide evidence of a comparable incubation period they do so by demonstrating chains of infection, as in the cases of priests who heard confessions at a hospital and became sick within several days. Some of those who served the sick remained unaffected, and some of those who segregated themselves in Jesuit residences contracted the disease, but the general pattern was the reverse; exposure to the sick increased the chances of infection. These chains of infection and the perception of the disease as contagious could on occasion indicate interhuman spread of the bubonic plague through *P. irritans*, so even if the classic model of plague—*Y. pestis, R. rattus,* and *X. cheopis*—does not work, at least the model proposed by the French flea school could fit the patterns observed by Jesuits. In short, all this evidence could produce a retrospective diagnosis that is likely and even probable.

Other evidence produces a different conclusion; namely, that if Jesuits did indeed encounter bubonic plague, the disease acted in a manner much different from modern observations of it. This "retrospective diagnosis" is in the category of "irrefutable." Jesuits documented a disease that was so contagious that on occasion interhuman spread via *P. irritans* could not explain some cases. Jesuits became infected after encounters with the sick that were too fleeting and too distant to result in the large transfer of human fleas necessary for infection. Even the proponents of the French human flea school argue that an epidemic of bubonic plague requires the initial presence of the black rat, and Jesuits made observations on the climatic conditions of wind, humidity, and temperature and reported on ominous astronomical phenomena but still failed to notice a single dead rat. The only animals mentioned in all the Jesuit accounts were the unbridled horses of Mario Beringucci's rhetoric, the pigs and horses eaten by peasants during a famine in Poland, mules for transport-ing the fleeing population of Seville, more mules captured by the Huguenots outside Avignon, dead cats in the Jesuit residence at Paris, and toads in the stinking houses of Coimbra. In addition to all this, the seasonality of the epi-demics does not fit the conditions preferred by that unholy trinity of culprits; Mediterranean Europe had epidemics in conditions of excessive heat and low humidity, while northern Europe had epidemics during the cool months of late autumn and early winter. On occasion both northern and southern Europe had epidemics during winter; according to the modern epidemiology of plague, the existence of an epidemic of the bubonic form during winter could develop into the even deadlier pneumonic form. Yet Jesuit accounts are as silent on the pneumonic form of the plague as they are on dead rats. The absence of the pneumonic form indicates that if indeed Jesuits encountered outbreaks of bubonic plague, the disease did not act according to modern medical observations; in other words, that a change has occurred either through the mutation of the plague bacillus or through a modification in the relationship between hosts. As a result of all these factors the retrospective diagnosis cannot be an irrefutable, probable, or even likely plague but must be "plague?"

——◆——

OUTBREAKS OF EPIDEMIC DISEASE IN JESUIT CORRESPONDENCE

ALL EPIDEMICS ARE OF pest unless otherwise indicated; when I name other diseases, I include pest only if the documents mention it along with the others. In order to be included in this chronology the evidence must indicate that an outbreak of disease affected the wider community and not just Jesuits.

Date	Place	Notes
Albania		
1576 May	Albania	
Austria		
1553 March–April	Vienna	
1560 November–December	Vienna	
1561 August–1562 April	Vienna	
1562 September–1563 April	Vienna	
1563 September–1564 April	Vienna	pest, epidemic, contagious disease, pestiferous fever
1563 September	environs of Innsbruck	
1564 April–December	Innsbruck	
1566 November	Innsbruck	

Date	Place	Notes
1569 November–1570 January	Vienna	
1570 July–1572 January	Vienna	pest, contagious epidemic
1571 November–1572 October	Graz	
1572 October	Vienna	
1575 March	Graz	epidemic of pestilential fever, acute and malignant fever
1575 July–December	Vienna	pest with malignant fever and dysentery
1576 August–1577 January	Vienna	epidemic of pest
1576 November	Graz	pest, contagious pestilence, dysentery
1577 June–November	Vienna	
1577 August–1578 January	Graz	
1580 August–September	Vienna	catarrh
1582 October–1583 January	Vienna	
1583 November–1584 May	Vienna	pest, contagious epidemic
1585 September–November	Graz	
1585	Vienna	pestiferous epidemic
1597 July–September	Vienna	pest, pestiferous epidemic, contagion
1598 October	Vienna	pest, epidemic
1599	Graz	fever and dysentery
1600 October	Graz	

Date	Place	Notes
Belgium		
1556 July–August	Tournai	pestilence
1564 August	Tournai	
1569 September	Namur	
1572 June–December	Tournai	
1572 July–August	Liège	
1574 May–October	Tournai	pest, contagious malady
1575 May	almost all of Belgium	
1575 July	Bruges, Tournai	
1578 September–October	Namur	contagion of pest
1578 September–January	Louvain	contagion of pest
1578 September–January	Liège	contagion of pest, pestilence
1579 June–September	Louvain	contagion of disease, pest
1579 August– 1580 January	Liège	dysentery, contagious disease
1583 October–November	Belgium	contagion of pest
1596 November	Liège	
1598	Liège	
Byelorussia		
1596	Nesvizh	epidemic
1599	Nesvizh	illness
Czechoslovakia		
1562 summer– 1563 February	Trnava	
1562 November– 1563 February	Prague	
1563 November	Kosice and environs	pestilence

Date	Place	Notes
1563 November	Bratislava	
1568 January	Prague	
1568 August–1569 January	Prague	
1570 October– 1571 January	Olomouc and environs	pest, contagious disease
1571 1st half of year	Prague	pestiferous fevers
1571 October– 1572 February	Olomouc	
1571 October– 1572 February	Brno	
1582 June–1583 January	Prague	contagious epidemic, pest
1582 August–September	Plzen	contagion
1582 September– November	Olomouc	
1583 summer	Brno	fevers
1583 December– 1584 January	Brno	
1584 May–August	Brno	new type of pest
1584 December– 1585 March	Olomouc	contagion, pest
1585 January–March	Brno	
1585 autumn	Prague	
1597 May	Jindrichuv Hradec (Neuhaus), Cesky Krumlov	
1597 October	Brno	pest or dysentery or whatever other disease, epidemic
1597–1598 February	Jindrichuv Hradec	epidemic
1598 July	environs of Chomutov	
1598 autumn	Prague	pestiferous epidemic

Date	Place	Notes
1598–1599	Cesky Krumlov	pestilence, pest
1599	Zillina	
1599 early	Olomouc	pestilence, pest
1599 September–October	Prague	
Egypt		
1562 April	Cairo	
1562 October	Alexandria	
1566	Alexandria	
England		
1570 summer	England	
1593 September	London	
France		
1553 July–1554 January	Paris and environs	
1557	Billom, Auvergne	varied and great diseases caused by raging weather
1561 July–September	Paris	
1562 April	Pamiers	
1562 July–1563 February	Paris and environs	
1562 September	Saint-Cloud	
1562 December	Paris	catarrh (coincides with pest)
1563 February	Toulouse, Rodez	coughs, headache, fevers, and an ache in the side
1563 September	Tournon	
1563 October	Toulouse, Perpignan	
1564 May–November	Lyon	
1564 July	environs of Paris, Picardy	

Date	Place	Notes
1564 August–October	Avignon	
1564 September	Clermont, Billom, Auvergne, Languedoc, Tournon	
1566 March	Avignon	
1566 June	Carpentras	
1566 September	Chambéry	
1568 July–1569 August	Verdun	
1570 June–July	environs of Chambéry	
1570 September	Paris and environs	many infirmities
1570 September	Toulouse	infirmity of fever and dysentery
1571 ended October	Cambrai	
1572 May	Cambrai	
1572 June	Rodez	contagious infirmity with great frenzy
1572 September	Douai	
1573 May–September	Toulouse	pestilential fever, a certain infirmity
1575 July	Douai, Saint-Omer	
1577 March–June	Lyon	
15⁻7 April	Le Puy-en-Velay, Montpellier, Dauphiné	
1577 April–May	environs of Tournon and of Chambéry	
1577 July–December	Chambéry	
1577 August–December	Avignon	fever and dysentery, disease, pestilential fever, malicious malady
1577 August–December	Pont-à-Mousson	

Date	Place	Notes
1577 September–October	Billom, Auvergne	dysentery and fever
1579 July–August	Douai	contagious disease
1579 July–September	Pont-à-Mousson	dysentery
1579 August–September	Pont-à-Mousson	
1580	Molsheim	epidemic of pestiferous contagion
1580 June	Lyon	coqueluche
1580 May–July	Burgundy	catarrh with fever, very sharp headache and stomachache
1580 September–1581 September	Avignon	pest, epidemic of disease
1580 autumn	Alsace	
1581	Lyon	pestilence, epidemic of pest
1581	environs of Tournon	
1581 March	Carpentras	
1581 March–August	Verdun	contagion, pestilence
1581 July–1582 January	Paris	pest, contagious epidemic
1581 August–September	Billom	pest, contagious and pestilential disease
1581 September–November	Douai	contagion of pest
1581 autumn–1583 March	Molsheim	pest, disease of pestilence, pestilential epidemic
1582	Lyon	
1582 January–February	Douai	contagion of pest
1582 June–September	Bourges	
1582 November–1583 January	Douai	contagion of pest
1583	Nevers	

Date	Place	Notes
1583 January	environs of Saint-Omer	contagion of pest
1584	Molsheim	epidemic of dysentery, pestilence
1584 July–September	Nevers	pest, contagion
1584 September–November	Paris	pest, epidemic
1585	Lyon	pestilence
1585	environs of Tournon, Avignon, Bordeaux	
1585 July–October	Pont-à-Mousson	pest, pestilence
1586	Avignon	
1586 February	Auvergne	contagion
1586 March–June	Rodez	disease, epidemic
1586 June–August	Lyon	
1586 July–August	Dijon	disease, pest
1586 July	Chambéry	
1587 January	Dole	
1587 July–October	Chambéry	epidemic, pestilence
1587 August–September	Bourges	pestilence, epidemic
1587 August–September	Verdun	pestilence
1587 August	Pont-à-Mousson, Dole, Dijon	pestilence
1588	Lyon, Pont-à-Mousson	
1588 July	Toulouse	pestilence, epidemic
1588 April–June	Billom	pestilence
1588 September	Verdun	
1596	Saint-Omer	infectious influenza
1596	Cambrai, Avignon	

Date	Place	Notes
1596 May	Chambéry and environs	pestilential disease, epidemic, pest
1596 September–October	Douai	
1596 September–1597 December	Saint-Omer	
1597	Molsheim	
1597	Besançon	pestilential disease, pest
1597 November–1598 August	Lille	
1598	Chambéry	
1598 August–September	Molsheim	contagion
1599	Chambéry	
1599 July– August	Lille	
Germany		
1546 October	Regensburg	
1552 December–1554 January	Cologne	pest and frenzy of the head (*capitis insania*)
1554	Cologne	
1562 August–1563 January	Munich	pest, pestilential epidemic
1562 November	Nürnberg	
1563 March–May	Munich	contagion
1563 June–1564 April	Augsburg	
1563 September–October	Bavaria	contagious and pestilential epidemic, pest
1563 September	Ingolstadt, Munich	
1563 October–November	Mainz	
1564 April	Munich, Ingolstadt	
1564 April–November	Cologne	
1564 August–1565 January	Trier	pest, plague

Date	Place	Notes
1564 August–December	Mainz	pestiferous disease, pest
1564 September– 1565 January	Augsburg	
1564 December	Munich	
1565 spring	Dillingen	
1565 September– 1566 January	Trier	
1566 June–July	Cologne	
1566 July–October	Trier	
1567 summer	Mainz	pestiferous air
1567 May–October	Trier	
1568 March	Cologne	
1570 November	Frankfurt an der Oder (environs)	
1571 February	Ingolstadt	I know not what kind of disease
1571 June	Munich	Hungarian disease
1571 autumn– 1572 February	Mainz	
1572	Baden-Baden	
1572 August–December	Munich	
1574 August–December	Cologne	
1574 September–October	Trier	
1574 October	Mainz, Speyer, Wurzburg, environs of Fulda	
1575	Cologne	
1575 July–August	Speyer	
1575 autumn	Fulda	pest, pestilential epidemic
1575 November	Mainz, Wurzburg	

Date	Place	Notes
1576	Cologne	
1576 June–July	Trier	
1576 August–1577 February	Mainz	
1576 October–1577 February	Cologne	
1577 September–November	Cologne	
1577 October–November	Wurzburg	
1580	Heiligenstadt	a pestilential disease
1580 August	Fulda, Mainz, Speyer	illness
1580 August	Cologne	pest, contagious disease of pest
1581 August–1582 February	Heiligenstadt	
1582 February	Speyer	
1582 July–1583 February	Mainz	
1582 September	Paderborn	
1582 November–1583 January	Koblenz, Speyer	
1583 October	Saxony	
1584 August	Trier	
1584 October	Fulda and environs	dysentery
1584 December	Fulda	
1585	Wurzburg	
1585 May–September	Cologne	pest, epidemic of contagion
1585 November–1586 March	Trier	epidemic of pest
1586 November–December	Augsburg	

Date	Place	Notes
1587 June–November	Trier	new disease, epidemic
1589 February	Hall	
1592	Landsberg	pestiferous epidemic
1592 July– 1593 January	Augsburg	pest, pestilential epidemic, pestiferous contagion
1596	Mainz	
1597	Koblenz, Erfurt	
1597	Paderborn	pestilential epidemic
1597	Speyer, Cologne	pestiferous contagion
1597	Heiligenstadt	pestilential disease
1597	Wurzburg	contagion (pestilence)
1597	Mainz	epidemic, pestilence
1597 August	Trier	pestilential disease, contagious disease
1597 September– December	Fulda	disease (pestilence)
1599 July	Regensburg	
Greece		
1570 July	Zakinthos	petechia or severe cold accompanied by general ill health (*mal di mazzucco*)
Italy		
1552 December	Rome	
1555 May–July	Venice	
1555 June–October	Padua	pest, pestiferous and deadly disease
1556 September– November	Bivona	

Date	Place	Notes
1556 September– 1557 January	Venice	
1557 January–March	Padua	
1557 April	Tivoli	infirmity with fever
1557 July	Loreto	petechia
1557 July	Bologna	infirmity of catarrh, fever, and headache
1557 July	Florence, Padua	infirmity
1557 July	Perugia	influenza
1557 July–August	Rome	influenza (catarrh and fever)
1557 summer	Loreto, Le Marche	a great infestation of the air, almost like half a pest
1557 September	Siracusa	sickness
1557 November– 1558 March	Ferrara	pest, type of pest caused by the influence of the air, varied diseases and illnesses
1557 December	Palermo	influenza
1558 January–March	Modena	a certain type of fever
1558 January	Florence	influenza
1558 July–September	Palermo	many infirmities, a contagious fever just like the pest
1558 summer–September	Siracusa	pestilential fevers and petechia
1560 August	Le Marche	general illnesses
1561 July–August	Palermo	many sick
1562 December	Rome	catarrh and fever = infection and influenza (type of pest)
1562 December	Nola	influenza of a general and pestiferous catarrh

Date	Place	Notes
1562 December	Naples	contagious catarrh
1562 December	Messina	catarrh
1563 January	Loreto	catarrh and fevers
1563 winter	Sassari	catarrh
1564 March	Chiavenna (north of Como)	
1564 October	Chivasso, Rivoli, Avigliano (Piedmont)	
1566 February	Naples	pestiferous fevers
1566 September–October	Rome	infirmity caused by the infection of the water
1568 summer–autumn	Tivoli	epidemic similar to that at Rome
1568 August–December	Rome	epidemic similar to that of 1566
1569 summer	Ferrara	great infirmity
1569	Venice	grave and contagious infirmity
1570 spring–summer	Brescia	petechia
1571 February–March	Loreto	pestilential fever, petechia
1572 March	Cagliari	a widespread disease
1575 June–1577 August	Messina	pest, contagious infirmity
1575 June–1576 May	Palermo	pest, smallpox in the beginning, many fevers, contagious disease
1575 June–August	Environs of Bivona including Sciacca, Palazzo Adriano, Bisacquino but not at Bivona	pest, epidemic, contagious disease
1575 July–1576 May	Monreale	pest, pestiferous infirmity

Date	Place	Notes
1575 October–1576 February	Bivona	
1575 November–1577 July	Venice	
1576 January–April	Trapani	
1576 April–May	Agrigento	
1576 April	Marsala	
1576 April	Padua	petechia
1576 April–1577 May	Mantua	
1576 May–August	Catania	
1576 June–1577 March	Reggio in Calabria, Siracusa	
1576 July–1577 July	Padua	pest = contagious disease
1576 July–August	Marignan (near Milan)	
1576 July–1577 December	Milan	pest, petechia
1576 August	Polizzi, Monza	
1576 August–1577 December	Brescia	surrounded Brescia from August but not definitely in the town until October
1576 September	Arona	the disease = pest
1576 October	Iseo	
1577 April–September	Pavia	
1577 May	Parma	
1577 May–September	Palermo	pest, contagious disease
1577 June–July	Inzago	
1577 July	Trezzo, Calabria	
1577 July–August	Vicenza	
1577 August	Susa, environs of Turin	
1577 August–September	Genoa	widespread disease of deadly tertian fever

Date	Place	Notes
1578	Caltagirone	
1578 June	Messina	
1579	Corsica	
1579 April–June	Catania	
1579–1580 April	Genoa	pest combined with acute and contagious fever
1580 May–July	Turin, Savoy, Piedmont	catarrh with fever, very sharp headache and stomachache
1580 summer	Milan	feverish catarrh
1580	Sicily	catarrh
1581	Province of Venezia	very dangerous infirmity
1582 November–December	Venice	epidemic
1584	Milan	pestilential fever
1584 June	Brescia	type of disease
1585	Siena	influenza of a malady
1585	Rome	various infirmities
1591 February–June	Rome	type of pest
1592 March–April	Messina	many maladies
1599–1600	Turin	pestilence
Lithuania		
1569 November	Lithuania	
1571 August–1572 April	Vilnius	contagion of pest, contagious disease
1572 August	Lithuania	
1580 February–April	Vilnius	very grave illnesses
1588 October–1589 August	Vilnius	
1592	Vilnius	pestiferous fever

Date	Place	Notes
Macedonia		
1576 May	Skopje	
Moldavia		
1588 September	Moldavia	epidemic of pest
Netherlands		
1574 August	Nijmegen	
1577 August–September	Maastricht	contagious disease, epidemic, pestilence, pest
1579 October	Maastricht	contagion
1598 August	Maastricht	
1599 July–August	Maastricht	
Poland		
1563 November	Poznan	
1564 July	Pultusk	
1566 January	Braniewo	pest, pestiferous contagion
1568 September	Poznan	
1569 October–December	Pultusk	
1571 September–1572 January	Pultusk	
1571 October–1572 March	Braniewo	
1572 January	Mazowsze (Masovia)	
1572 February	Brok	
1572 July–December	Pultusk, Poznan	
1572 August–November	Braniewo	
1577 December	Prussia	
1578 October–November	Poznan	
1578 November	Mazowsze	

Date	Place	Notes
1578 November	Prussia	pest, pestilential epidemic
1580 March–April	Jaroslaw	very serious illnesses
1580 September	Prussia	pest, pestilential epidemic
1580 September	Poznan	
1580 September	Mazowsze	pestilential epidemic
1580 September–October	Braniewo	pest, pestilence
1581 November–December	Braniewo	a catarrhal and contagious epidemic
1584 September	Braniewo, Pultusk	dysentery
1585 June	environs of Poznan	
1585 August	environs of Cracow	
1586 February	Poznan	
1586 August	Gniesno	
1586 August–October	Poznan	
1588 June–1589 February	Pultusk	pest, epidemic
1588 August–1589 February	Poznan	pest, pestilence, epidemic
1588 September	Warsaw, Prussia	epidemic of pest
1588 September–December	Jaroslaw, Kalisch	
1588 September–1589 January	environs of Braniewo	epidemic, pest
1588 September–1589 February	Cracow	
1589 August	Poznan	disease of pest
1591 August–September	Cracow	
1592 May–1593 January	Jaroslaw	
1592 July–1593 January	Lublin, Cracow	
1599 July	Braniewo	epidemic of dysentery

Date	Place	Notes
1599–1600 January	Cracow	contagion, pest
1600	Jaroslaw	
1600 August	Poznan	
1600 autumn	Cracow	pest, pestiferous epidemic
Portugal		
1557 November	Coimbra	catarrh (*romadizo*)
1557 December	Coimbra	fevers, like *modorra*, a pestilence without a name
1562 December–1563 January	Coimbra	cold (*romadizo*)
1569 March–1570 January	Lisbon	pestilence, pest
1569 September	environs of Evora	
1570	Bragança	pestilence
1570 January–March	Braga	
1571	Angra (Azores)	pestilence, pestiferous epidemic
1575 April–October	Coimbra	contagious disease
1575 May	Porto	contagious disease
1575 June	Bragança	contagious diseases
1575 June–July	Lisbon	contagious diseases
1575 October	Evora	contagious diseases
1577	Lisbon, Angra, Porto	contagious diseases
1577 August–November	Evora	deadly disease
1579 March–September	Lisbon	pest, pestilence
1580	Lisbon	pestilence
1580 May–June	Evora	
1580 July–August	Coimbra	pestilence
1581	Benavente	pestilence

Date	Place	Notes
1581 over by April	Coimbra	
1581 April	Porto	pestilence
1581 over by May	Evora	pestilence
1587 September–November	Lisbon	contagious disease
1591 probably late in the year	Evora	erysipilas = Saint Anthony's fire
1592 August	Evora	epidemic of diseases
1597	Lisbon	almost pestilential epidemic of diseases
1597	Braga	almost pestilential disease
1597 April	Evora	almost pestilential disease
1599	Evora, Porto, Bragança, Braga	
1599 March	Lisbon	
1599 April–July	Coimbra	
1599 August	Angra	
Romania		
1555	Transylvania	
1585	Suplac	
1585 November–1586 January	Oradea	
1586 April	Transylvania	
1586 April–September	Oradea	pest, Saint Anthony's fire
1586 May–September	Cluj	
1586 May–1587 January	Alba Iulia	
1586 July	Kolozsmonostor, Karánsebes, Marosvásárlely	
1587 October	Sicula	

Date	Place	Notes
Russia		
1588 September	Muscovy	epidemic of pest
Slovenia		
1599 June–January 1600	Ljubljana	
Spain		
1555 summer	Alcalá de Henares	a type of pest, many diseases
1557	Barcelona	great diseases
1557	Salamanca	illnesses
1557 March	Alcalá de Henares	fevers
1557 March	Gandia	contagious diseases
1557 April–December	Plasencia	continual grave illnesses, catarrh
1557 June	Murcia	modorra
1557 June–1558 September	Valencia	*modorrilla* and pest
1557 summer	Cordoba	modorra
1557 summer	Magdalena	savage diseases
1557 September–December	Alcalá de Henares	many serious illnesses
1557 October–1558 November	Barcelona	
1557 October	Burgos	illness
1558 June–November	Murcia	pestilence, pest
1559	Barcelona	pestilence
1559	Aragon	
1559 April–July	Murcia, Gandia	pest, plague
1559 May	Valencia	

Date	Place	Notes
1560 September–October	Barcelona	
1561 summer	Monterey	illness
1563 January–February	Seville	*romadizo* = influenza
1563 January–April	Murcia	catarrh
1564 March–April	Barcelona	
1564 March–September	Zaragoza	
1564 April	Valencia	tumors
1564 July–November	Logroño	
1565 May–August	Burgos	
1565 August	Valladolid	
1565 August–September	Bellimar	
1565 autumn	Valladolid	fevers
1566	Burgos	
1566 September	Seville	
1568 May–September	Seville	pest, disease of tumors, pestilence
1568 May	Andalusia	
1568 June	Utrera	
1568 July	Plasencia	pestilential infection
1569	Granada	modorra
1569 May–summer	Seville	
1569 June	Cádiz, Xerez de la Frontera, San Luca de Barrameda, Porto de Santa Maria	
1569 June	Cordoba	
1569 November	Valladolid	
1570 April–July	Seville	*modorra*, pest, disease of tumors

Date	Place	Notes
1570 July	Montilla	modorra
1571 April	Toledo	
1571 April–May	Cádiz	epidemic
1573 summer	León, Andalusia	sickness
1573 July–November	Seville	universal sickness
1574 August	Santander	tabardillo
1575 summer	Plasencia	illnesses
1575 July	Alcalá de Henares	tabardillo
1575 July–September	Medina del Campo	many illnesses
1578	Santiago	
1579 February–March	Granada	epidemic of disease
1586 March–November	Santiago	tabardillo
1587 January	environs of Girona	
1589 August–October	Barcelona	
1593 July	Alcalá de Henares	catarrh
1598	Province of Castille	
1598	Navalcarnero	pestiferous contagion
1599	Talavera	
1599 June	Seville	
1599 July–August	Alcalá de Henares	
1600	Tarragona	
1600 August	Granada	
Sweden		
1579 September–1580 March	Stockholm	pestilence, pest
1579–1580 winter	Stockholm	another disease coinciding with the pest

Date	Place	Notes
Switzerland		
1572 May	Geneva	
1574 July	Geneva	
1580 October	Luzern	
1585 September	Fribourg	
1585 October–November	Luzern	epidemic
1586	Fribourg	
1588	Fribourg	
1592 November–December	Fribourg	contagious diseases
1594 September–November	German Switzerland	
1594 October–November	Fribourg	
1594 November–December	Luzern	epidemic of diseases
1595	Fribourg	epidemic
1595	Luzern	
1596 March–April	Fribourg	
1596 September–December	Luzern	
1597 October	Fribourg	
1597 June–October	Luzern	
Turkey		
1576 September	Constantinople	
1592 September–December	Constantinople	
Ukraine		
1595	Lvov	

BIBLIOGRAPHY

Manuscript Sources

At Rome: Archivum Romanum Societatis Iesu
Aquitania (AQUIT)

    1 I, Epistolae generalium, 1571–1598

    15 I, Historia Provinciae Aquitaniae, 1583–1758

Austria (AUST)

    132, Austriae Historia, 1575–1599

Bohemia (BOH)

    192, Varia Historica Bohemiae, Saeculo XVI, XVII

Flandro Belgia (FL BELG)

    50 I, Flandro Belgiae Historia, 1542–1596

    50 II, Flandro Belgiae Historia, 1603–1641

Fondo Gesuitico

    644, Epistolae Selectae 1, A–Bly

    645, Epistolae Selectae 2, Bo–Chi

    646, Epistolae Selectae 3, Ci–Deq

    647, Epistolae Selectae 4, Der–Gho

    648, Epistolae Selectae 5, Gi–Mal

    649, Epistolae Selectae 6, Mon–Mro

    650, Epistolae Selectae 7, N–P

    650a, Epistolae Selectae 8, Q–Sav

    650b, Epistolae Selectae 9, Sca–Z

Fondo Gesuitico *continued*
    651, Epistolae Selectae, Ex Anglia, A–Z
    681, Miscellanea 6
Francia (FRANC)
    1 I, Epistolae generalium, 1573–1585
    10, Catalogi triennales, 1584–1611
    30, Historia, 1540–1604
Gallia (GAL)
    45, Epistolae generalium: Francia, 1576–1579; Aquitania, 1576–1580
    53, Quadrimestres et Annuae, 1560–1584
    61 I, Historia, 1554–1602
    61 II, Historia, 1599–1604
    62, Oeuvres et épreuves de la compagnie de Jésus en France depuis son origine jusqu'à nos jours. Documents generaux et particuliers
    63, suite
    64, Documenta ARSI quae ad tempus manserunt in archivio Prov. Lugdunensis, 1554–1761
    79, Epistolae Galliae, 1557–1561
    80, Epistolae Galliae, 1562–1564
    81, Epistolae Galliae, 1565–1568
    82, Epistolae Galliae, 1569
    83, Epistolae Galliae, 1570–1571
    84, Epistolae Galliae, 1572
    85, Epistolae Galliae, 1573
    86, Epistolae Galliae, 1574
    87, Epistolae Galliae, 1575
    88, Epistolae Galliae, 1576
    89, Epistolae Galliae, 1577
    90, Epistolae Galliae, 1578–1579
    91, Epistolae Galliae, 1580–1584
    92, Epistolae Galliae, 1585–1587
    93, Epistolae Galliae, 1588–1601
Gallo Belgia (GAL BELG)
    31, Gallo Belgiae Historia, 1579–1618
Germania (GERM)
    118, Fundationes Ass. Germaniae
    120, Epistolae P. Laurentii Maggii, 1563–1570
    121 I, Epistolae P. Laurentii Maggii, 1569–1580
    121 II, Epistolae P. Laurentii Maggii, 1580–1595

Germania (GERM) *continued*

122, Epistolae P. Laurentii Maggii, 1587–1604

133 I, Epistolae Germaniae, January–June 1571

133 II, Epistolae Germaniae, July–December 1571

134 I, Epistolae Germaniae, January–June 1572

134 II, Epistolae Germaniae, July–December 1572

135 I, Epistolae Germaniae, January–June 1574

135 II, Epistolae Germaniae, July–December 1574

136 I, Epistolae Germaniae, January–June 1575

136 II, Epistolae Germaniae, July–December 1575

137 I, Epistolae Germaniae, January–April 1576

137 II, Epistolae Germaniae, May–December 1576

138 I, Epistolae Germaniae, January–June 1577

138 II, Epistolae Germaniae, July–December 1577

138 A, Topical index by letter to GERM 133–138

139, Quadrimestres, 1558–1566

140, Lit. Annuae, 1566–1571

141, Lit. Annuae, 1572–1593

142, Epistolae Germaniae, 1556–March 1561

143, Epistolae Germaniae, April–December 1561

144, Epistolae Germaniae, 1562–1563

145, Epistolae Germaniae, 1564

146, Epistolae Germaniae, 1565

147, Epistolae Germaniae, 1566

148, Epistolae Germaniae, 1567

149, Epistolae Germaniae, 1568

150, Epistolae Germaniae, 1569

151, Epistolae Germaniae, 1570

152, Epistolae Germaniae, 1571–February 1573

153, Epistolae Germaniae, March–December 1573

154, Epistolae Germaniae, 1574

155, Epistolae Germaniae, 1575–March 1576

156, Epistolae Germaniae, April 1576–April 1578

157, Epistolae Germaniae, May 1578–December 1579

158, Epistolae Germaniae, 1580

159, Epistolae Germaniae, 1581–February 1582

160, Epistolae Germaniae, March–December 1582

161, Epistolae Germaniae, 1583

162, Epistolae Germaniae, January–May 1584

Germania (GERM) *continued*

163, Epistolae Germaniae, June–December 1584

164, Epistolae Germaniae, January–August 1585

165, Epistolae Germaniae, September 1585–April 1586

166, Epistolae Germaniae, May–December 1586

167, Epistolae Germaniae, January–September 1587

168, Epistolae Germaniae, October 1587–1590

169, Epistolae Germaniae, 1591

170, Epistolae Germaniae, 1592

171, Epistolae Germaniae, 1593

172, Epistolae Germaniae, January–July 1594

173, Epistolae Germaniae, August–December 1594

174, Epistolae Germaniae, January–June 1595

175, Epistolae Germaniae, July–December 1595

176, Epistolae Germaniae, 1596

177, Epistolae Germaniae, 1597

178, Epistolae Germaniae, 1598–1599

179, Epistolae Germaniae, 1600

185, Epistolae Germaniae, 1557–1558

186, Epistolae Germaniae, 1558

187, Epistolae Germaniae, 1559

Germania Superior (GERM SUP)

65, Germaniae superioris historia, 1592–1599

Hispania (HISP)

95, Epistolae Hispaniae Mixtae, 1557–1558

96, Epistolae Hispaniae, 1556–1559

97, Epistolae Hispaniae, 1560

98, Epistolae Hispaniae, 1561

99, Epistolae Hispaniae, 1562

100, Epistolae Hispaniae, 1563

101, Epistolae Hispaniae, January–September 1564

102, Epistolae Hispaniae, October 1564–December 1565

103, Epistolae Hispaniae, January–July 1566

104, Epistolae Hispaniae, August–December 1566

105, Epistolae Hispaniae, January–May 1567

106, Epistolae Hispaniae, June–August 1567

107, Epistolae Hispaniae, September–December 1567

108, Epistolae Hispaniae, January–July 1568

109, Epistolae Hispaniae, August 1568–January 1569

Hispania (HISP) *continued*

110, Epistolae Hispaniae, February–May 1569

111, Epistolae Hispaniae, June–September 1569

112, Epistolae Hispaniae, October–December 1569

113, Epistolae Hispaniae, January–March 1570

114, Epistolae Hispaniae, April–July 1570

115, Epistolae Hispaniae, August–December 1570

116, Epistolae Hispaniae, 1571–June 1572

117, Epistolae Hispaniae, July–November 1572

118, Epistolae Hispaniae, December 1572–May 1573

119, Epistolae Hispaniae, June–December 1573

120, Epistolae Hispaniae, January–April 14, 1574

121, Epistolae Hispaniae, April 15–July 1574

122, Epistolae Hispaniae, August–December 1574

123, Epistolae Hispaniae, January–April 1575

124, Epistolae Hispaniae, May–August 1575

125, Epistolae Hispaniae, September–December 1575

126, Epistolae Hispaniae, 1576–February 1579

127, Epistolae Hispaniae, March–June 1579

128, Epistolae Hispaniae, July–December 1579

129, Epistolae Hispaniae, 1580–March 1585

130, Epistolae Hispaniae, April–October 1585

131, Epistolae Hispaniae, November 1585–May 1586

132, Epistolae Hispaniae, June 1586–February 1587

133, Epistolae Hispaniae, March–September 1587

134, Epistolae Hispaniae, October 1587–1592

Volumes 95–134 have topical indices by letter

135, Epistolae Hispaniae, January–July 1593

136, Epistolae Hispaniae, August 1593–June 1594

137, Epistolae Hispaniae, July–November 1594

138, Epistolae Hispaniae, December 1594–July 1595

139, Epistolae Hispaniae, August 1595–1596

140, Epistolae P. Antonii de Corduba, 1564–1566; Epistolae P. Antonii de Araoz, 1562–1572

141, Epistolae Hispaniae, Quadrimestres et Annuae, 1564–1584

Historia Societatis (HIST SOC)

42, Defuncti, 1557–1623

Italia (ITAL)

    70a, Epist. Gener. pro Prov. Venet. et Medio. ad 14/11/1576 usque ad 5/3/1583

    107, Epistolae Italiae, 1555–March 1557

    108, Epistolae Italiae, April–June 1557

    109, Epistolae Italiae, July–October 1557

    110, Epistolae Italiae, October–December 1557

    111, Epistolae Italiae, January–March 1558

    112, Epistolae Italiae, April–July 1558

    113, Epistolae Italiae, August–December 1558

    114, Epistolae Italiae, January–June 1559

    115, Epistolae Italiae, July–December 1559

    116, Epistolae Italiae, 1560

    117, Epistolae Italiae, January–June 1561

    118, Epistolae Italiae, July–September 1561

    119, Epistolae Italiae, September–October 1561

    120, Epistolae Italiae, November–December 1561

    121, Epistolae Italiae, January–September 1562

    122, Epistolae Italiae, October 1562–May 1563

    123, Epistolae Italiae, June–December 1563

    124, Epistolae Italiae, January–July 1564

    125, Epistolae Italiae, August 1564–January 1565

    126, Epistolae Italiae, January–March 1565

    127, Epistolae Italiae, April–July 1565

    128, Epistolae Italiae, July–December 1565

    129, Epistolae Italiae, January–May 1566

    130, Epistolae Italiae, June–September 1566

    131, Epistolae Italiae, September–December 1566

    132, Epistolae Italiae, January–May 1567

    133, Epistolae Italiae, May–August 1567

    134, Epistolae Italiae, August–December 1567

    135, Epistolae Italiae, January–April 1568

    136, Epistolae Italiae, May–December 1568

    137, Epistolae Italiae, 1569

    138, Epistolae Italiae, January–May 1570

    139, Epistolae Italiae, June–September 1570

    140, Epistolae Italiae, October–December 1570

    141, Epistolae Italiae, January–September 1571

    142, Epistolae Italiae, September–December 1571

    143, Epistolae Italiae, 1572–1573

Italia (ITAL) *continued*

    144, Epistolae Italiae, January–September 1574

    145, Epistolae Italiae, September–December 1574

    146, Epistolae Italiae, January–April 1575

    147, Epistolae Italiae, April–June 1575

    148, Epistolae Italiae, June–September 1575

    149, Epistolae Italiae, October–December 1575

    150, Epistolae Italiae, January–April 1576

    151, Epistolae Italiae, April–August 1576

    152, Epistolae Italiae, August–December 1576

    153, Epistolae Italiae, January–May 1577

    154, Epistolae Italiae, May–August 1577

    155, Epistolae Italiae, September–December 1577

    156, Epistolae Italiae, 1578–1582

    157, Epistolae Italiae, 1583–April 1585

    158, Epistolae Italiae, May–December 1585

    159, Epistolae Italiae, 1585, De Legatione Japonica

    160, Epistolae Italiae, 1585–May 1592

    161, Epistolae Italiae, June 1592–1596

    162, Epistolae Italiae, 1597–September 1605

    171, ASS. ITALIAE, Relationes, Quadrimestres, etc.

Lithuania (LITH)

    38 I, Lithuaniae Historia, 1589–1649

Lugdunum (LUGD)

    28, Historia Provinciae Lugdunensis, 1575–1614

Lusitania (LUS)

    51, Lusitania, Annuae-Quadrimestres, 1557–1562

    52, Lusitania, Annuae-Quadrimestres, 1563–1570

    53, Lusitania, Annuae, 1574–1585, 1615–1644

    60, Epistolae Lusitaniae, 1556–1560

    61, Epistolae Lusitaniae, 1561–1565

    62, Epistolae Lusitaniae, 1566–1568

    63, Epistolae Lusitaniae, 1569

    64, Epistolae Lusitaniae, 1570–August 1572

    65, Epistolae Lusitaniae, September 1572–1573

    66, Epistolae Lusitaniae, 1574

    67, Epistolae Lusitaniae, 1575

    68, Epistolae Lusitaniae, 1577–1584

    69, Epistolae Lusitaniae, 1585–1586

Lusitania (LUS) *continued*

    70, Epistolae Lusitaniae, 1587–1589

    71, Epistolae Lusitaniae, 1591–1592

    72, Epistolae Lusitaniae, 1593–1594

    73, Epistolae Lusitaniae, 1595–1596

    74, Epistolae Lusitaniae, 1599–1655

Volumes 60–74 have topical indices by letter

    106, Lusitaniae Historia, 1540–1614

Mediolanum (MED)

    75, Annuae et Quadrimestres, 1557–1585

    76 I, Historia, 1554–1603

    79, Historia, 1551–1732

Neapolis (NEAP)

    72, Historia, 1551–1614

    193, Quadrimestres, Annuae, 1557–1584

Opera Nostrorum (OPP NN)

    159, Collectanea tractatuum moralis Theologiae

    244 I, Lettere originali del S. Card. Bellarmino, 1557–1603

    245, P. Roberti Bellarmini, Epistolae et acta, 1560–1621

    316, Antonio Possevino, De ritibus graecorum et de missionibus apud eos

    317, Antonio Possevino, Acta inter Caesarem et Poloniae Regem, 1583–1584

    324

    328, Possevini Epistolae, 1558, 1576–1580

    329 I, Possevini Epistolae, 1581–1583

    329 II, Possevini Epistolae, 1583

    330, Possevini Epistolae, 1584–1585

    331, Possevini Epistolae, 1586–1587

    332, Possevini Epistolae, 1588–1596

    333, Possevini Epistolae, 1597–1611

    339, Epp. Laur. Norvegi, Annuae Holmenses, Epp. Joa. Harlenii, Miscellanea [Svecia]

Polonia (POL)

    50, Polonia Historia, 1555–1600

    65, Polonia, Lithuania, Historia et Annuae, 1561–1621

    80, Epistolae Poloniae, 1577

Roma (ROM)

    126a, Quadrimestres, Annuae, 1557–1568

    126b I, Annuae, 1570–1585

    126b II, Annuae, 1578–1580

Roma (ROM) *continued*

    127 I, Historia, 1547–1593

    127 II, Historia, 1593–1600

    157 I, Historia Collegii Germanici, 1552–1584

    157 II, Historia Collegii Germanici, 1584–1625

    192, P. Hier. Benci Epistolae, 1580–1593

Rhenus Inferioris (RH INF)

    48, Rhenus Historia, 1578–1625; Rhenus Infer. Historia, 1626–1631

Sardinia (SARD)

    10 I, Sardiniae Historia, 1577–1616

    13, Sardiniae Epistolae, 1558–1565

    14, Sardiniae Epistolae, 1566–1573

    15, Sardiniae Epistolae, 1573–1585

    16, Sardiniae Epistolae, 1586–1596

    17, Sardiniae Necrologia, 1594–1700

Sicilia (SIC)

    181, Annuae, 1550–1561

    182, Annuae, 1562–1584

    183, Historia, 1555–1610

Toletana (TOLET)

    37a, Toletana Historia, 1547–1610

Venetia (VEN)

    100, Quadrimestres et Litterae Annuae, 1558–1571, 1584

    105 I, Veneta Historia, 1535–1591

    105 II, Veneta Historia, 1592–1624

PRINTED PRIMARY SOURCES

Bisciola, Paolo. *Relatione verissima del progresso della peste di Milano: Qual principiò nel mese d'agosto 1576 e seguì sino al mese di maggio 1577.* Ancona: Alessandro Benacci, 1577.

Bobadilla, Nicolás. *Bobadillae monumenta: Nicolai Alphonsi de Bobadilla, sacerdotis e Societate Jesu, gesta et scripta.* Madrid: Gabrielis Lopez del Horno, 1913.

Borgia, Francis. *Sanctus Franciscus Borgia quartus Gandiae dux et Societatis Jesu praepositus generalis.* 5 vols. Madrid: Augustini Avrial and Gabrielis Lopez del Horno, 1894–1911.

Brillmacher, Peter Michael. *Serta honoris et exultationis, ad catholicorum devotionem ornandam et exhilarandam.* Cologne: Apud Gervinum Calenium et haeredes Joannis Quentelii, 1589.

Broët, Paschase et al. *Epistolae P.P. Paschasii Broeti, Claudii Jaji, Joannis Codurii et Simonis Roderici Societatis Jesu*. Madrid: Gabrielis Lopez del Horno, 1903.

Canisius, Peter. *Beati Petri Canisii, Societatis Iesu, epistolae et acta*. Ed. Otto Braunsberger. 13 vols. Freiburg im Breisgau: Herder, 1896–1923.

Carayon, Auguste, ed. *Documents inédits concernant la Compagnie de Jésus*. Vol. 5, *L'Université de Pont-à-Mousson*. Poitiers: Henri Oudin, 1870.

Documenta Indica. Ed. Joseph Wicki and John Gomes. 18 vols. Rome: Monumenta Historica Societatis Iesu, 1948–.

Documenta Malucensia. Ed. Hubert Jacobs. 3 vols. Rome: Institutum Historicum Societatis Iesu, 1974–1984.

Epistolae mixtae ex variis Europae locis ab anno 1537 ad 1556 scriptae nunc primum a patribus Societatis Jesu. 5 vols. Madrid: Augustinus Avrial and R. Fortanet, 1898–1901.

Fracastoro, Girolamo [Hieronymi Fracastorii]. *De contagione et contagiosis morbis et curatione, Libri III*. Trans. Wilmer Cave Wright. New York: G. P. Putnam's Sons, 1930.

Hansen, Joseph, ed. *Rheinische Akten zur Geschichte des Jesuitenordens, 1542–1582*. Bonn: H. Berendt, 1896.

Lainez, Diego. *Lainii monumenta: Epistolae et acta patris Jacobi Lainii secundi praepositi generalis Societatis Jesu*. 8 vols. Madrid: Gabrielis Lopez del Horno, 1912–1917.

Litterae quadrimestres ex universis praeter Indiam et Brasiliam locis in quibus aliqui de Societate Jesu versabantur Romam missae. 7 vols. Madrid and Rome: Augustinus Avrial, La Editorial Ibérica, and A. Macioce e Pisani, 1894–1932.

Loarte, Baltasar. "A Curious Document: Baltasar Loarte S. I. and the Years 1554–1570." *Archivum Historicum Societatis Iesu* 45 (1976): 56–94.

Loarte, Gaspar. *Antidoto spirituale, contra la peste, dove si contengono alcun avisi, et rimedii spirituali, che possono giovare per la preservatione, et curatione di questo morbo*. (Genoa, 1577).

Loyola, Ignatius. *The Autobiography of St. Ignatius Loyola with Related Documents*. Ed. John C. Olin. New York: Harper and Row, 1974.

———. *The Constitutions of the Society of Jesus*. Ed. George E. Ganss. St. Louis: The Institute of Jesuit Sources, 1970.

———. *Sancti Ignatii de Loyola, Societatis Jesu fundatoris, epistolae et intructiones*. 11 vols. Madrid: Gabrielis Lopez del Horno, 1903–1911.

Monumenta antiquae Hungariae. Ed. Ladislaus Lukács. 3 vols. Rome: Institutum Historicum Societatis Iesu, 1969–1981.

Monumenta Brasiliae. Ed. Serafim Leite. 5 vols. Rome: Monumenta Historica Societatis Iesu, 1956–1968.

tre, Pierre, ed. *Les établissements des jésuites en France depuis quatre siècles.* 5 vols. Enghien: Institut Supérieur de Théologie, 1949–1957.

meau, Jean. *La Peur en Occident (XIVe–XVIIIe siècles): Une cité assiégée.* Paris: Fayard, 1978.

, Michael W. *The Black Death in the Middle East.* Princeton: Princeton University Press, 1977.

———. "Geographical Origin of the Black Death: Comment." *Bulletin of the History of Medicine* 52 (1978): 112–13.

out, Ignace. *Victimes de la charité: Catalogue des pères et frères de la Compagnie de Jésus, morts de maladies contagieuses contractées au service des malades.* Paris: M.-R. Leroy, 1907.

hr, Bernhard. *Geschichte der Jesuiten in den Ländern deutscher Zunge.* 4 vols. Freiburg im Breisgau: Herder, 1907–1928.

ncan, W. Christopher. "Cutaneous Manifestations of Infectious Diseases." In *Infectious Diseases: A Modern Treatise of Infectious Processes.* 2d ed. Ed. Paul D. Hoeprich. New York: Harper and Row, 1977.

er, Alan D. "The Influence of Bubonic Plague in England, 1500–1667." *Medical History* 22 (1978): 308–26.

kert, Edward A. "Boundary Formation and Diffusion of Plague: Swiss Epidemics from 1562 to 1669." *Annales de démographie historique* (1978): 49–80.

———. "Seasonality of Plague in Early Modern Europe: Swiss Epidemic of 1628–1630." *Reviews of Infectious Diseases* 2 (1980): 952–59.

l, Stephen R. "Immunity as a Factor in the Epidemiology of Medieval Plague." *Reviews of Infectious Diseases* 6 (1984): 866–79.

———. "Interhuman Transmission of Medieval Plague." *Bulletin of the History of Medicine* 54 (1980): 497–510.

———. "Three Days in October of 1630: Detailed Examination of Mortality during an Early Modern Plague Epidemic in Venice." *Reviews of Infectious Diseases* 11 (1989): 128–39.

———. "The Venetian Plague of 1630–1631: A Preliminary Epidemiologic Analysis." *Janus* 73 (1986–1990): 85–104.

Fejér, Josephus. *Defuncti primi saeculi Societatis Jesu, 1540–1640.* 2 vols. Rome: Institutum Historicum Societatis Jesu, 1982.

Flinn, Michael W. *The European Demographic System, 1500–1820.* Baltimore: Johns Hopkins University Press, 1985.

———. "Plague in Europe and the Mediterranean Countries." *Journal of European Economic History* 8 (1979): 131–48.

Monumenta Mexicana. Ed. Felix Zubillaga. 7 vols. Rome: Monumenta Historica Societatis Iesu, 1956–1981.

Monumenta Peruana. Ed. Antonio de Egana. 4 vols. Rome: Monumenta Historica Societatis Iesu, 1954–1966.

Nadal, Jerónimo. *Epistolae P. Hieronymi Nadal Societatis Iesu ab anno 1546 ad 1577.* 4 vols. Madrid: Augustini Avrial and Gabrielis Lopez del Horno, 1898–1905.

Parets, Miguel. *A Journal of the Plague Year: The Diary of the Barcelona Tanner Miguel Parets, 1651.* Ed. James S. Amelang. New York: Oxford University Press, 1991.

Polanco, Juan. *Polanci complementa: Epistolae et commentaria P. Joannis Alphonsi de Polanco e Societatis Jesu.* 2 vols. Madrid: Gabrielis Lopez del Horno, 1916–1917.

———. *Vita Ignatii Loiolae et rerum Societatis Jesu historia.* 6 vols. Madrid: Typographorum Societatis and Augustinus Avrial, 1894–1898.

[Possevino, Antonio]. *Cause et rimedii della peste, et d'altre infermità.* Florence: Appresso i Giunti, 1577.

Ribadeneira, Pedro. *Patris Petri de Ribadeneira Societatis Iesu sacerdotis confessiones, epistolae.* 2 vols. Madrid: Typis Gabrielis Lopez del Horno, 1920–1923.

Salmeron, Alfonso. *Epistolae P. Alphonsi Salmeronis Societatis Iesu.* 2 vols. Madrid: Typis Gabrielis Lopez del Horno, 1906–1907.

Skarga, Peter. *Listy Ks. Piotra Skargi T. J. z Lat 1566–1610.* Ed. Jan Syganski. Cracow: n.p., 1912.

Secondary Sources

Alexander, John T. *Bubonic Plague in Early Modern Russia: Public Health and Urban Disaster.* Baltimore: Johns Hopkins University Press, 1980.

———. "Reconsiderations on Plague in Early Modern Russia, 1500–1800." *Jahrbücher für Geschichte Osteuropas* 34 (1986): 244–54.

Amundsen, Darrel W. "Medical Deontology and Pestilential Disease in the Late Middle Ages." *Journal of the History of Medicine* 32 (1977): 403–21.

Appleby, Andrew B. "The Disappearance of Plague: A Continuing Puzzle." *Economic History Review,* 2d ser., 33 (1980): 161–73.

———. "Epidemics and Famine in the Little Ice Age." In *Climate and History: Studies in Interdisciplinary History,* 63–83. Ed. Robert I. Rotberg and Theodore K. Rabb. Princeton: Princeton University Press, 1981.

Ariès, Philippe. *Centuries of Childhood: A Social History of Family Life.* New York: Vintage Books, 1965.

———. *The Hour of Our Death.* Harmondsworth: Penguin Books, 1983.

Astrain, Antonio. *Historia de la Compañia de Jesús en la Asistencia de España.* 7 vols. Madrid: Sucesores de Rivadeneyra, 1902–1925.

Audoin-Rouzeau, Frédérique. "La peste et les rats: Les réponses de l'archéozoologie." In *Maladies et société (XIIe–XVIIIe siècles): Actes du colloque de Bielefeld, novembre 1986*, 65–71. Ed. Neithard Bulst and Robert Delort. Paris: Editions du CNRS, 1989.

Bahmanyar, M., and D. C. Cavanaugh. *Plague Manual*. Geneva: World Health Organization, 1976.

Baltazard, M. "Déclin et destin d'une maladie infectieuse: La peste." *Bulletin of the World Health Organization* 23 (1960): 247–62.

Beier, Lucinda McCray. *Sufferers and Healers: The Experience of Illness in Seventeenth-Century England*. London: Routledge and Kegan Paul, 1987.

Beloch, Karl Julius. *Bevölkerungs-geschichte Italiens*. 3 vols. Berlin: Walter de Gruyter, 1937–1940.

Benedictow, Ole Jøregen. "Morbidity in Historical Plague Epidemics." *Population Studies* 41 (1987): 401–31.

Biraben, Jean-Noël. "Current Medical and Epidemiological Views on Plague." In *The Plague Reconsidered: A New Look at Its Origins and Effects in Sixteenth- and Seventeenth-Century England*. Local Population Studies Supplement. Matlock, Derbyshire: "Local Population Studies" with the S.S.R.C. Cambridge Group for the History of Population and Social Structure, 1977.

———. *Les hommes et la peste en France et dans les pays européens et méditerranéens*. 2 vols. Paris: Mouton, 1975–1976.

———. "Les pauvres et la peste." In *Etudes sur l'histoire de la pauvreté*, 505–18. Ed. Michel Mollat. Paris: La Sorbonne, 1974.

———, and Jacques Le Goff. "The Plague in the Early Middle Ages." In *Biology of Man in History*, 48–80. Ed. Robert Forster and Orest Ranum. Baltimore: Johns Hopkins University Press, 1975.

Bloomfield, Arthur L. "A Bibliography of Internal Medicine: Plague." *Stanford Medical Bulletin* 15 (1957): 3–13.

Boero, Giuseppe. *Risposta a Vincenzo Gioberti sopra le lettere di S. Carlo Borromeo*. Rome: Marini e Marini, 1849.

Bradley, Leslie. "Some Medical Aspects of Plague." In *The Plague Reconsidered: A New Look at Its Origins and Effects in Sixteenth- and Seventeenth-Century England*. Local Population Studies Supplement. Matlock, Derbyshire: "Local Population Studies" with the S.S.R.C. Cambridge Group for the History of Population and Social Structure, 1977.

Braudel, Fernand. *The Structures of Everyday Life: The Limits of the Possible*. London: Collins, 1981.

Brodrick, James. *The Progress of the Jesuits (1556–1579)*. London: Longmans, Green, 1946.

———. *Saint Peter Canisius*. Chicago: Loyola University Press, 1962.

Brossolet, Jacqueline, and Andreina Zitelli. "La disinfez[...] peste, 1348–1797. 2d ed. Venice: Marsilio Editori, 19[...]

Butler, Thomas. "A Clinical Study of Bubonic Plague." *A[...]* (1972): 268–76.

———. "Plague and Tularemia." *Pediatric Clinics of N[...]

Cabourdin, Guy. *Terre et hommes en Lorraine (1550–1635)* [...] 1977.

Calvi, Giulia. *Histories of a Plague Year: The Social and th[...] ence*. Berkeley: University of California Press, 1989.

Canalis, A., and P. Sepulcri. "Prescrizioni mediche uffic[...] governo in Venezia nella peste del 1575–1576." *Annali* [...] 1201–14.

Carmichael, Ann G. "Contagion Theory and Contagion Pr[...] Milan." *Renaissance Quarterly* 44 (1991): 213–56.

———. *Plague and the Poor in Renaissance Florence*. Cam[...] sity Press, 1986.

———, and Arthur M. Silverstein. "Smallpox in Europ[...] Century: Virulent Killer or Benign Disease?" *Journal* [...] *and Allied Sciences* 42 (April 1987): 147–68.

Cartwright, Frederick F. *A Social History of Medicine*. London: [...]

Cavanaugh, Dan C., and James E. Williams. "Plague: Some [...] ships." In *Fleas: Proceedings of the International Confere[...] R. Traub and H. Starcke. Rotterdam: A. A. Balkema, 1980[...]

Christian, William A. *Apparitions in Late Medieval and Renai[...] Princeton University Press, 1981.

Cipolla, Carlo M. *Cristofano and the Plague: A Study in the Hi[...] the Age of Galileo*. London: Collins, 1973.

———. *Faith, Reason, and the Plague in Seventeenth-Centur[...] nell University Press, 1979.

———. *Fighting the Plague in Seventeenth-Century Italy*. M[...] Wisconsin Press, 1981.

———. *Public Health and the Medical Profession in the Ren[...] Cambridge University Press, 1976.

——— and Dante E. Zanetti. "Peste et mortalité différentielle." [...] *phie historique* (1972): 197–202.

Crosby, Alfred W. *Ecological Imperialism: The Biological Expansion* [...] Cambridge: Cambridge University Press, 1986.

Davis, David E. "The Scarcity of Rats and the Black Death: An Ecol[...] *nal of Interdisciplinary History* 16 (1986): 455–70.

Fosseyeux, Marcel. "Les saints protecteurs contre la 'male' mort au Moyen-Age et à la Renaissance." *Bulletin de la Société Française d'Histoire de la Médecine* 19 (1935): 339–49.

Fouqueray, Henri. *Histoire de la Compagnie de Jésus en France des origines à la suppression (1528–1762).* 5 vols. Paris: Librairie Alphonse Picard et Fils, 1910–1925.

Franco, Antonio. *Imagem da virtude em o noviciado da Companhia de Jesus no Real Collegio de Coimbra em Portugal.* 2 vols. Evora and Coimbra: Na Officina de Universidade and No Real collegio das artes da Companhia de Jesu, 1719.

—————. *Imagem da virtude em o noviciado da Companhia de Jesus do Real Collegio do Espirito Santo de Evora do Reyno de Portugal.* Lisbon: Na Officina real deslandesiana, 1714.

—————. *Imagem da virtude em o noviciado da Companhia de Jesus na corte de Lisboa.* Coimbra: No Real collegio das artes da Companhia de Jesu, 1717.

Garcia Villoslada, Riccardo. *Storia del Collegio Romano, dal suo inizio (1551) alla soppressione della Compagnia di Gesù (1773).* Rome: Apud sedes Universitatis Gregorianae, 1954.

Gilmont, Jean-François. *Les écrits spirituels des premiers jésuites: Inventaire commenté.* Rome: Institutum Historicum Societatis Iesu, 1961.

Giuffré, Liborio. "L'epidemia d'influenza del 1557 in Palermo e le proposte per il risanamento della città fatte nel 1558 da G. F. Ingrassia." *Archivio storico siciliano* 15 (1890): 179–92.

Gottfried, Robert S. *The Black Death: Natural and Human Disaster in Medieval Europe.* New York: The Free Press, 1983.

—————. *Epidemic Disease in Fifteenth-Century England: The Medical Response and the Demographic Consequences.* New Brunswick: Rutgers University Press, 1978.

Goubert, J.-P. "Twenty Years On: Problems of Historical Methodology in the History of Health." In *Problems and Methods in the History of Medicine,* 40–56. Ed. Roy Porter and Andrew Wear. London: Croom Helm, 1987.

Greenwood, Major. *Epidemics and Crowd-Diseases: An Introduction to the Study of Epidemiology.* London: Williams and Norgate, 1935.

Harney, Martin. *The Jesuits in History: The Society of Jesus through Four Centuries.* Chicago: Loyola University Press, 1962.

Henderson, John. "Epidemics in Renaissance Florence: Medical Theory and Government Response." In *Maladies et société (XIIe–XVIIIe siècles): Actes du colloque de Bielefeld, novembre 1986,* 165–86. Ed. Neithard Bulst and Robert Delort. Paris: Editions du CNRS, 1989.

Hirst, Leonard Fabian. *The Conquest of Plague: A Study of the Evolution of Epidemiology.* Oxford: Clarendon Press, 1953.

Kilbourne, Edwin D. *The Influenza Viruses and Influenza.* New York: Academic Press, 1975.

Klairmont, Alison. "The Problem of the Plague: New Challenges to Healing in Sixteenth-Century France." *Proceedings of the Fifth Annual Meeting of the Western Society for French History* 5 (1977): 119–27.

Koenig, John. "The Origins of the Crisis Procession in the Early Middle Ages." Unpublished paper presented at the conference of the Australasian Historians of Medieval and Early Modern Europe at Adelaide on September 27, 1991.

Kroess, Alois. *Geschichte der böhmischen Provinz der Gesellschaft Jesu.* 2 vols. Vienna: Ambr. Opitz, 1910–1927.

Laburu, J. A. de. *La salud corporal y San Ignacio de Loyola.* Bilbao: Mensajero del Corazón de Jésus, 1956.

La Cava, A. Francesco. *La peste di San Carlo: Note storico-mediche sulla peste del 1576.* Milan: Editore Ulrico Hoepli, 1945.

Laforce, F. Marc, et al. "Clinical and Epidemiological Observations on an Outbreak of Plague in Nepal." *Bulletin of the World Health Organization* 45 (1971): 693–706.

Lamalle, Edmond. "L'archivio di un grande ordine religioso: L'Archivio Generale della Compagnia di Gesù." *Archiva Ecclesiae* 24–25 (1981–1982): 89–120.

Le Roy Ladurie, Emmanuel. "A Concept: The Unification of the Globe by Disease (Fourteenth to Seventeenth Centuries)." In *The Mind and Method of the Historian*, 28–83. Chicago: University of Chicago Press, 1984.

Livi-Bacci, Massimo. "The Nutrition-Mortality Link in Past Times: A Comment." In *Hunger and History: The Impact of Changing Food Production and Consumption Patterns on Society*, 95–100. Ed. Robert I. Rotberg and Theodore K. Rabb. Cambridge: Cambridge University Press, 1983.

Martin, A. Lynn. *The Jesuit Mind: The Mentality of an Elite in Early Modern France.* Ithaca: Cornell University Press, 1988.

————. "Vocational Crises and the Crisis in Vocations among Jesuits in France during the Sixteenth Century." *Catholic Historical Review* 71 (1986): 201–21.

Matossian, Mary Kilbourne. "Did Mycotoxins Play a Role in Bubonic Plague Epidemics?" *Perspectives in Biology and Medicine* 29 (1986): 244–56.

————. *Poisons of the Past: Molds, Epidemics, and History.* New Haven: Yale University Press, 1989.

McNeill, William H. *Plagues and Peoples.* Garden City, N.Y.: Anchor Books, 1976.

Meissner, W. W. *Ignatius Loyola: The Psychology of a Saint.* New Haven: Yale University Press, 1992.

Meuvret, J. "Demographic Crisis in France from the Sixteenth to the Eighteenth Century." In *Population in History: Essays in Historical Demography*, 507–22. Ed. D. V. Glass and D. E. C. Eversley. London: Edward Arnold, 1974.

Meyer, K. F. *Disinfected Mail.* Holton, Kan.: Gossip Printery, 1962.

Mollaret, Henri H. "Presentazione della Peste." In *Venezia e la Peste, 1348–1797.* 2d ed. Venice: Marsilio Editori, 1980.

Mols, Roger. *Introduction à la démographie historique des villes d'Europe du XIVe au XVIIIe siècle.* 3 vols. Louvain: Publications Universitaires de Louvain, 1954–1956.

Morrison, Alan S., Julius Kirshner, and Anthony Molho. "Epidemics in Renaissance Florence." *American Journal of Public Health* 75 (1985): 528–35.

Muchembled, Robert. "Le corps, la culture populaire et la culture des élites en France (XVe–XVIIIe siècle)." In *Leib und Leben in der Geschichte der Neuzeit,* 142–53. Ed. Arthur E. Imhof. Berlin: Duncker und Humblot, 1983.

Müller, Wieslaw. "Les jésuites en Pologne aux XVIe et XVIIe siècles." In *Les jésuites parmi les hommes aux XVIe et XVIIe siècles,* 323–30. Association des publications de la Faculté des lettres et sciences humaines. Clermont-Ferrand, 1987.

Nadal, J., and E. Giralt. *La population catalane de 1553 à 1717: L'immigration française et les autres facteurs de son développement.* Paris: S.E.V.P.E.N., 1960.

Niero, Antonio. "Pietà ufficiale e pietà popolare in tempo di peste." In *Venezia e la Peste, 1348–1797.* 2d ed. Venice: Marsilio Editori, 1980.

O'Malley, John W. *The First Jesuits.* Cambridge, Mass.: Harvard University Press, 1993.

Paget, Stephen. *Ambroise Paré and His Times, 1510–1590.* New York: G. P. Putnam's Sons, 1899.

Palmer, Richard J. "The Church, Leprosy and Plague in Medieval and Early Modern Europe." In *The Church and Healing,* 79–99. Ed. W. J. Sheils. Oxford: Basil Blackwood, 1982.

Pas, J. de, and M. Lanselle. "Documents sur la peste de 1596 à Saint-Omer." *Bulletin de la Société Française d'Histoire de la Médecine* 23 (1928): 206–16.

Pastor, Ludwig von. *History of the Popes from the Close of the Middle Ages.* 40 vols. London: Routledge and Kegan Paul, 1949–1953.

Patterson, K. David. *Pandemic Influenza, 1700–1900: A Study in Historical Epidemiology.* Totowa, N.J.: Rowman and Littlefield, 1986.

Pérez Moreda, Vicente. *Las crisis de mortalidad en la España interior (siglos XVI–XIX).* Madrid: Siglo Ventiuno Editores, 1980.

Poland, Jack D. "Plague." In *Infectious Diseases: A Modern Treatise of Infectious Processes,* 1227–37. Ed. Paul D. Hoeprich. Philadelphia: Harper and Row, 1983.

———— and Allan M. Barnes. "Plague." In *CRC Handbook Series in Zoonoses,* 1:515–59. Ed. James H. Steele. Boca Raton, Fla.: CRC Press, 1979.

Pollitzer, R. *Plague.* Geneva: World Health Organization, 1954.

————. "A Review of Recent Literature on Plague." *Bulletin of the World Health Organization* 23 (1960): 313–400.

———— and Karl F. Meyer. "The Ecology of Plague." In *Studies in Disease Ecology*, 433–501. Ed. Jacques M. Mays. New York: Hafner Publishing, 1961.

Poncelet, Alfred. *Histoire de la Compagnie de Jésus dans les anciens Pays-Bas*. 2 vols. Brussels: M. Lamertin, 1927–1928.

————. *Nécrologe des jésuites de la province Flandro-Belge*. Wetteren: J. de Meester, 1931.

Porter, Roy. *Disease, Medicine and Society in England, 1550–1860*. London: Macmillan, 1987.

Post, John D. "Famine, Mortality and Epidemic Disease in the Process of Modernization." *Economic History Review*, 2d ser., 39 (1976): 14–37.

————. *Food Shortage, Climatic Variability, and Epidemic Disease in Preindustrial Europe: The Mortality Peak in the Early 1740s*. Ithaca: Cornell University Press, 1985.

Postan, Michael M. "Malthusian Pressure and Population Decline." In *The Black Death: A Turning Point in History?* 56–59. Ed. William M. Bowsky. New York: Holt, Rinehart and Winston, 1971.

Preto, Paolo. "Peste e demografia: L'età moderna: Le due pesti del 1575–77 e 1630–31." In *Venezia e la Peste, 1348–1797*. 2d ed. Venice: Marsilio Editori, 1980.

————. *Peste e società a Venezia nel 1576*. Vicenza: Neri Pozza Editore, 1978.

Prosperi, Adriano. "Clerics and Laymen in the Work of Carlo Borromeo." In *San Carlo Borromeo: Catholic Reform and Ecclesiastical Politics in the Second Half of the Sixteenth Century*, 112–38. Ed. John M. Headley and John B. Tomaro. Washington: Folger Books, 1988.

Pugh, Wilma J. "Social Welfare and the Edict of Nantes: Lyon and Nîmes." *French Historical Studies* 8 (1974): 349–76.

Pullan, Brian. "Catholics and the Poor in Early Modern Europe." *Transactions of the Royal Historical Society*, 5th ser., 26 (1976): 15–34.

————. "Due organizzazioni per il controllo sociale." In *La memoria della Salute: Venezia e il suo ospedale dal XVI al XX secolo*, 13–24. Ed. Nelli-Elena Vanzan Marchini. Venice: Arsenale, 1985.

————. "Plague and Perceptions of the Poor in Early Modern Italy." In *Epidemics and Ideas: Essays on the Historical Perception of Pestilence*, 101–23. Ed. Terence Ranger and Paul Slack. Cambridge: Cambridge University Press, 1992.

————. *Rich and Poor in Renaissance Venice: The Social Institutions of a Catholic State, to 1620*. Cambridge, Mass.: Harvard University Press, 1971.

Pyle, Gerald F. *The Diffusion of Influenza: Patterns and Paradigms*. Totowa, N.J.: Rowman and Littlefield, 1986.

Rackham, James. "*Rattus Rattus:* The Introduction of the Black Rat into Britain." *Antiquity* 53 (1979): 112–20.

248

Riley, James C. *The Eighteenth-Century Campaign to Avoid Disease*. London: Macmillan, 1987.

—————. *Sickness, Recovery and Death: A History and Forecast of Ill Health*. Iowa City: University of Iowa Press, 1989.

Rinaldi, Stefania Mason. "Le immagini della peste nella cultura figurativa veneziana." In *Venezia e la Peste, 1348–1797*. 2d ed. Venice: Marsilio Editori, 1980.

Roberts, R. S. "The Use of Literary and Documentary Evidence in the History of Medicine." In *Modern Methods in the History of Medicine*, 36–56. Ed. Edwin Clark. London: Athlone Press, 1971.

Rodenwaldt, Ernst. *Pest in Venedig, 1575–1577: Ein Beitrag zur Frage der Infektkette bei dem Pestepidemien West-Europas*. Heidelberg: Springer, 1953.

Rodrigues, Francisco. *História da Companhia de Jesus na Assistência de Portugal*. 4 vols. Pôrto: Apostolado da Imprensa, 1931–1950.

Saint-Eloy, Madeleine. "Quand la peste régnait à Nevers, 1399–1628." *Bulletin de philologie historique* (1966): 335–66.

Scaduto, Mario. *Catalogo dei gesuiti d'Italia, 1540–1565*. Rome: Institutum Historicum Societatis Iesu, 1968.

Schofield, Roger S. "An Anatomy of an Epidemic: Colyton, November 1645 to November 1646." In *The Plague Reconsidered: A New Look at Its Origins and Effects in Sixteenth- and Seventeenth-Century England*. Local Population Studies Supplement. Matlock, Derbyshire: "Local Population Studies" with the S.S.R.C. Cambridge Group for the History of Population and Social Structure, 1977.

Schove, D. J. "Chronology and Historical Geography of Famine, Plague, and Other Epidemics." In *Proceedings of the XXIII International Congress of the History of Medicine, 2–9 September 1972*, 1265–72. London: Wellcome Institute of the History of Medicine, 1974.

Schullian, Dorothy M. "A Manuscript of Dominici in the Army Medical Library." *Journal of the History of Medicine and Allied Sciences* 3 (1948): 395–99.

Shrewsbury, J. F. D. *A History of Bubonic Plague in the British Isles*. London: Cambridge University Press, 1970.

—————. "The Plague of Athens." *Bulletin of the History of Medicine* 24 (1950): 1–25.

Sigerist, Henry E. *Civilization and Disease*. Ithaca: Cornell University Press, 1944.

Slack, Paul. "The Disappearance of Plague: An Alternative View." *Economic History Review*, 2d ser., 34 (1981): 469–76.

—————. *The Impact of Plague in Tudor and Stuart England*. London: Routledge and Kegan Paul, 1985.

—————. Introduction to *Epidemics and Ideas: Essays on the Historical Perception of Pestilence*, 1–20. Ed. Terence Ranger and Paul Slack. Cambridge: Cambridge University Press, 1992.

————. Introduction to *The Plague Reconsidered: A New Look at Its Origins and Effects in Sixteenth- and Seventeenth-Century England.* Local Population Studies Supplement. Matlock, Derbyshire: "Local Population Studies" with the S.S.R.C. Cambridge Group for the History of Population and Social Structure, 1977.

Sogner, Sölvi. "Nature and Dynamics of Crises (Including Recent Crises in Developing Countries)." In *The Great Mortalities: Methodological Studies of Demographic Crises in the Past,* 311–44. Ed. Hubert Charbonneau and André Larose. Liège, Belgium: International Union for the Scientific Study of Population; Ordina Editions, 1980.

Sommervogel, Carlos. *Bibliothèque de la Compagnie de Jésus.* 9 vols. Paris: Alphonse Picard, 1890–1900. Supplementary volumes 10–12 published at Paris and Louvain: Alphonse Picard and Editions de la Bibliothèque SJ, 1919–1960.

Sournia, Jean-Charles. "Discipline du diagnostic rétrospectif." In *Maladies et société (XIIe–XVIIIe siècles): Actes du colloque de Bielefeld, novembre 1986,* 57–64. Ed. Neithard Bulst and Robert Delort. Paris: Editions du CNRS, 1989.

Tacchi Venturi, Pietro, and Mario Scaduto. *Storia della Compagnia di Gesù in Italia.* 4 vols. Rome: Società Editrice Dante Alighieri and Edizioni La Civiltà Cattolica, 1938–1974.

Thomas, Keith. *Religion and the Decline of Magic: Studies in Popular Beliefs in Sixteenth- and Seventeenth-Century England.* Harmondsworth: Penguin Books, 1973.

Thorndike, Lynn. "The Blight of Pestilence on Early Modern Civilization." *American Historical Review* 32 (1927): 455–74.

Twigg, Graham I. *The Black Death: A Biological Reappraisal.* London: Batsford Academic and Educational, 1984.

————. "The Black Death in England: An Epidemiological Dilemma." In *Maladies et société (XIIe–XVIIIe siècles): Actes du colloque de Bielefeld, novembre 1986,* 75–98. Ed. Neithard Bulst and Robert Delort. Paris: Editions du CNRS, 1989.

————. "The Role of Rodents in Plague Dissemination: A Worldwide Review." *Mammal Review* 8 (1978): 77–110.

Velimirovic, Boris, and Helga Velimirovic. "Plague in Vienna." *Reviews of Infectious Diseases* 11 (1989): 808–26.

Wright, A. D. "The Borromean Ideal and the Spanish Church." In *San Carlo Borromeo: Catholic Reform and Ecclesiastical Politics in the Second Half of the Sixteenth Century,* 188–207. Ed. John M. Headley and John B. Tomaro. Washington: Folger Books, 1988.

Ziegler, Philip. *The Black Death.* Harmondsworth: Penguin Books, 1970.

Zitelli, Andreina, and Richard J. Palmer. "Le teorie mediche sulla peste e il contesto veneziano." In *Venezia e la Peste, 1348–1797.* 2d ed. Venice: Marsilio Editori, 1980.

INDEX

Index

Charity (*continued*)
  Jesuits as victims of, 186-88, 201ff.
  and pest, 38-39
  and public reputation, 191
  victims of, 186-88, 201
Chaulet, Jacques, 52
Chauliac, Gui de, 3, 6, 9
Children, mortality rates, 158
China, rat mortality and plague, 11
Chivasso, 133
Christians, attitudes to death, 98
Christian, William A., 202
Christocentricism, of Jesuits, 103-4, 202
Church attendance, from fear, 147-48
Cipolla, Carlo, 131, 144
Cities and countries. *See also* appendix on pp. 207-30 for chronological listing of pest epidemics, by country and city.
  with epidemic diseases.
    -Aegean islands (plague), 12
    -Africa (plague), 11
    -Alba Julia, 124, 128
    -Alcalá de Henares, 72, 120, 186-87
    -Americas, 72, 73n84
    -Amsterdam (plague), 16
    -Andalusia, 61
    -Angra, 21
    -Aragon, 120, 189
    -Asia, 72, 72n84; (plague), 11
    -Athens (plague), 6
    -Augsburg, 92, 96, 102, 149, 160, 162t
    -Australia (plague), 2
    -Avigliano, 133, 163
    -Avignon, 3, 52-55, 70, 76, 83, 95, 121-22, 163t, 191-92, 195
    -Avila, 66
    -Baden-Baden, 157
    -Barcelona, 118, 121, 147, 149, 158, 167, 192t
    -Bivona, 62, 193
    -Bologna, 65-66, 139, 141-43
    -Bourges, 179
    -Braga, 127, 159, 179
    -Braganca, 178
    -Braniewo, 21, 106, 126, 135, 154
    -Brazil, 21, 23, 72
    -Brescia, 25, 64, 93, 127, 151-52, 154, 156, 160-63, 176, 180, 187, 190
    -Brno, 62, 86, 118, 129
    -Brok, 108
    -Burgos, 130, 187
    -Cairo, 162t

Cities and counties
  with epidemic diseases (*continued*)
    -Calabria, 118
    -Chambéry, 94, 101, 160, 163t, 187
    -China (plague), 11
    -Chivasso, 133
    -Cluj, 55-57, 84, 86, 189
    -Cochin, 72
    -Coimbra, 29, 65-66
    -Cologne, 67, 96, 97, 99, 154, 156, 162-63t, 177
    -Constantinople, 162-63t
    -Cracow, 146-47, 152, 163t,
    -Dijon, 156
    -East Asia (plague), 11
    -East Indies, 72, 72n84
    -England, 8, 95; (plague), 7
    -Europe (plague), 7
    -Evora, 64, 70
    -Ferrara, 70, 97, 120, 126, 166, 178, 187
    -Flanders, 69
    -Florence, 65-66
    -Forlì, 133
    -Fribourg, 158
    -Fulda, 61, 67
    -Gandia, 164
    -Genoa, 180
    -Germany, 122, 134-35
    -Granada, 177
    -Graz, 44-45
    -Heiligenstadt, 158
    -Hindustan (plague), 11
    -Hong Kong (plague), 2
    -India, 73n84; (plague), 2
    -Ingolstadt, 64
    -Inzago, 163t,
    -Italy, 67, 71, 81, 83-84, 122, 133, 141
    -Klausenburg. *See* Cluj.
    -Kolozsmonostor, 84, 86n139
    -Kolozvar. *See* Cluj.
    -Krain duchy, 57
    -Le Marche, 62
    -Liège, 122-23
    -Lisbon, 86, 96, 123, 127, 150, 162-63t, 176, 191
    -Ljubljana, 57-58
    -Loreto, 61, 66, 187
    -Luzern, 187
    -Lyon, 95, 101-2, 127, 136, 151, 159, 163t, 165, 178, 191
    -Maastricht, 180, 194
    -Mainz, 67, 149

254

COLOPHON

———

Design and typography by Tim Rolands
Cover and title page by Teresa Wheeler

Text is set in Minion, designed by Robert Slimbach
and released by Adobe in 1989.
Display is set in Mantinia, designed by Matthew Carter.

Printed and bound by Edwards Brothers, Ann Arbor, Michigan

SIXTEENTH CENTURY JOURNAL PUBLISHERS, INC.
MC 111-L NMSU • Kirksville MO 63501-4211
Tel. 816-785-4665 • Fax 816-785-4181 • ISBN Prefix 0-940474

Ardolino, Frank. **Apocalypse and Armada in Kyd's Spanish Tragedy.** vol. 29. IISBN 0-940474-31-X. $35

Brink, Jean R., ed. **Privileging Gender in Early Modern England.** vol. 23. 250 pp. incl. Idx. SBN 0-940474-24-8 .... $35

Brunelle, Gayle. **The New World Merchants of Rouen: 1559-1630.** vol. 16. 190 pp. Illus., Idx. Bib. ISBN 0-940474-17-4 .... $35

Burnett, Amy. **The Yoke of Christ: Martin Bucer and Christian Discipline.** vol. 26. approx. 250 pp. Idx. ISBN 0-940474-28-X. $35

Christensen, Carl C. **Princes and Propaganda: Electoral Saxon Art of the Reformation.** vol. 20. 149 pp. Idx. ISBN 0-940474-21-2 ...... $35

Coats, Catherine Randall. **Subverting the System: D'Aubigne and Calvinism.** vol. 14. 136 pp. Idx. ISBN 0-940474-03-4 .... $35

Dick, John R., and Ann Richardson. **Tyndale and the Law.** vol. 25. 250 pp. Idx. ISBN 0-940474-24-8. .... $35

Eurich, S. Amanda. **The Economics of Power: The Private Finances of the House of Foix-Navarre-Albret during the Religious Wars.** vol. 24. 245 pp. Idx. ISBN 0-940474025-5. ...... $35

Fix, Andrew C., and Susan C. Karant-Nunn. **Germania Illustrata: Essays On Early Modern Germany Presented To Gerald Strauss.** vol. 18. 167 pp. Idx. Bib. ISBN 0-940474-19-0 ...... $35

Friedman, Jerome. **Regnum, Religio et Ratio: Essays Presented to Robert M. Kingdon.** vol. 8. 86 pp. Bib. ISBN 0-940474-08-5. ...... paper $25

Geiger, Gail. **Filippino Lippi's Carafa Chapel: Renaissance Art in Rome.** vol. 5. 240 pp. 80 b&w Illus. Idx. Bib. ISBN 0-940474-05-0 .... $50

Graham, W. Fred, ed. **Later Calvinism: International Perspectives.** vol. 22. 564 pp. Idx. ISBN 0-940474-23-0 .... $45

Lindberg, Carter, ed. **Piety, Politics, And Ethics: Reformation Studies in Honor Of George W. Forell.** vol. 3. 210 pp. Idx. Bib. ISBN 0-940474-03-4 .... $35

Loeschen, John R. **The Divine Community: Trinity, Church and Ethics in Reformation Theologies.** vol. 1. 238 pp. Idx., Bib. ISBN 0-940474-01-8 .... $35

Martin, A. Lynn. **Plague? Jesuit Accounts of Epidemic Disease in the Sixteenth Century.** vol. 28. ISBN 0-940474-30-1 .... $35

Mentzer, Raymond. **Sin and The Calvinists: Morals Control and the Consis- tory in the Reformed Tradition.** vol. 32. 206pp. Idx. ISBN 0-940474–34–4 .... $35

Pabel, Hilmar M. **Erasmus' Vision of the Church.** vol. 33. 170 pp. incl Idx. ISBN 0-940-474-35-2 .... $35

Ryding, Erik S. **In Harmony Framed: Musical Humanism, Thomas Campion, and the Two Daniels.** vol. 21. 136 pp. Idx. ISBN 0-940474-22-0 .... $35

Safley, Thomas Max. **Let No Man Put Asunder: The Control of Marriage in the German Southwest 1550-1600.** vol. 2, 210 pp. Idx. ISBN 0-940474-02-6. .... $35

Schilling, Heinz. **Civic Calvinism in Northwestern Germany and the Netherlands 16th-19th Centuries.** V vol. 17. 167 pp. Idx. Bib. ISBN 0-940474-18-2 .... $35

Schnucker, R.V., ed. **Calviniana: Ideas and Influence of Jean Calvin.** vol. 10. 288 pp. Idx. Bib. ISBN 0-940474-10-7. .... $35

Sessions, Kyle, & Philip Bebb, eds. **Pietas Et Societas: New Trends in Refor- mation Social History.** vol. 4.240 pp. Idx. ISBN 0-940474-04-0 .... $35

Smeeton, Donald. **Lollard Themes in the Reformation Theology of William Tyndale.** vol. 6. 240 pp. Idx. Bib. ISBN 0-940474-06-9 ..... $35

Spalding, James C., ed. **The Reformation of the Ecclesiastical Laws of England, 1552.** vol. 19. 274 pp. Illus. Idx. ISBN 0-940474-20-4. .. $35

Thorp, Malcolm R., & Arthur J. Slavin, eds. **Politics, Religion and Diplomacy in Early Modern Europe: Essays in Honor of DeLamar Jensen.** vol. 27. ISBN 0-940474-29-8. ..... $35

Tracy, James. **Luther and the Modern State of Germany.** vol. 7. 108 pp. Idx. ISBN 0-940474-07-7. .... $35

[Vermigli] **A Bibliography of the Works of Peter Martyr Vermigli.** John Patrick Donnelly, SJ, Robert M. Kingdon, Marvin W. Anderson, eds. vol. 13. 36 pp. Idx. ISBN 0-940474-14-X. $50

Vermigli, Peter Martyr. **Early Writings: Creed, Scripture, Church.** Ed. Joseph C. McLelland; tr. Mariano Di Gangi; biographical intro. Philip McNair. *The Peter Martyr Library no. 1.* vol. 30. ISBN 0-940474-32-8. .... $35

Vermigli, Peter Martyr. **A Dialogue on the Two Natures in Christ.** Ed. and tr. John Patrick Donnelly, S.J. *The Peter Martyr Library no. 2.* vol. 31. ISBN 0-940474-33-6. .... $35

Vermigli, Peter Martyr. **Prayers from the Psalms.** Ed. and tr. John Patrick Donnelly, S.J. *The Peter Martyr Library no. 3.* vol. 36. ISBN 0-940474-36-0. .... $35

Williams, George Huntston. **The Radical Reformation.** 3rd ed. vol. 15. 513 pp., updated Bib. 5 Idxes ISBN 0-940474-27-1 paper $50 / ISBN 0-940474-15-9. .... $125